The Handbook of Technical Analysis

A Comprehensive
Guide to Analytical
Methods, Trading
Systems and
Technical Indicators

DARRELL R. JOBMAN
EDITOR

IRWIN
Professional Publishing®
Chicago • London • Singapore

ISBN 1-55738-597-1

Printed in the United States of America

BB

  3 4 5 6 7 8 9 0

JB

TABLE OF CONTENTS

PREFACE

After being the editor of a publication such as *Commodities/Futures* magazine for 15 years, I guess some things about trading are bound to rub off. Every month I heard about new trading strategies or new applications for old strategies and how people have traded successfully— and unsuccessfully. I had a chance to see simple concepts that make trading look so easy and complex formulas and diagrams that probably are traded just as successfully if you can figure them out.

For those who expect someone exposed to hundreds of good trading ideas to have discerned at last the secret to trading success, this book may be a disappointment.

Editors tend to learn a little about a lot but usually know a lot about only a little and, often, don't really know much about anything. And, certainly, not much about everything. This applies especially to trading, where there are a number of routes to success and no magic answers, despite what you may hear.

As an editor, my goal was to find people with the best trading ideas, convince them to share their knowledge with readers and then present this material in the most understandable way possible. While I have studied markets and have traded myself, I cannot claim to have made a million dollars trading, as some have, and I do not claim to be any kind of analytical genius, as others are. At best, I am only a filter, attempting to tap the best sources to share a full range of technical analysis ideas with you in this volume.

Because books on trading often serve as a reference and are seldom read from front cover to back like a novel, I've tried to make each chapter a self-contained unit. In actual trading, however, you can't put things in nice little containers. So it is with this book: Many topics relate to other areas—seasonals to cycles or vice versa, market sentiment to market structure to chart patterns, etc. Nothing in technical analysis can be taken in isolation, and technical analysis is only one aspect of trading.

And, as you'll be reminded a number of times throughout the book, technical analysis is an art, not a science, so don't expect any definitive rules on trading success.

After you have read and studied and, hopefully, learned all the various aspects of technical analysis in this book, you will still have one challenge: Sorting out those things that fit *you* best and putting them together into a system and a style *you* can trade profitably. No trader can include every facet of technical analysis in a trading plan, so you don't have to feel you're missing the boat if you ignore many approaches in this book.

Fortunately, there is no one right way trading has to be done; there are many roads to trading success. But you do have to have a map—a plan that shows *your* route. When you do build your plan, I hope you have gained enough from this volume to incorporate something from each of its four major sections.

Darrell Jobman
Waterloo, Iowa

ACKNOWLEDGMENTS

Special thanks for this book must go to Merrill J. Oster and *Futures* magazine—first, for giving me the break to be editor of *Commodities/Futures* magazine to learn about this amazing trading business and, second, for allowing me to use articles and illustrations from the magazine. All material from the magazine is copyrighted, and permission for its use has been granted by the publisher.

As the futures and options industry's major publication since 1972, the magazine has always been a great source of information and ideas for traders, large and small. Permission to tap into its archives to use a few of its best resources was a significant help in rounding out some areas of this volume.

Second, I must acknowledge the contributions of the magazine's other editors, writers and staff members over the years. Their names won't show up at the top of chapters, but they were the ones who did much of the research and writing and helped to provide me with the background necessary to put together a book such as this. Through the years, they were a source of education and inspiration.

Third, of course, special thanks must go to the contributors to this volume who are among the many well-known traders and analysts in the futures and options industry who have written for the magazine over the years. They are the experts—the ones with the trading ideas and the experience and, thankfully, the willingness to share what they know with others. Other sources probably could have been chosen, but these are some of the people to whom I was exposed during my magazine years, and I am grateful for the opportunity to have worked with, and learned from, each of them.

INTRODUCTION

WHY TECHNICAL ANALYSIS?

Let's assume you've decided to become a trader in the copper market, and you want to know everything there is to know about copper.

The supply of copper obviously is a critical factor, so you set out on a mission to find out everything you can about production. You discover that, while the United States is one of the world's major producers, Chile, Canada, Russia, Zaire, Zambia and Peru also produce significant shares of the world's copper output. So the scope of your study has to become worldwide if you are to get a good grip on total copper supplies.

You know conditions in Russia have changed dramatically in the last few years. You have heard about improvements in Chile's economy. Somewhere you have read a report suggesting that the AIDS disease would decimate the labor supply for the mines and smelters in central Africa. And what about this report that governments, which now control a significant portion of world production, might reduce copper shipments as a way to increase prices and bring in more revenue for the government coffers? And what about talk of a mine shutting down because of a labor dispute? Or the latest figures showing huge copper stocks available for delivery at the London Metal Exchange?

Your research turns up some useful statistics about historical copper production, but you're having a problem getting a handle on the current situation. How much copper is available today? How would any of the events above—or dozens of other things you can imagine—impact the market tomorrow?

Supply, far-flung as it is, is not an easy item on which you can get a fix, especially if you are not in that industry. So you turn to the other side of the equation, the demand side. Again, you have loads of statistics—are they really accurate?—indicating what past consumption has been. But consumption is not the same thing as demand, and you won't get very far into your research before you learn that the state of the U.S. economy, just to mention one key country, is an important factor in this market.

In addition to copper statistics, now you have to become an economic expert to put some perspective on housing starts, capacity utilization, durable goods orders and numerous other economic reports. And then what happens to demand if a new use is found for copper or if the U.S. Mint decides to quit making copper pennies?

It won't take much research to conclude that demand is an even more elusive element to quantify than supply.

As an outsider, you may find it almost impossible to get an accurate reading of all the fundamentals involved in the copper market. You probably do not have the time and resources to get all of this information anyway so you may decide to concentrate on just a few of the factors that seem to be most significant. First, you have to determine what those factors are; then you have to weigh any changes in those factors to calculate how they would affect the value of copper.

Of course, even if you were an insider and had perfect statistics for every supply and demand factor, a lot of other market participants don't. Their perceptions and opinions might be far different from yours and their deduction of value might be well off the mark of what the current supply-demand figures suggest.

Being a "fundamentalist" interested in supply and demand poses several tremendous challenges: First, getting timely, reliable information and, second, calculating the market impact of so many factors if you had the information. However, in a free-market setting, there is one element that incorporates every change in a fundamental factor, big or small, and every interpretation of those factors. What's more, this element is not a secret limited to insiders but is readily available to all, without regard to their knowledge of copper fundamentals.

This element is price. Everything that is on the line during a specific period of time in a market is included in the line that is price.

This is the realm of the "technician," who doesn't see much sense in chasing down fundamental information when it's all included and distilled into just one item, price. The fundamentals ultimately drive the market and determine the price, of course, but instead of trying to assess supply and demand and all the other factors that make up a market, technical analysis studies the action of prices and the market itself. Technical analysis looks at price and what it has done in the past and assumes it will perform similarly in the future under similar circumstances.

"Each price represents a momentary consensus of value of all market participants—large commercial interests and small speculators, fundamental researchers, technicians and gamblers—at the moment of transaction," Dr. Alexander Elder has written in *Trading for a Living*, one of the best recent books on trading.

At that fleeting moment of transaction, the bullish and bearish forces are equally balanced. But, an instant later, someone—or many someones—may decide that price is higher or lower than they perceive the value should be or will be in the future. Motivated by greed—the desire to enhance their bank account—or fear—trying to preserve or lock in what they've got—market participants buy or sell. No matter where your perch in the marketplace is, you can't know all the motivations that prompt buy/sell decisions. But these hundreds and thousands of decisions do leave tracks—prices and price patterns. Studying these tracks is the art known as technical analysis.

Analysts have come up with a number of ways to look at price and market action. This handbook covers a broad spectrum of technical analysis approaches and places them into four major categories:

❑ **Price and presentation: Charts.** While bar charts are the most widely known method for presenting prices and price change, they aren't the only chart form. Any handbook on technical analysis has to begin with bar chart formations, of course, but candlestick charts, point-and-figure charts and Market Profile are among other ways traders visualize price action.

❑ **Price and pace: Indicators.** Often, it is not price itself or chart formations that are most important but how fast or how slow or how far from "normal" the price movement is. The momentum of price change, reflected in a variety of technical indicators, has become a vital input for many traders, especially since personal computers have become an integral part of technical analysis.

❑ **Price and participants: Sentiment.** Sometimes a more significant clue to market direction lies in who is trading and what they are thinking. Some analytical approaches focus on volume and open interest, the commitment of major players to their positions or the opinions of experts to gauge how traders view the current market and what they might do next.

❑ **Price and projection: Structure.** Experienced traders realize that price patterns, indicators and sentiment based on past market action may be helpful in the future—if they can interpret them correctly. But some find more comfort in seeing a structure to markets as revealed by cycles and seasonal patterns or in longer-term natural patterns popularized in the studies of R.N. Elliott, Fibonacci or W.D. Gann. Rather than waiting for price to set the pattern, they see a framework and a pattern already set into which prices will fall.

Technical analysis obviously cannot be sliced into four pieces as neatly and as cleanly as that because there is a good deal of overlap in some areas—chart formations may be part of an Elliott Wave structure produced by participants with a particular psychological mindset, for example. The subject could be diced another way into trend-following and trend-reversing approaches. But we'll use the framework outlined above to present the ideas and methods of some of the top technical analysts involved in futures trading today.

SECTION 1

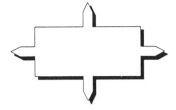

PRICE AND
PRESENTATION:
CHARTS

CHAPTER 1

CHART (AND ART) FORMS

Plotted on a grid, a dot representing the price of a commodity or financial instrument provides the trader with several valuable pieces of information: a value and a time at which that value occurred—in the example on page 4, $380 per oz. for April gold futures at the Commodity Exchange in New York on Oct. 31. (Figure 1.1)

Yet, without any other data, it's like being at the "You are here" sign at a large shopping mall with no diagram to tell you where "here" is. Or it's like waking up on a raft in the middle of the ocean with no clue where you are or where you are headed.

Is the price high? Or low? How high? How low? Is the price going up? Or down? Is an ounce of gold really worth more historically? Or less?

An isolated price, with no other clues and no experience on which to rely, is not very useful if you want to be a trader. Even just one more price at one more time point would tell you something: The trend is up or down or sideways. If you have some way to record each new price as you get it, you're on the way to being able to analyze whether the latest price is fair compared to what has happened to prices previously.

Many traders use charts of some type to depict this price action. A chart is simply a picture of price history—a roadmap of prices and a

FIGURE I.I   COMEX APRIL GOLD FUTURES

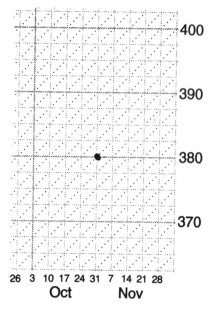

tool many analysts use to envision where prices might go based on what they have observed in the past. No matter what a market has done, it can do only one of two things in the future: continue what it has been doing or change. As the sum of all trading decisions by all market participants—the mass psychology—shifts, prices shift and, over time, price patterns form as a result of these shifting opinions carried out in trading actions. Looking at similar patterns in the past, you may be able to surmise what a market is likely to do next because of the way the trading crowd has reacted in similar circumstances in the past.

This is the "technical analysis" of prices and price action as opposed to an analysis of value based on supply-demand or fundamental factors. Prices can be presented in several ways, depending on the source of your price data, your time frame for trading and the type of chart that says something to you.

Close-only charts—Only the close for a time period is significant. You simply plot the closes, such as on the April gold price example, and connect the dots. The line you get may be sufficient in some cases, but in today's trading, close-only charts are typically used for one-price-a-day situations such as cash prices (see Figure 1.2), spread charts that track the difference in prices between two contracts or basis charts that show the difference between cash and futures prices.

FIGURE 1.2

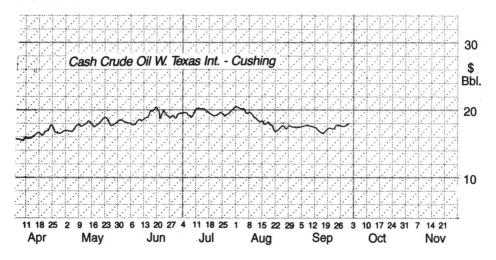

Source: Commodity Price Charts

Bar charts—By far the most common type of chart, traditional bar charts focus on the high, low and closing prices for a time period. The period may be one minute, one day or one month, but the price patterns that develop and the way they are analyzed are the same for all time periods.

Point-and-figure charts—Only the highs and lows are significant; the opening and closing prices have no bearing on how these charts are plotted. Time also is not a factor as it is on other charts.

Candlestick charts—The opening price is a key feature on these charts, especially in relationship to the closing price. The high and low prices for the time period are part of the chart but are not nearly as significant as the range between the open and close.

Market Profile—Every price tick is evaluated. As prices reach different levels during different times of the day, they form certain shapes and patterns that suggest a particular type of trading day.

The following chapters in the first section of this book go into more detail about these charts. However, several points need to be emphasized before going any further:

First, whole books—big textbooks—have been written on each of these charting styles. As a handbook, this volume covers only the major points. As the essence of technical analysis, however, it is important that you have some understanding of charts.

Second, what you "see" on a chart may not be what other traders "see." Constructing a chart is relatively mechanical and straightforward; reading what it says is an art, no matter what type of chart you are using. Sometimes interpreting this chart art may require as much creativity as deciphering some pieces of modern art.

Third, a price chart alone may not be enough to make a trading decision. Anyone can point to a price chart in hindsight and say, "If you had bought at the bottom here and sold at the top here, you could have made . . ." A visual analysis of a chart is only one trading tool. In today's computer world, you may want inputs other than a simple chart to trigger a trading decision. That's what the other three sections of this handbook are about.

FIGURE 1.3   HOW PRICES LOOK ON CHARTS—ONE DAY'S ACTION

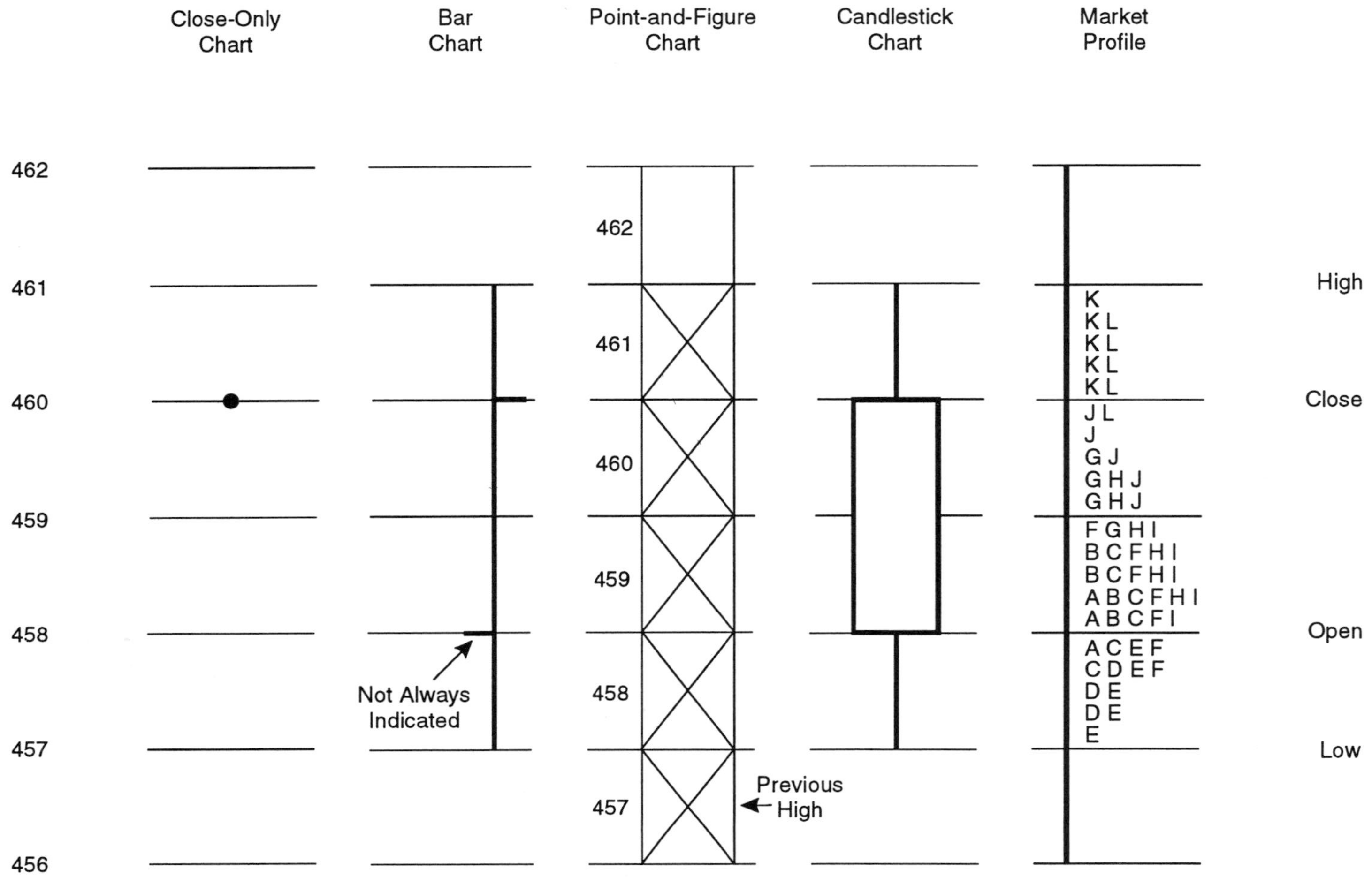

CHAPTER 2

BAR CHART BASICS

Drop a traditional bar chart in front of almost any novice who doesn't know a thing about trading—even your spouse—and they can probably tell you the trend of prices at a glance. If they can't, odds are pretty good the market is in such a sideways move or congestion phase that it may not be very attractive for you to trade anyway. But, when a market does break out into one of those long extended moves you sometimes see on a chart, even a nontrader can recognize it as an opportunity.

The bar chart is, by far, the most popular method traders use to see how this price action looks. We've already indicated that a bar for any given time period—a minute, a day, a month—shows the high price for the period at the top of the bar, the low price for the period at the bottom of the bar and the closing price at the end of the period indicated by a horizontal line on the right side of the bar. Sometimes the opening price is indicated by a horizontal line on the left side of the price bar. We've also already stated that every factor in the marketplace during the time period the bar covers—every fundamental, every perception, every fear—is incorporated in that one price bar.

Put a series of these bars for a number of time periods together side by side, and you have a chart. Looking from right to left on a chart, there is no mystery about where the trends or the sideways moves are. They are pretty easy to spot when you look back at past price action. When you look ahead, from left to right, however, it's quite a different matter as you hit the right side of the chart. Technical analysis—the study of price and its action in the past—can help you make some intellectual guesses about the future, but there are no guaranteed answers, no matter how many charts from the past you've examined.

Whole textbooks have been written on bar chart analysis, and many books on trading cover this aspect of technical analysis in some manner. What follows is relatively standard fare on bar chart analysis. It's intended to take some of the mystery out of charting for the beginning technical analyst and provide a basis for discussing charts in other chapters.

For organizational purposes, this chapter will look first at trendlines and continuation patterns and then at reversal formations. You probably won't be surprised to learn that sometimes a pattern can turn out to be either, and it is only in hindsight that you can identify the clues. As with any art, only practice will help you here.

TRENDLINES

"Trade with the trend" is a basic tenet of successful trading. So identifying the trend is where bar chart analysis begins. If a chart does nothing else for you, it is valuable for showing you the trend, even if you are one of those people who remain convinced that a lot of technical analysis is hocus-pocus stuff. For many traders, the trading strategy is simple: As long as the trend is intact, stay with it.

An uptrend is a continuous series of higher highs and higher lows; a downtrend is a series of lower highs and lower lows. To see where a market may be going on a bar chart, connect the lows with a straight line to form the trendline in an uptrend; if the market is going down, draw the trendline across the highs to give you the most important line on the chart.

Nearly every bar chart displays trends of some type. The December crude oil chart has several, most notably the downtrend line (A) from above $19 per barrel in October to below $16 in March and the uptrend line (B) from the low under $15 in late March to well over $19 again in late July (Figure 2.1 on page 12). Another uptrend line connecting the bottoms in June and July (C) is approximately a 45-degree line, considered to be a significant angle by chartists.

The longer the trendline and the more times prices touch it, the more reliable it is and the more "support" it offers the market when prices test it. In a downtrend, the trendline drawn across the descending highs is a point of "resistance"—a line likely to turn back price advances until the market becomes strong enough to break above it as it did here in early April.

The major trendlines on the oil chart have at least three points of contact, as drawn. Remember, chart analysis is an art, and there is some latitude in picking vital points and drawing the lines. Some analysts view the close as the most valuable price and use only closes for trendlines, ignoring the highs or lows that define the trendline points for other analysts. That would give slightly different levels of support and resistance and a little different view on where the breakouts occur. That's part of the art of chart analysis.

The first spurt away from the bottom produces a steep short-term trendline on the crude oil chart, typical as a market breaks out of an old trend. But the steeper the trendline, the harder it is to maintain, and the market quickly settles into a steadier, sustainable climb. Once trendline B is broken, you could establish another trendline at a lower level (D) as a support area once a new low seems to be in place. This low, by the way, can be projected as we'll explain in the retracement discussion below.

Another feature of a trendline on bar charts is that a parallel line (E) often develops and produces a well-defined "channel," a relatively nar-

FIGURE 2.1

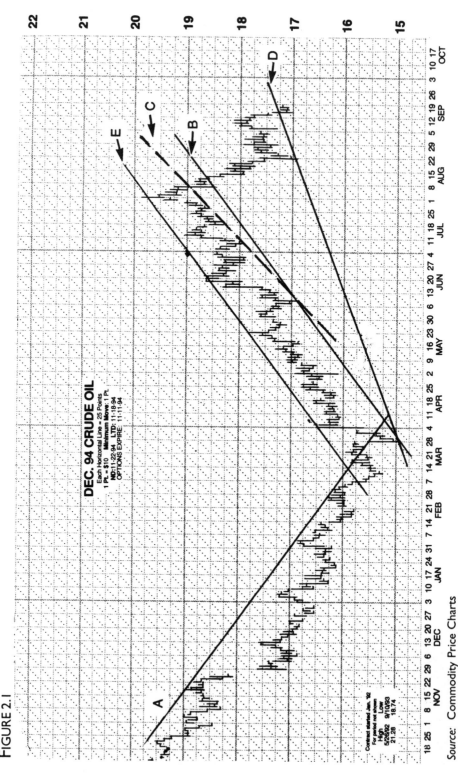

Source: Commodity Price Charts

row band of price action within two parallel trendlines. Once a channel is established, close followers of the market might use "breakouts" of the channel to establish positions: A break above the top of the uptrend channel would suggest an even stronger market than has existed, offering a buy opportunity; a break below the channel indicates weakness and a possible sell signal.

Or you might assume after a while that the most likely course of action is for prices to stay within the channel: Buy when prices approach the bottom of the channel, sell when they get near the top of the channel. Stay alert for channel breakouts, however.

Another type of "trend" or "channel" formation is a sideways move. December gold futures prices stayed within a $25 per oz. channel for much of 1994, including weeks on end in a range of less than $10 (Figure 2.2 on page 14). Tops (A and B) and bottoms (C and D) seem to have the market confined between about $380 and $405 per oz. Traders who are convinced this is a sideways market use the top of the channel or trading range to sell and the bottom to buy, assuming the market will reverse its course at those resistance and support points to stay within the range whenever either trendline is tested.

The width of the channel will help you determine whether this is a viable strategy to trade. The $25 range in gold equals $2,500 per contract, an amount you might find worth pursuing if you capture only part of a move. In some cases, the range is so narrow that your account could get chewed up by gyrations within the channel, even when you've determined correctly what type of market it is. For example, cattle futures traded sideways within about a half-cent range or only $200 per contract for weeks in 1994. It's difficult to get positioned in a market like that and is not an attractive situation for any trader except perhaps for someone who wants to sell options.

Lackluster as it may seem to be, you need to watch a sideways formation especially carefully: The longer a market moves sideways, the more

FIGURE 2.2

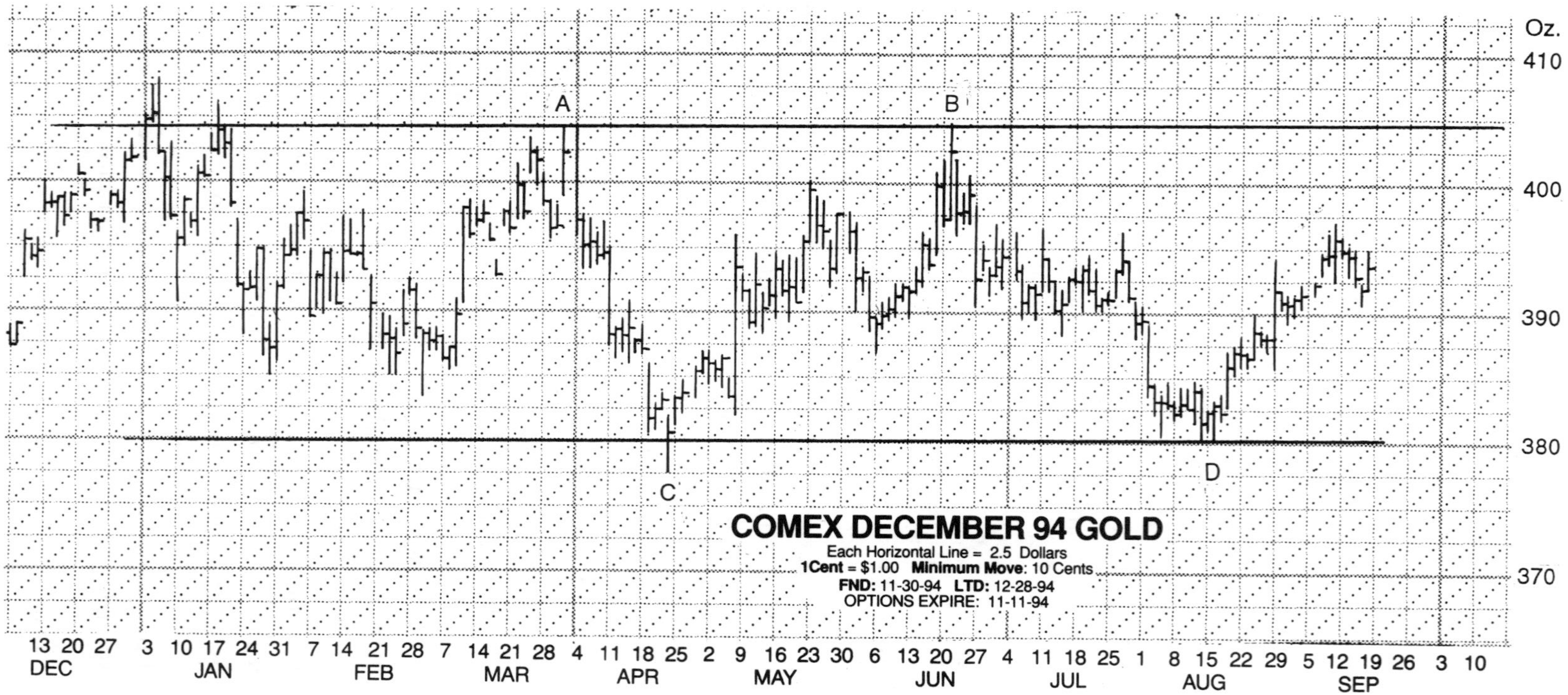
Oz.
410
400
390
380
370
A
B
C
D
COMEX DECEMBER 94 GOLD
Each Horizontal Line = 2.5 Dollars
1Cent = $1.00 Minimum Move: 10 Cents
FND: 11-30-94 LTD: 12-28-94
OPTIONS EXPIRE: 11-11-94
13 20 27 3 10 17 24 31 7 14 21 28 7 14 21 28 4 11 18 25 2 9 16 23 30 6 13 20 27 4 11 18 25 1 8 15 22 29 5 12 19 26 3 10
DEC JAN FEB MAR APR MAY JUN JUL AUG SEP

Source: Commodity Price Charts

energy it tends to store up. When the market breaks out from a double, triple or multiple top or bottom of a trading range, the pent-up energy can produce a significant move in the direction of the breakout.

CONTINUATION FORMATIONS

If the first thing you look for on a bar chart is the trend, your second question probably will be something like, "Okay, there's the trend. Now, will it continue or reverse?" Your logical followup questions might be, "And, if the trend continues, how long or how far will it continue? If the trend reverses, how far or how long will the reversal be?" Technical analysis will give you some clues, but keep in mind that this is a subjective art and the answers are not absolute.

Markets seldom go straight up or down. In most cases, a trend will be interrupted by "congestion areas," "pauses" or "resting periods" as prices react against the main trend, perhaps for days or even a few weeks. As bears and bulls sort out the dominant psychological force in the marketplace, chart patterns may develop that suggest a turn in direction or a continuation of the larger trend already in place. Even when a trend remains intact, you may find countertrend moves you want to trade, depending on your trading style.

Bar chart patterns that suggest a move will continue include "symmetrical triangles" or "pennants," "ascending triangles" and "descending triangles" and "flags." Sometimes one formation will evolve into another. You can see some examples of these patterns on the same crude oil chart as we used to show trendlines (to reduce clutter, the major trendlines aren't shown). These aren't the only examples of formations on these charts nor even the best—your eye may pick out some others.

The names pretty well describe how the formations look. Much depends on where these patterns occur on the overall chart picture. With triangles in general, prices tend to trade in a narrower and narrower range or coil before springing out with another strong move. The evi-

FIGURE 2.3

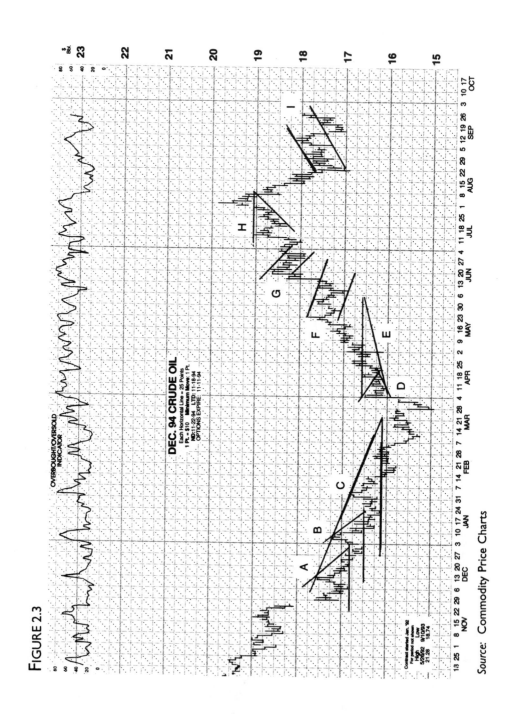

Source: Commodity Price Charts

dence of such a formation is more conclusive if the level of trading volume generally follows the same pattern as the the level of prices. CAUTION: A breakout may not be in the direction of the prevailing trend; triangles also can be reversal formations.

The breakout of an ascending or descending triangle that develops during a trend usually is through the flat side of the triangle (A, B, C, E, H on oil chart). In a descending triangle, prices are pressed down to the baseline several times and rally less each time until they break below the baseline. After the break, prices frequently come back to the baseline to retest it, but it may become the new ceiling (in a descending triangle) or support floor (in an ascending triangle) as it turns back prices. This is the adjustment period for traders as they start to accept a new price level.

A pennant or symmetrical triangle reflects uncertainty and a time for traders to pause and catch up with the market. A series of lower highs and higher lows winds chart action into a tight little coil pattern at the apex of the triangle. When the market springs out of the pennant, the breakout often comes on a wide range day and in the same direction as the trend leading into the pennant. This is one of the more reliable chart patterns.

A flag formation is a short-term trend against the prevailing trend—a bear flag with lower highs and lower lows in a larger bullish trend (F and G on the crude oil chart) or a bull flag with higher lows and higher highs in an overall bearish move (I on the crude oil chart). The best examples come after a sharp move that actually looks like a "flagpole" on which to anchor the flag (G is a better example than F on the oil chart). The market seems to need a rest for a bit to sort out what it's done after making a quick spurt up or down and, in effect, is assessing whether the move is real. Once it has consolidated its forces, it is ready for the next phase of its original trend.

MEASURING A CONTINUATION TREND

Anticipating a question you may have at this point: Yes, it is possible to read too much into a bar chart and to imagine a pattern that coincides with or reinforces your market bias. As market action is unfolding, it frankly is often very difficult to determine the current chart pattern. Price action on the crude oil chart after H looks a lot like earlier action on the chart, but it turned out to be a top (at least for the time shown) while action at D, E, F, and G developed into triangles and flags that continued the uptrend.

When you're in the middle of F, it is difficult to recognize it as a flag and not a potential top. However, don't give up on technical analysis at this point. As this formation develops, you get several valuable pieces of information:

1. Early in the countertrend move, it's not clear what will happen. If you had a tight uptrend line drawn on the April-May lows, you may even have been stopped out of a long position when prices dropped below the trendline in the third week of the counter move. As the countertrend price points became evident—first a low, then a lower high, then a lower low—a flag began to look like a possibility but still wasn't a foregone conclusion.

    Even without knowing what the emerging formation was, however, you at least had logical places to put stops, no matter what happened—a buy stop at the upper line, a sell stop below the lower line or the low point of the countertrend. You may have had an opinion about the next move based on your other analysis, but on the bar chart evidence alone, you still don't know whether this is a flag in an overall uptrend or the top of the uptrend after three weeks. All you do know is that your stops can put you in a position to get onboard a move in either direction.

2. Once the breakout above the top line has occurred and your stop has gotten you long, analysis of what is evidently a flag formation can give you a clue about a second important item of concern—how far the uptrend might continue. This is not an exact science either, but formations such as pennants and flags tend to occur about halfway through a move. The "length" of the flagpole also can be used to project the next move.

Look at the crude oil chart again (Figure 2.4), beginning with the pennant/symmetrical triangle labeled D on the previous chart. The flagpole created by the upward spike off the bottom measures about 160 points (vertical line J). Add that amount to the breakout point at $16.30 per barrel near the apex of the triangle, and you get a target of $17.90 (vertical line K). After prices break above triangle D, they fall back to retest the area and then almost drop below the triangle lows in early May before moving up nearly to the target projected by the symmetrical triangle.

Similarly, the less well-defined flagpole leading into the flag formation F measures about 175 points (vertical line L). Added to the point where prices break out above the flag, the projection is for a high around $19.30 (vertical line M). Likewise, the 125-point flagpole for flag formation G (vertical line N) sets a target for the high above $19.50 (vertical line O).

The concept can be applied to the downside as well. The slide from the top to the beginning of what appears to be a bear flag formation (I) covers approximately 300 points (vertical line P). Subtract that amount from the point where prices break out below the bottom of the flag, and the projected low is in the $14.50 vicinity (vertical line Q). Likely? At the time of the breakout in September, all you could say is that, based on technical analysis studies of flag formations in the past, that's what it looked like. A month later, you might wonder whether you even had a flag formation (Figure 2.5).

FIGURE 2.4

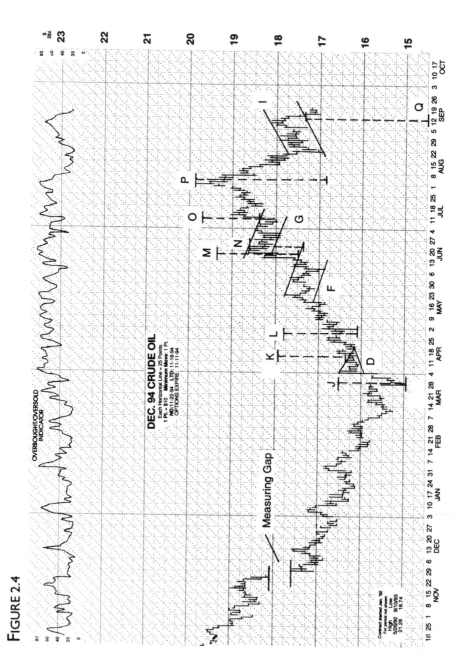

Source: Commodity Price Charts

FIGURE 2.5

Source: Commodity Price Charts

You can do similar calculations with ascending and descending triangles. Figure out the difference between the high and the base (support area) of a descending triangle and subtract that figure from the base to get a downtrend target after prices break below the base. In an ascending triangle, find the difference between the low at the start of the triangle and the baseline (resistance area) and add that amount to the baseline to get an upside target after prices break above the baseline.

MEASURING GAPS

Another continuation formation amounts to nothing—that is, there actually is no formation but a "gap" or a price level where no trading takes place in a running market. This can be a "measuring gap."

To a fundamentalist, that's a point at which something so dramatic has happened that no one wants any part of the market at the current price level. The supply or demand situation has changed so drastically that prices jump to a totally new level with no buying or selling at the intervening prices.

To a technician, a measuring gap performs somewhat the same function as a pennant or symmetrical triangle, typically marking the halfway point in a move between a bottom and top or vice versa. The most visible gap on the crude oil chart is the unusually large gap in November (Figure 2.4). Prices had been near $20 and were close to $18 at the time of the gap—a $2 drop. To calculate an objective based on this measuring gap, subtract $2 from the bottom of the gap—$17.50 minus $2 puts a downside target in the $15.50 area.

As you might expect in this subjective world, gaps are fairly common on bar charts, and not every gap means something. Some measuring gaps may turn out to be exhaustion gaps that indicate a reversal, not a continuation, of the trend. But a correctly diagnosed measuring gap can be helpful in projecting a price objective.

REVERSAL FORMATIONS

Like a surfer looking for the big wave, the chart trader's dream is to catch a big trend early and stay onboard for a long ride. That would seem to be relatively easy to do when you look at a bar chart in hindsight. But, as we have already mentioned, what looks like a continuation formation may turn into a reversal signal instead. When the big one does come along, it may not look that attractive initially and traders often find it hard to catch the wave.

As the previous section indicated, price patterns along the way sometimes suggest a move will continue and even offer clues about how far it could go. Obviously, however, trends do not continue forever. What you need are signals that tell you when one trend is ending and another is beginning so you can establish a new position or exit an old one if you have been riding a trend. Technical analysis also reveals those signals, but, again, remember the caveat: Chart analysis is an art and not a science. It is quite likely not all traders will read a chart precisely the same way.

To discover reversal patterns, you'll have to start at exactly the same place as you do for finding continuation patterns—the trend revealed by the trendline, the straight line drawn across the bottoms of price action as an uptrend records a series of higher lows and higher highs or, if it is a downtrend, the straight line drawn across the tops as the market establishes lower highs and lower lows.

As long as the integrity of a trendline is maintained, the trend continues, and position traders may find it risky to go against the trend. In the battle between market bulls and bears, a trendline often becomes a crucial support/resistance factor in determining whether a trend will continue or reverse. The more a trendline is tested and the more points of contact on the trendline, the stronger it is. But all trendlines are penetrated at some point. When that happens, what had been support often becomes stout resistance and vice versa.

Breaking a trendline is the simplest, most basic chart reversal pattern. It could be a false move or a trap, of course, but a trendline break usually signals some new market action you need to watch—a new trend in the opposite direction, a pause or short-term congestion in the direction of the longer trend or perhaps just a shift to a sideways market.

If the crude oil chart here looks familiar, it should: It is the same chart used earlier in the chapter to show continuation patterns (Figure 2.6). After trending down for nearly six months (A), crude oil prices finally bolted above the downtrend line with several wide-range days, forming the "flagpole" that was discussed above in the section on continuation formations. Then, after trending upward for four months, prices broke below the major uptrend lines (B and C), again with wide-range days. It may look almost too simple, but penetrating trendlines of such duration is one of the most significant bar chart reversal formations.

RETRACEMENTS

One subject that needs to be interjected here is the matter of "retracements" or "corrections."

When a trendline has been broken and a new trend begun, chart analysts naturally would like to have a way to project how far the new trend might go and at what point might this new trend be reversed. The section on market structure will go into this topic in more detail, especially in the discussion of Fibonacci numbers and ratios, but this is an important item to introduce here because it is a key part of the analysis of either the continuation or the reversal pattern.

Every time the market acts, it usually reacts, the amount of the reaction depending upon the market's strength or weakness. A flag is an example of a relatively minor reaction against the main trend action as a move continues on its way.

Perhaps the most common possibility for a reaction observed on a number of bar charts is a 50 percent retracement or a "correction" that takes back 50 percent of the market's previous move (Figure 2.7). There is no magic about 50 percent—some use eighths of a previous move or Fibonacci ratios or Gann techniques—but this is a chart point where experience tells some analysts to expect new support or new resistance to turn the new, shorter trend around.

FIGURE 2.6

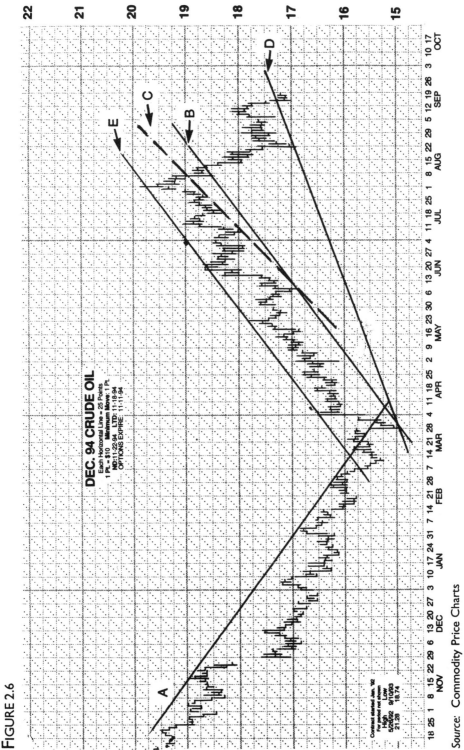

Source: Commodity Price Charts

FIGURE 2.7

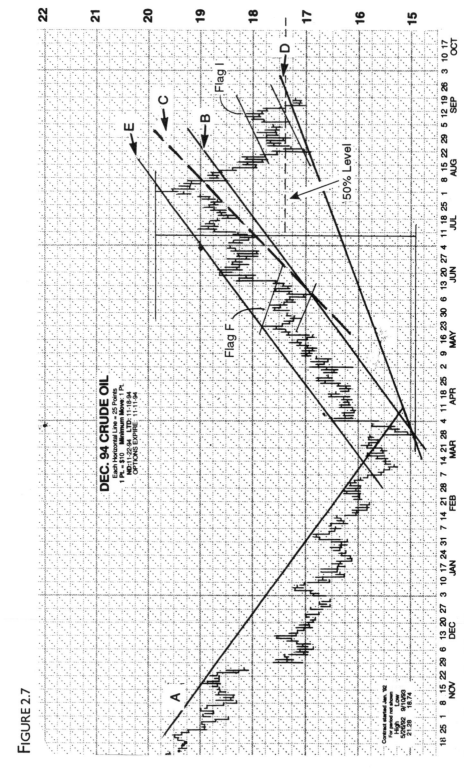

Source: Commodity Price Charts

The major uptrend on the crude oil chart took prices up about $5 per barrel from a little below $15 to almost $20. After prices gave up 25 percent of that move and broke below the major uptrend lines, analysts might look to a 50 percent retracement as the next possible level for support. Also note that the pause (flag I) in the downtrend developed at about the same price level as the pause (flag F) in the uptrend about three months earlier.

Retracement levels can be a clue to continuation or reversal pattern targets. Another related possibility for calculating either a continuation or reversal target is the "measuring gap," discussed above as a continuation pattern because it usually occurs about halfway through a move. If the gap on the crude oil chart at the $17.50-$18 area is a measuring gap, we have already mentioned the continuation pattern's objective would be the $15.50 vicinity—not only the objective for that major move but also the place to watch for the next major turn. One trader's continuation clue may be the basis for another's reversal prediction.

In addition, the measuring gap can also provide a reversal target of another type. Gaps sometimes are tough to "fill"—that is, getting price action to take place at the level where no buying or selling occurred earlier. As markets struggle to get through a gap area, the gap itself sometimes acts as a support or resistance area. Because the measuring gap, by definition, is at the 50 percent retracement level, there may be a couple of arguments for expecting at least some reversal action at this point in the ensuing April-July uptrend, as is suggested by the flag/pause labeled F on the crude oil chart.

KEY REVERSAL

One chart feature that is mentioned often in market commentaries is a "key reversal"—in an uptrend, a market drives to new highs and then closes on or near the low and below the previous period's low; in a downtrend, the market hits new lows and then turns around to close on or near the high and above the previous period's high. While they may be popular in technical trader talk, the problem is key reversals are not very reliable. Some would say they are no better than 50-50 in projecting actual turns.

ISLAND REVERSAL

An "island reversal," which may take several days to develop, tends to be a more reliable bar chart reversal pattern. The price action in an island reversal formation is isolated from what happens before or after that period and usually stands out on a bar chart (Figure 2.8).

FIGURE 2.8

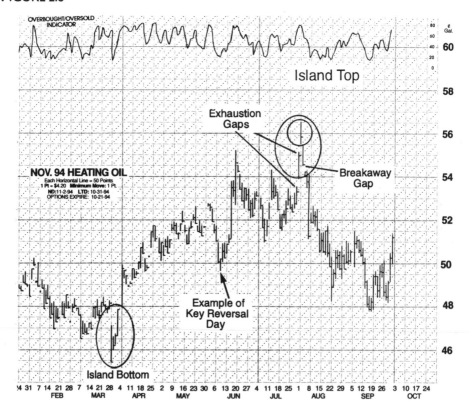

Source: Commodity Price Charts

On the left side going into the formation is an "exhaustion gap," a price level where no trading takes place as traders seem to put everything into one last gasp to continue the trend. The "island" is a bar or several bars that push to a new high or low before closing on a low or high. On the right side is a "breakaway gap," a familiar sight as a market begins to move away from the previous trend and picks up steam, sometimes almost appearing to panic to get away from the old price level.

The crude oil chart we have been using almost produced that type of pattern at the very bottom and the very top. The pattern shows up more clearly on the heating oil chart.

MULTIPLE TOPS, BOTTOMS

Another market axiom suggests, "Sell double or triple tops; buy double or triple bottoms." That assumes, of course, that the concept of support/resistance is driving the market. In that case, whenever prices approach the previous tops or the top of a channel or sideways market, sell; whenever prices approach the previous bottoms or the bottom of a channel or sideways move, buy.

Look back at the gold chart in the continuation formation section (page 14). Selling at A and B and buying at C and D look like good moves, treating the extremes of the channel as reversal targets. But what do you do on the next thrust to a channel line? Will it be the one that breaks out and turns everything around? One approach is that, until a market proves otherwise, treat the shorter moves as reversal opportunities. However, as we cautioned above, you need to be especially nimble if you want to trade these situations: A breakout from a sideways pattern can produce an explosive move in either direction, and what was an extended continuation pattern can become a big reversal move. This is where your money management skills become most important.

Vs AND SAUCERS

Some volatile markets tend to spike up or down and then react in the opposite direction almost immediately in a reversal action that looks like a "V" on a bar chart (Figure 2.9). Others seem to take forever to establish what look like rounding or saucer tops or bottoms. It's hard to catch a V top or bottom, and the saucer top or bottom may be so slow in developing that it will try any trader's patience.

The silver chart features plenty of V-type reversal formations as prices race up and down $3,000 per contract several times within a few weeks. The crude oil chart bottom and top also look like Vs. You have to know your market and use other aspects of technical analysis to get good positions in these types of markets.

On the other hand, copper moved gently lower and then higher over a period of several months before it came out of its rounding bottom (Figure 2.10). Note that as the market moved above the right lip of the saucer, it left a gap as it jumped to higher ground and never looked back.

HEAD-AND-SHOULDERS

Perhaps it's just the name that makes it memorable, but "head-and-shoulders" tops or bottoms are among the best-known chart reversal formations. Sometimes traders stretch to see a head-and-shoulders, and a picture-perfect one is hard to find. However, when a real head-and-shoulders shows up on a chart, the breaking of a "neckline" does tend to provide a good indication the market will follow through in the direction of the breakout.

In a head-and-shoulders top, the market drives to a high and then reacts downward in what may be a flag continuation formation to form the "left shoulder." Then it propels itself back up to a new high to form the "head." As prices fall to complete the head, they hit a low

FIGURE 2.9

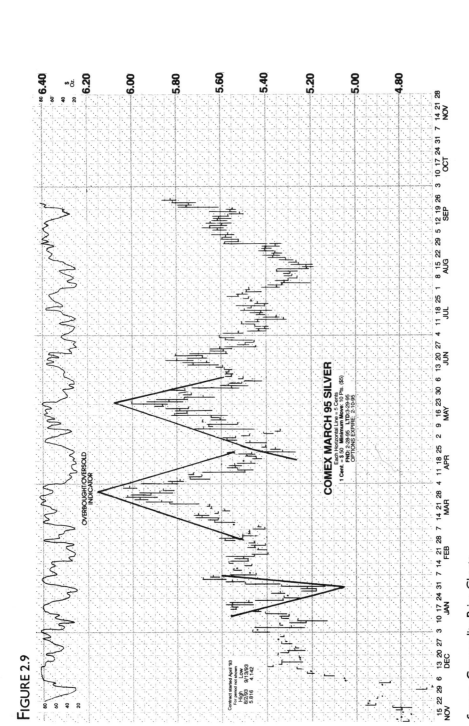

COMEX MARCH 95 SILVER
Each Horizontal Line = 5 Cents
1 Cent = $50 Minimum Move: 10 Pts. ($5)
FND: 2-28-95   LTD:3-29-95
OPTIONS EXPIRE: 2-10-95

OVERBOUGHT/OVERSOLD
INDICATOR

Contract started April '93
For period not shown
High   8/2/93   5.816
Low   9/13/93 4.142

Source: Commodity Price Charts

FIGURE 2.10

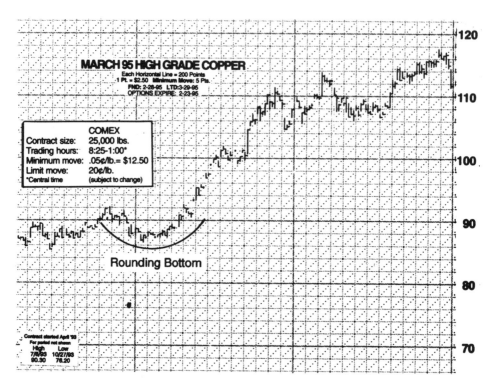

Source: Commodity Price Charts

reasonably in line with the bottom of the move between the left shoulder and the head. Then the market reacts higher again in what may be another flag formation to form the "right shoulder." The top of the right shoulder is somewhat close to the top of the left shoulder but not as high as the head.

The neckline connecting the two lows formed by the shoulders is the key point. As prices move down from the right shoulder and penetrate below this neckline, that's the signal to sell. Some analysts measure the distance from the top of the head to the neckline and project that the bottom will be the same distance below the neckline.

To be a true head-and-shoulders, the formation should come at the end of an extended move, and the pattern of trading volume should be roughly the same as the pattern of prices.

The head-and-shoulders isn't always pretty or exact, as the examples illustrate (Figures 2.11 and 2.12). On the daily cocoa chart, the left

FIGURE 2.11

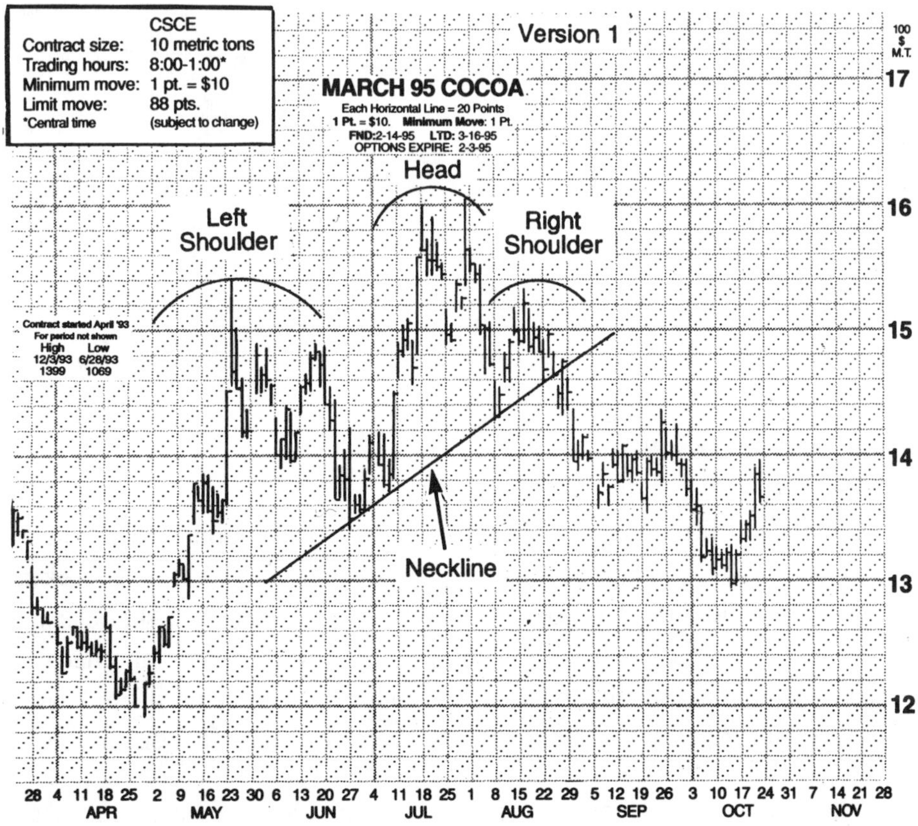

Source: Commodity Price Charts

FIGURE 2.12

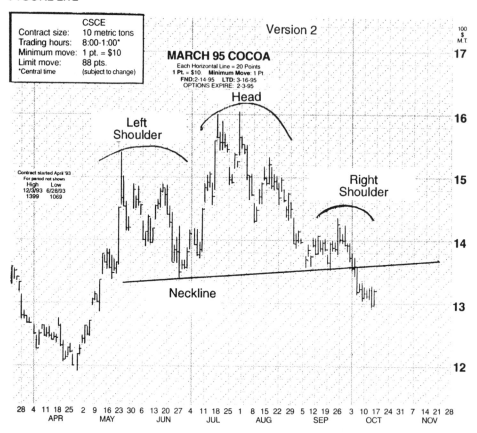

CSCE	
Contract size:	10 metric tons
Trading hours:	8:00-1:00*
Minimum move:	1 pt. = $10
Limit move:	88 pts.
*Central time	(subject to change)

Version 2

MARCH 95 COCOA

Each Horizontal Line = 20 Points
1 Pt. = $10   Minimum Move: 1 Pt
FND:2-14-95   LTD: 3-16-95
OPTIONS EXPIRE: 2-3-95

Head

Left
Shoulder

Right
Shoulder

Contract started April '93
For period not shown
High   Low
12/3/93 6/28/93
1399   1069

Neckline

28 4 11 18 25 2 9 16 23 30 6 13 20 27 4 11 18 25 1 8 15 22 29 5 12 19 26 3 10 17 24 31 7 14 21 28
APR   MAY   JUN   JUL   AUG   SEP   OCT   NOV

Source: Commodity Price Charts

shoulder is a little messy, the head includes a double top, and the neckline is at quite an angle in version 1. But, when the neckline is broken, the price action is what you would expect for a head-and-shoulders. If you "see" the chart a little differently, you might make out another version of a head-and-shoulders with a more horizontal neckline (Figure 2.12). This is just one example of how subjective chart analysis can be.

Using this reversal formation to project a low after the breakout, measure the distance from the top of the head to the neckline and subtract that figure from the point where the breakout of the neckline occurs. On version 1 of the daily cocoa chart, that puts the bottom target at $1,260 per metric ton. Version 2 would put the bottom projection below $1,100, which coincides with the previous bottoms.

The weekly cocoa chart gives you another look at the head-and-shoulders formation in the making (Figure 2.13). It reveals that the earlier bottoms comprised the neckline of what had all the appearances of being another head-and-shoulders top, but it failed to complete the breaking of the neckline. Sometimes you may "see" such obvious formations shaping up, but you need to remain flexible. One advantage of chart analysis is that, even when your formation "fails" to materialize, you can use it to gauge market sentiment and develop appropriate trading strategies for the new conditions. On the cocoa chart, failure of a possible head-and-shoulders to follow through to lower levels indicated a stronger market and higher prices.

FIGURE 2.13

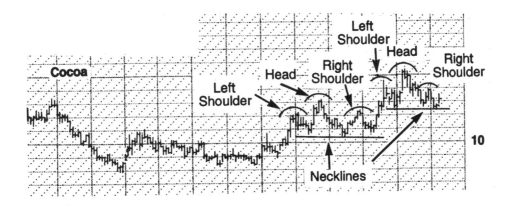

Source: Commodity Price Charts

FIGURE 2.14

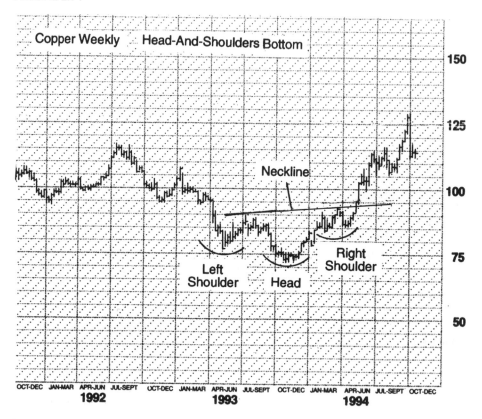

Source: Commodity Price Charts

The weekly copper chart shows that the same principles of a top apply to head-and-shoulders bottoms (Figure 2.14).

MS AND WS, 1-2-3 SWINGS

"M" tops and "W" bottoms that aren't perfect can also be reliable chart reversal patterns. They look quite similar to the double tops or bottoms described above, but the right side of the letter doesn't extend as far as the left side. Ms and Ws also resemble the head-and-shoulders formation but are missing a shoulder. Some analysts identify this formation as a 1-2-3 swing and have based advisory services on tactics for trading these swings.

In an M top such as on the weekly T-bond chart (Figure 2.15), prices hit a high, drop to a reaction low (1), rally back to a high that is not quite as high as the previous high (2) and then fall again. When prices drop below the reaction low, that's the signal to sell (3), placing a stop at the secondary high (2).

FIGURE 2.15

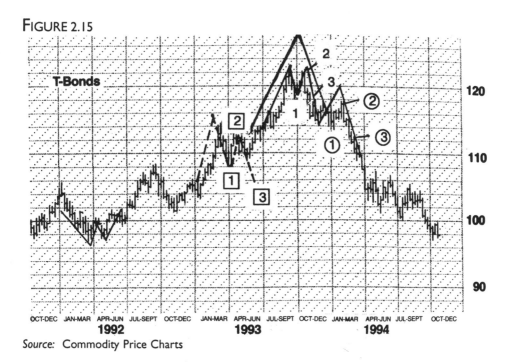

Source: Commodity Price Charts

In this case, two Ms have been superimposed at the top on the chart, using the virtual double top at 122 for the tops of the M for one and combining these two tops into one broader top on a larger M. On the larger M, the slide to below 114 is the reaction low ①, and the weak bounce to 117 is the secondary high ②. The sell signal (or the place to have a sell stop) occurs when prices fall below the reaction low ① under 114 again ③. Once short, the protective stop would be placed at about 118 above the secondary high ②.

When the high at 2 goes higher than the previous high or if 3 does not drop below 1, you negate the M formation and come up with a different plan. A top and an M appeared to be forming in the first half of 1993 (dashed lines) on the weekly T-bond chart. However, your sell stop below the reaction low around 108 ⒈ would not have been activated as prices in a possible leg ③ did not go below the reaction low ⒈ . In fact, as prices moved above the secondary high②, it looked more like a W bottoming formation, and your stop might have been a buy stop instead above the secondary high.

The same 1-2-3 count principles apply to a W bottom: Prices on the daily Kansas City wheat chart (Figure 2.16) drive to a low, bounce back to a reaction high (1), drop off again but not below the first low (2) and then move up above the reaction high (1), providing a buy

FIGURE 2.16

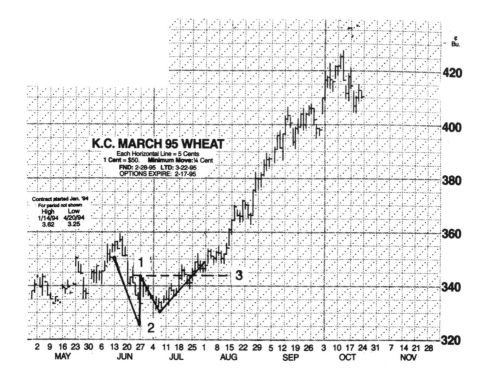

signal (3). Once long, the protective sell stop is placed below the secondary low (2).

RETESTS

Whenever prices penetrate a trendline or the boundaries of a chart formation, note that the market often comes back to the key breakout lines and points to retest them before taking off. This are-you-really-sure-you-want-to-do-this action quite often gives you several opportunities to position yourself at the breakout point, but it also can be a tricky area to trade. Market action may become more volatile as traders react differently to the breakout. Or it may spiral into congestion as the market sorts out what it wants to do. Either way, price action at significant breakouts often is enough to try a trader's patience—and bank account.

Sometimes the best-laid plans of the technical analyst work like a charm. But, remember, this is an art, not an exact science. That's the dilemma you face when you're operating at the hard right edge of the chart without the benefit of hindsight.

CHAPTER 3

BAR CHART APPLICATIONS

Bar chart analysis will permeate much of the discussion throughout this book so you'll see many other examples of bar chart techniques in practical applications. You can also read much more about bar chart analysis in textbooks devoted specifically to that subject.

Over the years, *Commodities/Futures* magazine has printed hundreds of charts and numerous chart-related articles, many dealing with current market situations. This chapter presents highlights from three articles that seem to me to be especially interesting.

The first deals with one of the most perplexing problems and intriguing challenges in technical analysis: When is a chart pattern really a chart pattern, and when is it "successful"? What constitutes a flag formation? How many times do various formations occur? How many times do they "work"? As subjective as chart analysis is, how can you quantify its results, even with today's computers? That was the theme of an article in one of the first issues of *Commodities* in 1972, and it remains an issue for analysts today. That's why I think you'll be interested in Curtis Arnold's article, "Pattern Probability."

The other two articles focus on bar chart analysis for short-term trading and trading during congestion periods, subjects of particular interest to a growing number of more active traders using real-time analytical services. They were written in a paper chart era a few years ago by John Hill and his daughter, Holliston Hill Hurd, but many of the techniques translate well to the live screen.

PATTERN PROBABILITY

By Curtis Arnold

Curtis Arnold is the developer of the Pattern Probability System, a professional money manager and an author. His company, London Financial Inc., is based in Jupiter, Fla. This article appeared in the August 1994 issue of Futures *magazine. It is reproduced with permission.*

Like a modern-day Columbus, a trader charts and navigates based on what he has learned from books and articles. All traders accept the notions uncritically, believing, "If it's written down, it must be true." But then we tear open our daily statement, unfold it and wince. We look back to our monitor and wonder what went wrong.

After a decade of trading, my quest for answers led me on a search for meaningful research on chart patterns. The truth is little original research had been published in this area in 50 years. Modern texts are replete with references to classical chart patterns—often with accompanying guidelines explaining their predictive value. But, curiously, nearly all these texts say the same things.

I found that most authors simply paraphrase the conclusions in Edwards and Magee's *Technical Analysis of Stock Trends.* First published in 1948, it is the chartist's "bible." A single original research source that has been paraphrased by modern commodity authors ad infinitum may be cause for concern for futures traders.

This book was based on stock charts, not commodity charts. In fact, the authors stated their research was not applicable to commodities due to inherent market differences. Yet, countless traders, possibly unaware of the original caveat, have applied the conclusions gained from stock chart research to commodity trading with abandon. Having traded both stocks and commodities, I agreed with Edwards and Magee's sentiment that commodities do not behave like stocks, but a scientific test was required.

Strict definitions were needed to determine success or failure. Patterns had to be quantified mathematically—no eyeballing. Stops and exits had to be defined. After a year of research, evidence piled up supporting my original hypothesi: Classical chart patterns in themselves have little predictive value.

Why did some patterns work perfectly some of the time and not at all on other occasions? It hit me. I was studying each pattern as if it existed in a vacuum. It was only when I placed a pattern in a market scenario or in a particular market structure that the pattern delivered consistent results. Examining each pattern's performance in an uptrend versus a downtrend, I found astonishing differences.

Edwards and Magee explained uptrends and downtrends as mirror images of each other. To them, an ascending triangle in an uptrend offered the same implications as a descending triangle in a downtrend. This is not the case for commodities. Two significant differences exist in reliability between the two—(1) the ascending triangle produces a far higher probability of success than the descending triangle; (2) in commodities, uptrends and downtrends exhibit distinctly different behavior characteristics as do the price patterns within them (due to price pressures unique to futures markets resulting from the trading behaviors of speculators and commercials).

The answer to why patterns sometimes work and sometimes don't came when isolating those market scenarios that must exist before a pattern can be expected to exhibit a high probability of success. Specifically, the patterns were required within the context of an existing trend. Implementing trend filters (simple moving averages), we discriminated between those patterns that occurred within well-defined trends and those that did not.

Success and failure must be strictly defined for a pattern to be useful in actual trading. The pattern breakout becomes the obvious entry point. But what's next? Initial stops must be defined. Just as in real trading, an unlimited amount of risk cannot be assumed in hopes the pattern eventually will work. Finally, assuming the trade does progress favorably, it must be determined when to label it a success.

For each pattern, the probability of success for any upcoming trade is determined as well as the risk/reward ratio. Those patterns that rated high on both scales were selected to become part of the Pattern Probability System (PPS).

HIGHLY RATED PATTERNS

Using the Pattern Probability System, some chart patterns prove to be more reliable indicators in either uptrends or downtrends. A breakdown of the more popular types:

IN UPTRENDS	IN DOWNTRENDS
Symmetrical triangle	Symmetrical triangle
Rectangle	Rectangle
Ascending triangle	Minor tops:
Falling wedge	Double top
Rising wedge	Descending triangle

In addition to the initial components of PPS—trend filters, an entry system and an exit system—a fourth, the money management system, was added. Here, in detail, are the components:

Trend filters—The research clearly indicates patterns show higher probabilities of success when found in established trends. Trend filters simply require an established trend be in place before a pattern is considered for an entry. Moving averages are a simple and consistent way to filter trends. The specific length of the moving average is not that important. PPS dictates only that a signal to enter long occurs above the 28-day moving average and that a signal to enter short occurs below the 28-day moving average.

Entry system—The core of the system, the entry system, consists of the patterns themselves. Their purpose is to enter into the trade with minimal risk. To go long, ascending triangles, rectangles and falling wedges are employed in uptrends. To go short in downtrends, double tops, head-and-shoulder tops and descending triangles are traded only after a minor rally has occurred. The symmetrical triangle, unique among the patterns, is the only one that is traded both in uptrends and downtrends. The rising wedge, though found infrequently, is significant because it is the only pattern that allows the PPS trader to go counter-trend—going short while still in an uptrend. There is no pattern to go long in a downtrend.

Exit system—In PPS, as in many other systems, the exit system may be the most critical component of the entire system. Unlike the entry system that has just one decision to make—when to get in—the exit system must make a critical decision every day: Stay in or get out. And each day the odds change. How much open profit is at risk versus how much potential is still in the trade? These questions are difficult to answer. PPS employs separate algorithms depending on whether the trade is new or has been in progress for some time.

A new trade will fall in the dominion of the "initial stop." This stop, determined by the size and shape of each individual pattern, is placed at the time the trade is entered. If that "mechanical stop" presents too much risk, for example, during a time of high volatility, a money management stop will override it. If price then moves in the right direction or time passes without a significant price move, a "breakeven stop" takes over, reducing risk to zero as quickly as possible.

When a trade has been in progress for some time, the second algorithm—designed to lock in profit—comes into play. This algorithm consists of two subsystems. Current market conditions determine which subsystem is moved into place that day. These subsystems, one price-based and the other time-based, will cause the stop to move sideways, trail at a fixed increment or jump to chart-determined price points.

Remember, an exit system doesn't exist in a vacuum. It must complement your entry system. If your goal is to catch big trends, after you exit, you must have a way to reenter the trade if the trend continues. When PPS is stopped out of a trade, it enters a "reentry alert mode" that will activate a reentry signal should the market suddenly regain strength before a new pattern has the opportunity to form.

PPS trades a diversified, dynamic portfolio that changes constantly. About 30 markets are monitored. The trend filters eliminate trades in markets that are not already in powerful trends. Because the system is only interested in catching large moves, it sacrifices very little by requiring trend confirmation before entering the market.

The market sectors that PPS monitors are interest rates, currencies, metals, grains, softs, fibers and petroleum. Stock indexes and meats are not traded. Systems compatible with the most commodities do not generally work well in stock indexes, which tend to exhibit a "back and fill" nature (support and resistance areas are breached only to see the market quickly retrace into the congestion area). Also, the volatility and contract size would dictate a risk beyond our established limits. The meat complex also is unkind to technically based trend-following approaches.

The logic of PPS is based on four tenets of successful trading: Trade with the trend, cut losses short, let profits run and use good money management. Each component of the system corresponds to one of the tenets: (1) Trend filters dictate that trades are taken only in the direction of the trend; (2) initial and breakeven stops force losses to be cut short; (3) the trailing nature of the exit system allows profits to run; (4) the 2 percent maximum loss per trade rule satisfies prudent money management guidelines and works to assure the account will be able to survive drawdowns.

FIGURE 3.1

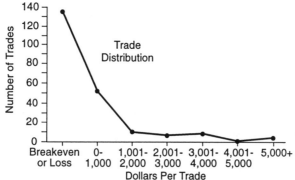

The majority of PPS trades result in breakevens or small losses.

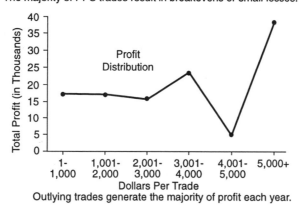

Outlying trades generate the majority of profit each year.

Take a minute to examine some historical charts. You'll find that every year, among those 30 markets, there will be several major moves—at least three, sometimes more. Most trend-following systems will assure that you catch those moves when they occur. The strength of PPS lies in its tight control of losses. The smaller moves, in the $1,000-$3,000 range, normally offset the numerous small losses taken as the system "nibbles" at trends. The outlying trades, in the $5,000-$10,000 range, however, generate the majority of profit each year.

Most of the top traders in the world are described as "blend" traders—that is, they trade primarily with a mechanical system, perhaps 95 percent of the time, but aware that any mechanical system has limitations, they also have a "skill factor" so 5 percent of the time they might employ other means in their trading decisions.

PPS methodology incorporates additional considerations as well, such as internal market composition (open interest breakdowns), basis and spread relationships and first notice/option expiration considerations to vary trade aggressiveness.

USING CONGESTION AREA ANALYSIS TO SET UP FOR BIG MOVES

By Holliston Hill Hurd

Holliston Hill Hurd is the daughter of John Hill (see page 58) and a well-known technical analyst and money manager in her own right. Information for this section is from her article printed in Futures *magazine in April 1985, supplemented by more current charts. It is reproduced here with permission. As an explanation of some bar charting basics, it is as applicable today as it was then.*

Every market, whether it be gold or soybean futures, IBM stock or the Dow Jones Industrial Average, goes through periods of time when neither the bulls nor the bears are in complete control.

In fact, these indecisive periods, known as "congestion areas" or periods of "accumulation" and "distribution," account for as much as 85 percent of the trading time of even the most active contracts. Being able to recognize the different kinds of congestion areas and knowing what they will lead to can help you reap great profits.

A congestion area forms because a market cannot make up its mind which direction it wants to go. Congestion areas are pauses in the market action as many traders step aside to see what will happen next.

While the market is in the congestion area, it fluctuates within a rather well-defined price range. Typically, these areas signal either a continuation of the previous market direction or a reversal in prices. Congestion area analysis can be applied to stocks or commodities or to any time period, whether it be a five-minute, hourly, daily, weekly or monthly price chart.

Markets have definite stages: a runup phase, accumulation, a rundown period and distribution. Accumulation and distribution, or line congestion areas, account for most of the trading time. Despite commodities' reputation for big moves, runs occupy only about 15 percent of the time. That's when the potential for the most profit is available—if you can predict when a market is beginning its run.

FIGURE 3.2

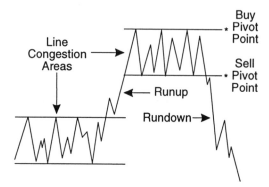

The market is indecisive when the forces of supply and demand keep prices between support and resistance points in a particular trading range. As these forces push from both the top and bottom, they help to form the line congestion area. Once either supply or demand becomes stronger and support and resistance lines are broken, a reversal is imminent. The more time spent in a line congestion area and the larger the congestion area, the more dramatic the run usually will be.

A reversal out of this area would signify that a top or bottom has been established. A close outside the line congestion area would help confirm that a true breakout has occurred. But the technician must beware of false breakouts. Very often, shakeouts, called "springs" and "upthrusts" (or "jabs"), will occur prior to a big move in the opposite direction (see Figure 3.3). Springs and upthrusts pop through a line marking one end of a trading range, then bounce in the other direction through the opposite line, signaling a price reversal.

FIGURE 3.3

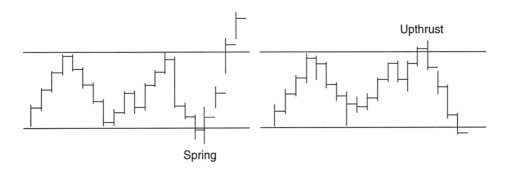

Still looking at the big picture, runs are filled with small congestion areas. Often a runup will form a series of reverse "L" formations, and a rundown will form a series of "L" formations. (The December 1994 S&P 500 stock index futures contract (Figure 3.4) provides an example of these patterns in a runup and rundown.)

In studying these formations, you might notice that the lengths of the real runs, signified by "X," are close to being equal. In addition, the width of the congestion areas, signified by "Y," are also about equal. In a long run, two or more of these segments could be averaged to predict the next segment in the move. (The S&P futures market is generally more erratic and volatile than other markets, but in a more typical market, the "X" and "Y" often are also close to being equal in size. Thus, the technician could use either the real run or the small congestion area to predict the extent of the next segment.)

However, it is important to know the different kinds of small congestion areas that occur so you can anticipate the end of a move and predict a reversal. There are five kinds of small congestion areas.

The first two are the descending and ascending congestion channel areas (see Figure 3.5). These patterns can occur after either a rundown

FIGURE 3.4

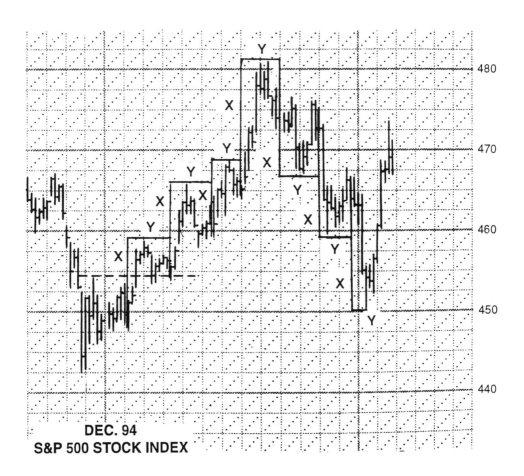

DEC. 94
S&P 500 STOCK INDEX

Source: Commodity Price Charts

FIGURE 3.5

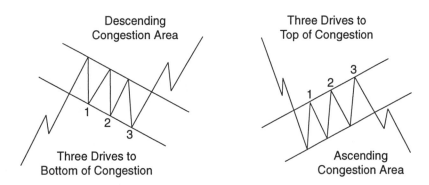

or during a runup. Often, these two kinds of congestion areas form with three drives to the top or bottom in the congestion area before the breakout occurs. The descending congestion area (some call it a flag) frequently signals a move to the upside; the ascending congestion area typically signals an imminent move to the downside when the trendline is broken.

Three of the small congestion areas are in the form of triangle formations. (All three types are visible on the copper chart—see Figure 3.6.) Triangles usually are pauses in a runup or rundown. The market will break out of the pattern and continue in the same direction it was going before the triangle was formed.

The diminishing triangle is constructed when the market makes a correction. It is distinguished by smaller and smaller range days moving out to the apex of the triangle. But a breakout usually occurs before the apex is formed.

The support triangle is found most often in a downmove. The market reaches a support point it cannot break through. Prices bounce off this level two or three times but rally less and less each time. If the market can break through the support level, a breakout is possible.

The opposite of this triangle is the resistance triangle. The resistance triangle usually occurs in an upmove and has a line of resistance forming the top of the triangle. This occurs because the market tests this resistance level several times and falls back down less and less each time. A rise above the resistance level might mean a breakout.

However, breakouts must meet certain criteria to be true breakouts. Predicting such breakouts is the goal of congestion area analysis. Here are some factors you should observe to have a true breakout:

❑ Increased volume. Either the bulls or bears have won out, and a market decision has been made. People on the sidelines get back into the market, increasing volume.

❑ Because false breakouts occur often, a close above or below the congestion area is necessary for confirmation.

❑ Two or three days of follow-through price action should accompany the breakout.

❑ A significant move above or below the pivot point of the particular congestion area is needed (see pivot points indicated on diagrams).

❑ No immediate move back into the congestion area price range should occur within four to six days.

Once you have defined congestion areas and breakouts on the charts, how can you use this analysis to profit? The hardest part, first of all, is recognizing a congestion area and knowing which kind it is. Looking at the overall picture can help you here. If the market has just had a major move down, a bottom is likely to form. In that case, look for corrective, indecisive price action. During a run, look for pauses—triangles—or for some kind of reversal signal such as congestion channels.

FIGURE 3.6

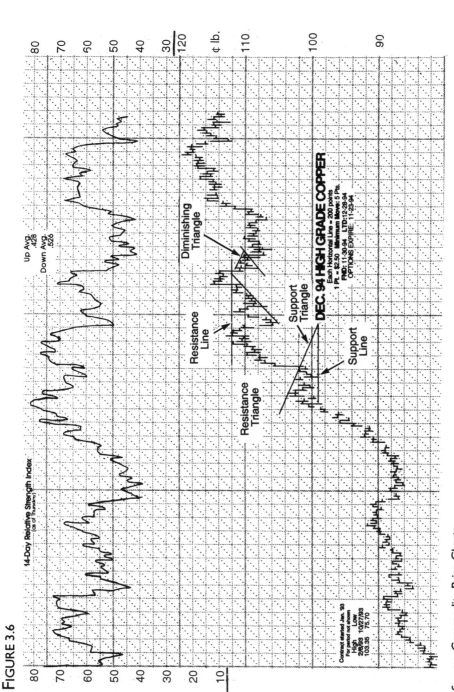

Source: Commodity Price Charts

If you identify a line congestion area, watch for springs, upthrusts and reversal periods to signal breakouts. Take a position when a support or resistance level is broken. Put a stop-loss at the midrange of the congestion area or at the support or resistance level. A reversal along with a stop-loss would be smart in the event the breakout is false and is really a spring or uptrhrust, suggesting a move in the opposite direction is imminent.

When you identify descending or ascending congestion areas, take a position when the market crosses the channel line or the pivot point line. A move above or below the left pivot line signifies a stronger breakout. The stop on this trade should be put at the right pivot point line (see Figure 3.7).

Diminishing triangles are often indecisive. Buy or sell on a move above or below the corners of the triangle. Put a stop-loss and a possible reversal at the opposite corner.

When a support or resistance triangle forms, buy or sell when the market crosses the respective line. Put a stop-loss and reversal at the pivot point line drawn off the top or bottom of the triangle, depending on which kind of triangle you have.

FIGURE 3.7

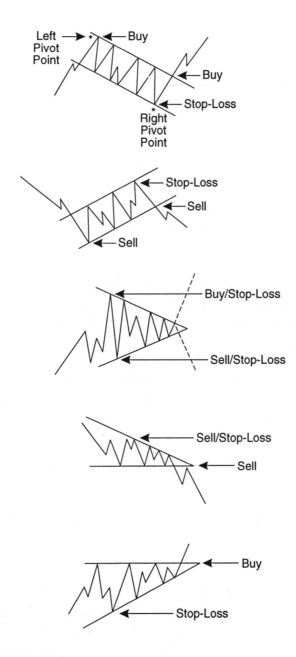

SHORT-TERM CHART REVERSAL PATTERNS

By John R. Hill

The following comes from an article written by John R. Hill in the February 1979 issue of Commodities *magazine as adapted from Hill's book,* Stock and Commodity Market Trend Trading by Advanced Technical Analysis. *Hill is chairman of Futures Truth Co. in Hendersonville, N.C. Originally a chemical engineer, he was able to use profits from futures trading to set up companies to study market action in great detail, develop trading software and manage money. Hill and his associates have probably analyzed and tested more trading methods and systems since the late 1950s than any other organization. Reports of their research on how systems actually performed in the marketplace are published in the bi-monthly* Futures Truth *newsletter.*

Reversal signals on a bar chart may be based on only a few days of price action. However, a word of caution is in order: You should always look at these signals in the context of the overall chart pattern and other indicators and should not use them alone.

If you see any of the following patterns forming against the prevailing trend, it initially indicates only the beginning of a congestion period. For a true reversal, you need more evidence. Always look for follow-through action to verify the signal or for other signs that the signal may be invalid and that trading positions based on them should be abandoned.

Here are nine very basic chart patterns that signal a change in trend:

1. Island reversal

For a sign of topping action, the high, low and close of the period preceding and the period following the high day are entirely below the range of the high day. The last day's action should reverse at least two closes, and the close should be below the opening and mid-range for that day. (On the bottom, of course, the lows on the preceding and following days should both be higher than the high on the low day.)

FIGURE 3.8   ISLAND REVERSAL

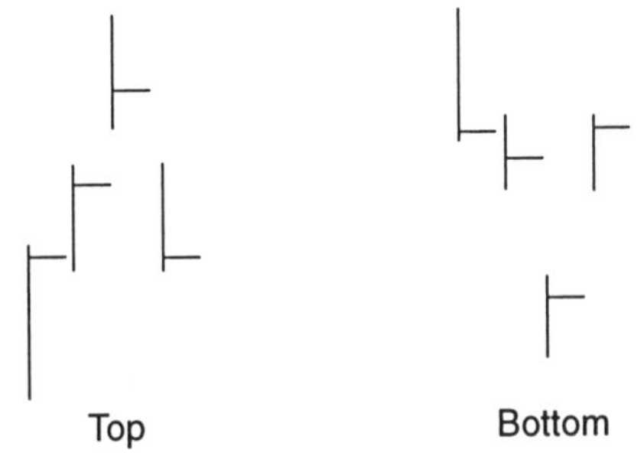

Top   Bottom

This is one of the strongest types of formations. The "island" can be one or many days. It represents a drastic change in sentiment and leaves one side trapped. This losing side will generally cover either on this day or on the next reaction.

2. **Reversal gap**

This is also known as a breakaway gap. In a bottom formation, the low on the last day is entirely above the preceding day's action. The close should reverse at least two closes and close above the opening price and the mid-range for the day.

FIGURE 3.9   REVERSAL GAP

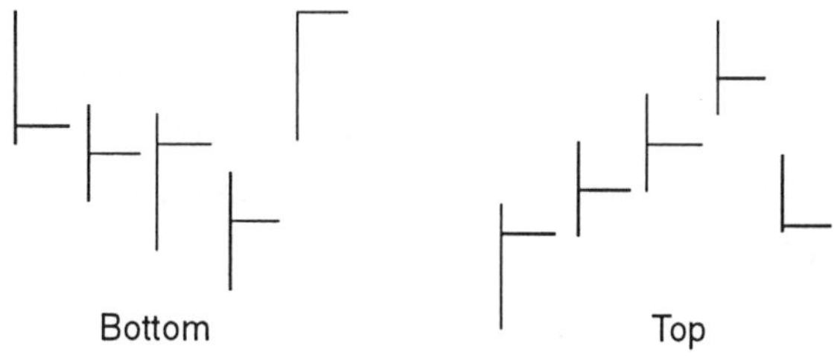

Bottom   Top

Reversal gaps can be one of the strongest indicators of a reversal in trend and are seldom false. They suggest a sudden strong change in sentiment. This signal is at its best when preceding market action shows a narrowing price range and volume has been drying up.

3. Pattern gap

This pattern is similar to the reversal gap except that the low for the last day extends down into the previous day's range (in the bottom formation). The low is above the previous day's close. The close is above the previous day's high and above the opening and mid-range of the last day. The close should also reverse at least two closes.

FIGURE 3.10   PATTERN GAP

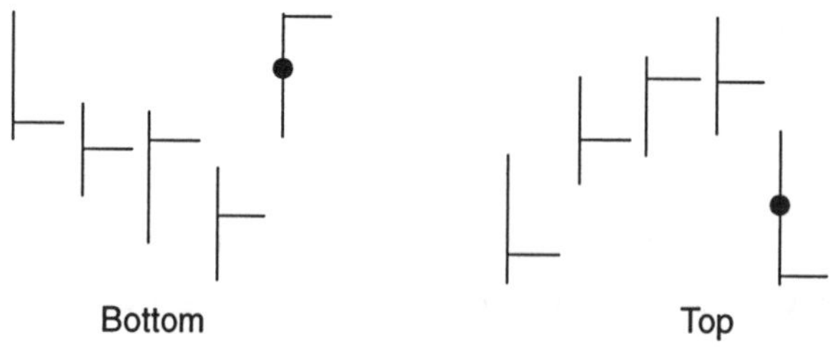

Bottom   Top

4. Three-day high reversal

Three days of relatively narrow price ranges are followed by a day with a wide range and a close that is above the high of the previous three days (in a bottom formation). The close should be above the opening and mid-range.

FIGURE 3.11   THREE-DAY HIGH REVERSAL

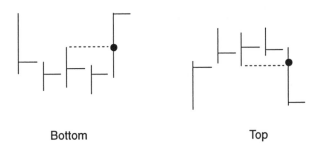

Bottom   Top

5.   Three-day close reversal

The close is above the previous three closes (in a bottom formation).
The high is above the high of the previous three days, and the low is
above the low of the last three days. The close should be above the
opening and the mid-range, and the range should be larger than the
average range of the previous three days.

FIGURE 3.12   THREE-DAY CLOSE REVERSAL

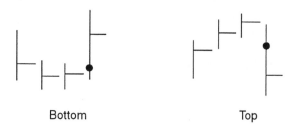

Bottom   Top

6. Four-day close reversal

A close on the fifth day is above the four previous closes (in a bottom formation). The close should also be above the opening and mid-range for the day. The four closes should be in close proximity to each other.

FIGURE 3.13   FOUR-DAY CLOSE REVERSAL

Bottom   Top

Not Valid

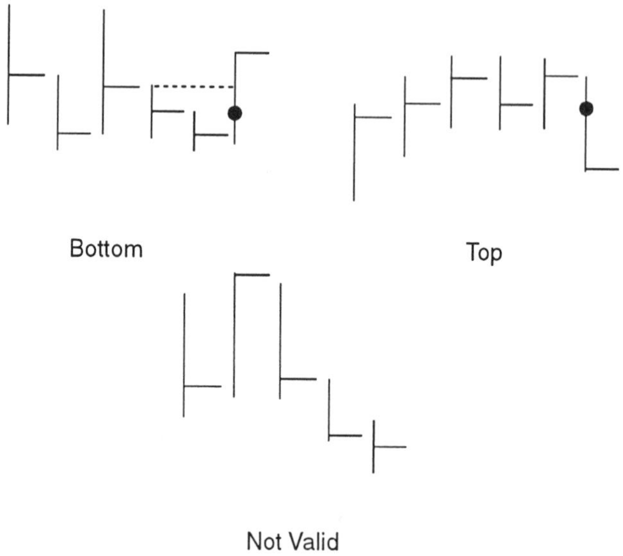

7. Top or bottom tails

In a bottoming formation, the market closes higher for three days in the top part of the trading range each day. On a top, the market closes lower for three days near the bottom of the trading range.

FIGURE 3.14   TOP OR BOTTOM TAILS

Bottom   Top

On a top, such a formation indicates supplies coming in. The first time it does this is not too significant. However, if this happens two or more times, it indicates important supply influence. It is a greater sign of weakness if each successive tail is at a lower level and volume picks up.

8. **Narrow range after advance or decline**

This formation requires a narrow range day following a sharply accelerated price movement. After the narrow range day, an opposite movement then takes place with a widening range.

In a topping formation, the close on the last day should be below mid-range, below the opening and below the low of the top narrow range day. At least two closes should be reversed. If a market is moving up and then has a sharply accelerated movement followed by a narrow range day, it indicates buyer power is exhausted temporarily. There is a vaccuum as nervous shorts have all covered. A temporary end of the move is almost assured if you have action as shown after a narrow range day. This is a case of supply overcoming demand.

FIGURE 3.15   NARROW RANGE AFTER ADVANCE OR DECLINE

Bottom   Top

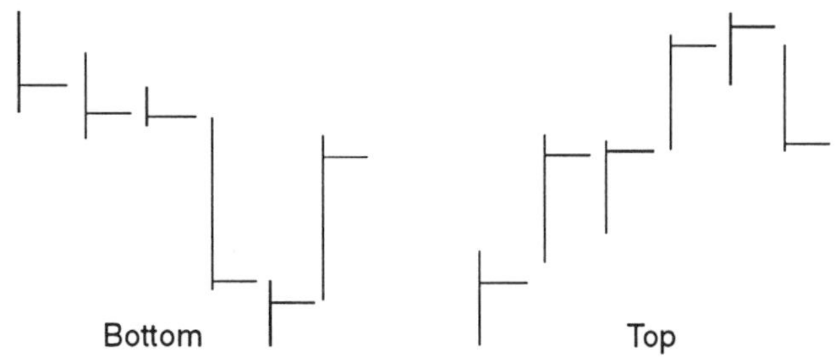

9. **New five-day highs and closes**

The market makes new highs for five successive days (in this case, ignore inside days). Closes should accompany the new highs upward.

This indicates a shifting of momentum to the upside. The market is generally a purchase on the first reaction.

FIGURE 3.16   NEW FIVE-DAY HIGHS AND CLOSES

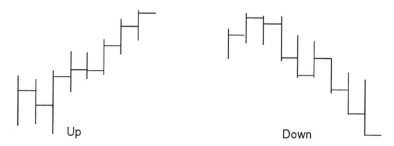

UPTHRUST REVERSAL PATTERNS

Of course, sometimes price action that appears to be a change in trend leads to bull and bear traps. These traps can be avoided and used to your advantage.

FIGURE 3.17   UPTHRUST REVERSAL PATTERNS

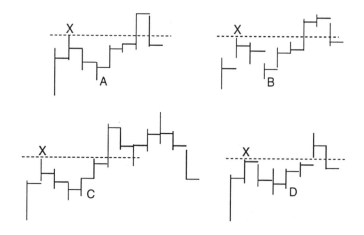

One example is the upthrust reversal pattern. Requirements for this pattern include:

❑ The market must have a prior pivot point (X on the charts).

❑ Market action takes the price above the pivot point.

❑ A widespread reversal ensues as follows:

   1. Two previous closes are reversed.

   2. The close is below the pivot point.

   3. The close is below the opening and mid-range.

   4. The range should be greater than for the previous day's action.

   5. It is best when heavy volume is present on the breakout, which would indicate abundant supply.

A. In this example, one day's action breaks above a previous rally top, volume shows an increase, and the close is above a previous rally top. However, on the following day, the market may open slightly higher and then proceed to sell off the rest of the day, closing near the bottom, below the previous day's low.

B. It takes two days for the supply forces to overcome demand in this example. On the first day, you have breakout action above a previous rally top. The second day is generally characterized by heavy volume and a narrow range or spread. On the third day, supply forces win the battle. The commodity sells off all day, and the daily range increases. The close is on or near the low of the day and below the close of the day when the move broke out of the formation.

C. In this example, the commodity exceeds a previous rally top by a good margin—and all the technicians talk about the big breakout. However, there is no follow-through the next day. This is followed by a number of inside days (inside the range of the breakout day).

You may see an attempt to go through the top, but when this fails, the demand forces give up. You have a day of heavy supply action, which sells back down below the rally top, closes at or near the bottom and below the low of the breakout day.

D. In this case, the previous rally top is exceeded by a gap. The day's action shows a narrow range and heavy volume, indicating abundant supply. Demand forces give up the following day. The daily range increases, and the close is at or near the low, below the rally top and below the close on the day just preceding the breakout.

SPRING REVERSAL PATTERNS

Spring reversal patterns provide similar action on the bottom. The requirements for these patterns follow those of upthrust reversal patterns:

❑ The market must have a prior pivot point.

❑ Price action takes place below the pivot point.

❑ A widespread reversal ensues as follows:

FIGURE 3.18   SPRING REVERSAL PATTERNS

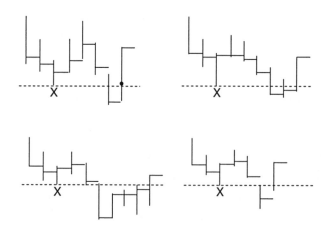

1. Two previous closes are reversed.

2. The close is above the pivot point.

3. The close is above the opening and mid-range.

4. The range should be greater than for the previous day's action.

When a market goes below a previous minor low and then springs up to a new high on widening ranges and increasing volume, it indicates good quality demand and should be bought on the first reaction. It suggests the entire recent market action has been a process of accumulation.

CHAPTER 4

THE LONG-TERM ANALYSIS DILEMMA

Stock market traders who want a historical view of a particular stock can pick up a long-term chart of that stock and get an accurate picture of its price for as long as the company has existed. There may be adjustments for stock splits or other reasons, but it's relatively easy to get a continuous price series for stocks.

The same is true for a stock index, although there may be notations or wobbles where stocks have been added or deleted due to mergers or economic factors, or for cash prices of most commodities and financial instruments.

But futures pose a special problem for an analyst who wants to apply traditional analytical techniques to several years of historical price data at once. That's because futures contracts continually expire, leaving no continuous price series other than the cash price for the underlying commodity or instrument.

The most commonly used long-term weekly or monthly bar charts for futures are based on prices of the spot or nearest futures month until it expires. As one month expires, the chart picks up prices for the next futures contract month until it expires, then moves on to the next month, etc. A number of chart services provide such nearest futures price series charts.

The major problem, however, is that these charts sometimes have huge price changes when the nearby contract expires and the chart is forced to shift to the next delivery month. The weekly Eurodollar chart (Figure 4.1), for example, seems to show significant price collapses at the end of each quarter in 1994. Prices indeed were declining, but much of what looks like a small crash can be attributed to changes in futures contract months as the nearest futures month expired.

FIGURE 4.1   EURODOLLAR CHART

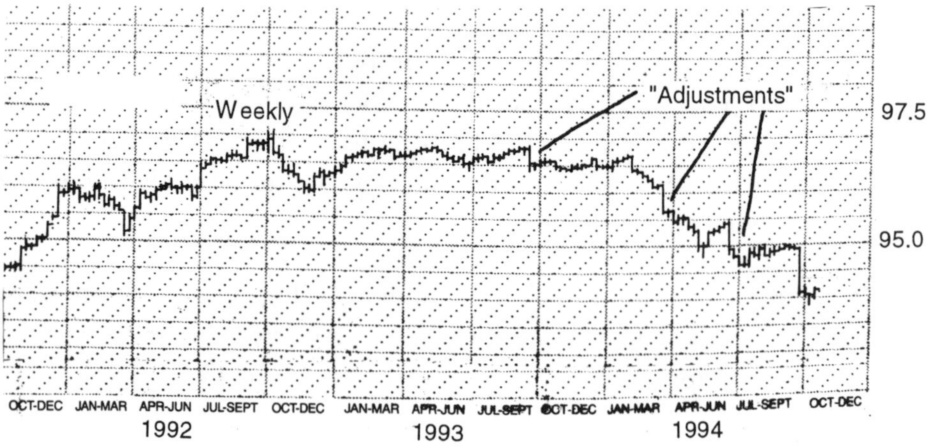

Source: Commodity Price Charts

In some cases, these changes may not be too significant in the overall scheme of analysis. For commodities such as pork bellies, where the next futures month after August is February, or the grains, where the shift in contract months may reflect two totally different crop seasons, the price changes can be dramatic. For the long-term technical analyst, these drastic changes in price can distort trading-model results by triggering incorrect signals.

To resolve some of these problems and to produce a better long-term picture of futures prices, several approaches attempt to produce a smooth representation of long-term futures prices without the distortions caused by the transition from one contract month to the next. The best-known is the "perpetual contract." Another is the "continua" future.

While these "contracts" smooth out price changes, they do require you to keep another set of figures. Also, keep in mind these are derived contracts, not real contracts with actual tradable numbers. After doing your analysis on these charts, you have to transfer all of your conclusions to an actual futures contract to implement any trading decision. The translation from theory to reality may not be exact.

These approaches do address the perplexing problems of long-term technical analysis on futures charts, but they may not be the final answer.

THE PERPETUAL CONTRACT

By Robert Pelletier

Robert Pelletier is president of Commodity Systems Inc. (CSI) in Boca Raton, Fla., for many years a leading supplier of data on futures and stocks. The following is taken from an article by Pelletier, the developer of the perpetual contract, in the March 1983 issue of Commodities *magazine. Reproduced with permission.*

The perpetual contract is calculated as a time-weighted average of the two distinct futures contracts (excluding the thinly traded contracts) that surround a given period of time in the future. Traders with a sharp pencil and graph paper can compute it themselves every day, or they can get data by phone.

Daily and historical data on this simulated time series from two futures contracts combine to provide a perpetual contract which does not expire. It can be in the center of liquidity, reflects constant carrying charges and interest rates and may provide a simultaneous flavoring of old and new crop futures. You remain in the center of trader activity by moving from one contract to the next when open interest becomes greater than the previous contract.

The concept of the perpetual contract is not new. Banks quote interest rates as forward obligations for time periods 30, 60 or 90 days in the future. The London Metal Exchange similarly quotes forward prices for metals such as copper, tin, lead or zinc on a 90-day forward basis, and some foreign currencies are often based on constant time forward periods. The perpetual contract permits all commodities to be analyzed in the same way.

The perpetual contract may be calculated for periods from 2 to 11 months in the future. It can be used to analyze the market from a traditional long or short view. It also can be used to evaluate spread opportunities.

If you want to use the perpetual contract for technical trading purposes, you probably want to follow signals developed by the perpetual that roughly coincides with the delivery month you choose to trade. In other words, if you are accustomed to trading contracts from two to four months to maturity, then you should follow the two-, three- or four-month forward perpetual contract.

Use shorter-term perpetuals for metals, currencies, government debt instruments and other nonagricultural items. It is highly desirable to monitor market action close to delivery in these markets.

Longer time-forward perpetuals are better for agricultural products because you may want to observe the combined effects of both old and new crops simultaneously. In markets where, historically, there is a pronounced difference between old and new crop price movement, perpetuals should be used sparingly. Such use requires analyzing both close and further out perpetuals. You may uncover spread opportunities using the difference between any two perpetual contracts.

Avoid perpetual contracts for monthly periods forward less than the maximum elapsed time between any pair of adjacent delivery months. Any currency or financial futures should not use a two-month perpetual, for example, because active delivery months of these futures are spaced three months apart. Similarly, perpetual contracts should not be less than six months forward for pork bellies because of the six-month gap in active deliveries between the August and February contracts.

To illustrate how to calculate a perpetual contract, assume you're analyzing Comex copper futures on Aug. 11. Three months forward (actually 91 calendar days to the computer) would be Nov. 10. The active contracts expiring immediately before and after that date are the September and December futures contracts (there are contracts for the intervening months, but volume usually is light and they are not recommended for trading).

Assume closing prices on Aug. 11 are $1.09 per lb. for September futures and $1.1110 per lb. for December futures. Using a simple graph which has price and time axis, plot those prices on the dates when the futures contracts expire. Then connect the two closing prices with a straight line. Where a vertical line from the previously selected three-months-ahead date intersects with the straight line is the price quote for the perpetual contract.

The graphically computed three-month forward price of $1.1004 per lb. (see Figure 4.2) is slightly closer to the September futures price because Nov. 10 is slightly closer to Sept. 28, the September contract expiration date, than to Dec. 28, December's expiration date.

FIGURE 4.2   CALCULATING A PERPETUAL CONTRACT

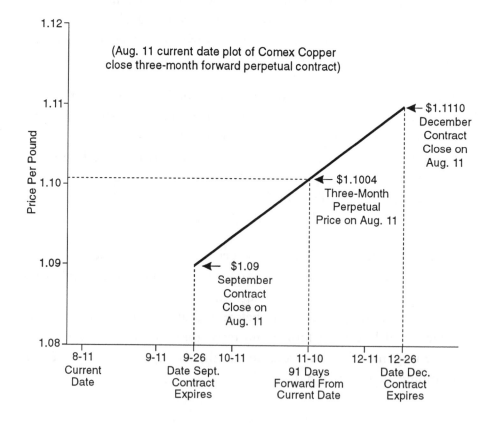

The same graphical calculations must be performed for the opening, high and low prices to get a complete picture of the perpetual contract.

Although the perpetual contract means tracking another set of figures, here are some reasons why you may find the effort worthwhile:

❑ Replaces nearest futures prices contracts (with their potentially drastic differences in prices) as a medium for analysis.

❑ Substitutes as a stationary market barometer. You can control the forward positioning of your market barometer by choosing any appropriate perpetual contract from 2 to 11 months ahead. Because of the inherent stationarity of the resulting time series, you can monitor the market where volume and liquidity are nearly constant and let the more active contracts tell you when trades should be made.

❑ Uncovers market opportunities with minimal effort. You can monitor and compare several markets by using only one time series for each. This relaxes the need to process many different contracts of each commodity because only one perpetual contract produces the desired objective.

❑ Simplifies spread trading. Traditional spread traders have too little data upon which to base a decision because they have to wait until both contracts are trading. The nature of spread analysis shortens even further the time for a price series to be analyzed. Perpetual contracts can be used to analyze the strength or weakness of near and distant contracts simultaneously, a distinct advantage to spread traders. You do not have to restart the analysis exercise every time the nearby contract expires. The perpetual contract immediately assesses which contract is stronger.

❑ Allows flexibility. To compute stops, buy or sell points or objectives, you only need to apply the same differentials computed with the perpetual contract to the actual futures contract you wish to trade. You follow only the signals given by the perpetual contract. Knowing simply to be long or short leaves you free to concentrate on market strategy and choose the most suitable contract to trade.

❑ Helps pick trades with the most promising profits. Conventional contracts of different commodities do not always coincide closely enough to allow an adequate study of profit potential from the various trade alternatives. The ever-present problem of contract longevity also may cut your analysis short. The ability to compare commodities on the same forward basis over an extended period of time makes the perpetual contract an attractive alternative.

❑ Allows economical use of data. The perpetual contract can begin at any time in the past, even before the first day of trading of the contract in which you will take a position. Therefore, you never lose any data getting started. Moving average systems for conventional contracts, for example, need at least as many days of data input at the start as the largest moving average used in the system before that system's signals can be traded.

Of course, the perpetual contract also has some disadvantages:

❑ Price data cannot be found in newspapers. Prices generated must be computed and, therefore, are not published by exchanges or newspapers.

❑ Account equity calculations are approximate. Because perpetual contract prices are not actual futures prices, you cannot accurately compute account equity changes. You can only approximate figures.

❑ Intraday stops and objectives are difficult to assess. If you use the perpetual contract to compute trading points, you must do so on an approximate basis. If the perpetual contract requires a sell-stop 50 points below the current day's close, then the futures contract in which the position is actually held should also require a 50-point stop below its close. Because of the subtle averaging process required when calculating the perpetual contract, the 50-point stop could be in error by 5 percent or more, and care must be taken when making such projections.

THE CONTINUA CONTRACT

By Donald Jones

Donald Jones is president of CISCO (Commodity Information Services Co.), a commodity data and research service in Chicago. The following is extracted from an article by Jones and Norman Strahm in the November 1983 issue of Futures *magazine. Reproduced with permission.*

The continua future adjusts prices of each futures contract uniformly so that on the day of the switch the adjusted settlement of the contract being abandoned exactly matches the adjusted settlement of the same day of the next futures contract.

All prices within each contract are adjusted by the same amount—the "cumulative shift." This system retains all the basic relationships between prices within a commodity, as well as correctly reflecting equity changes in a switch from one contract to another.

In the design or application of an automatic trading model, price data is used to accomplish two functions: (1) generate buy and sell trade signals and (2) calculate equity changes implied by the trade signals. The same data series need not be used to perform both functions.

For instance, trade signals for T-bonds might be generated from an index formed from several Treasury instruments, but the equity consequences of trading T-bonds would have to be calculated using appropriate T-bond prices. However, it is extremely convenient to use the same data series to perform both functions.

All three versions of continuous data (nearest futures, perpetual and continua contracts) could be used for the first function, but only the continua data series accurately performs the second.

An analyst's goal may be to extract the "signature" of a commodity—a cyclic time period, an optimal stop point, a characteristic reversal pattern, etc. This is accomplished by studying the past behavior of the commodity over sufficiently long periods so that the significant events that go into the commodities' signature are all experienced.

Included, of course, would be periods of high volatility, periods of low volatility, periods of flatness, periods of trending, short-term squeezes, etc. Because signatures are generally poorly defined over the time frame of one futures contract—say, a year or less—several futures contracts of data are needed to extract them. Overcoming the noise (random fluctuation) which masks the signature requires long strings of data.

In some instances, extracting the signature is made easier by some averaging or data-smoothing process such as an averaging over several different delivery months. As an illustration, you can find a cyclic periodicity more easily from an oscillator than from raw data. That's because the averaging process reduces the noise without distorting the period as long as the time scales of the moving average filters are far from the time scale of the cycle.

In other cases, an averaging process can be expected to destroy some of the desired information. A signature obtained from smoothed data, such as data filtered through a moving average or averaged like the perpetual data, may be suspected of lacking important features. For instance, if stops are to be used in trading real life contracts, a determination of ideal stops using averaged data can be very misleading.

The perpetual contract employs an averaging process over the first two liquid futures months. The continua contract has no such averaging. However, if it is desired, several versions of averaging can be incorporated.

One scheme recognizes that the continua contract is "spread-adjusted" continuous data. The amount of spread adjustment in the switching process is just the value of the spread between the settlement prices of two contracts on the day of the switch.

To make the result less sensitive to the particular value of the spread on that one day, the analyst effectively may wish to switch, say, one-tenth of a contract each day for 10 successive days. Equivalently, the continuous price series then reflects the equity of a long position of 10 contracts in which one contract is switched each day for 10 days (prices, however, are expressed on a one-contract basis).

A different sort of averaging is accomplished with a series which represents one (or several) contracts in each of, say, two, three or four expiration months. Each contract is switched from the nearby month to the next unused expiration month.

As these schemes illustrate, when averaging is desired, a trade-off is necessary in that the continua contract reflects multiple positions rather than a single position. These schemes incorporate the continua futures philosophy that the price series is most useful if it actually shows carrying charges and reflects the equity of some particular trading sequence just as a normal bar chart reflects the equity of a continuously held long position. Neither the nearest futures nor the perpetual contract reflect the equity of any trading sequence.

To show explicitly how the continua data are developed, we will use an example starting with December T-bill futures and rolling successively into the March and then the June contracts. The respective settlements are:

December	Nov. 30	91.65
March	Nov. 30	91.11
March	Feb. 28	92.12
June	Feb. 28	92.19

Starting with the December contract through Nov. 30, the cumulative shift is zero, and there is no change in prices. On Nov. 30. roll into the

March contract. The cumulative shift is 0.54 (the December contract price of 91.65 minus the March price of 91.11). All March prices are incresed by that amount through Feb. 28, when the adjusted settlement is 92.66 (actual price of 92.12 plus 0.54). On the same day, the June settlement is 92.19 for a new shift of 0.47 (92.66 minus 92.19). This procedure continues for as long as the continua data file is to be developed.

Because all translations are merely additions or subtractions, it is an easy matter to adjust all prices so the latest futures contract has its actual (unshifted) value and the further back ones are shifted. This can be accomplished by merely taking the latest cumulative shift and adjusting all prices in the array by that amount.

You might wish to do this to make prices fit the chart of the latest futures contract. In any case, all charts of all futures of continua data have exactly the same form as their raw data counterparts because there is only a uniform translation up or down.

The continua approach is very convenient for the trader who does not have access to a computer. The most complex operation is an addition or subtraction, and the same quantity is used for an entire futures array. This system is even more appropriate for computer-based analysis because a huge amount of data can be covered.

CHAPTER 5

POINT-AND-FIGURE CHARTS: PRICE WITHOUT TIME

Bar charts are clearly the most widely used type of chart, but another way to depict prices is the point-and-figure chart. While bar charts have one price bar showing the high-low-close for each time period, the point-and-figure chart does not have a time element, and it places no emphasis on the open or close as other charts do. On these charts, time is irrelevant; it is only the specific price points for the high or the low of the time period that matter.

Initially, this style of charting may look more complex than trying to decipher bar chart formations, but it may actually make your trading decisions easier because point-and-figure charts give you specific prices at which to buy and sell without having to interpret signals from a formation.

Price action on a point-and-figure chart is indicated by a series of Xs and Os within boxes on graph paper—a vertical column of Xs when the market is going up, another vertical column of Os when it is moving down. Unlike a bar chart, which has a bar for each time period, you may go days or even weeks without making any entry at all on a point-and-figure chart.

To start a point-and-figure chart, two of the most crucial decisions you must make come right at the beginning:

❑ What value should you give to each box or price unit?

❑ How many boxes or price units should it take to indicate a reversal from the Xs of an uptrend to the Os of a downtrend?

Each contract you trade will have different values, depending on a variety of factors. Once you get into point-and-figure charting, you will probably want to optimize each of these factors, keeping in mind that the optimum values are quite likely to change as market conditions change.

Let's assume it's the beginning of 1994 and you make a resolution to start a point-and-figure chart for the December Eurodollar futures contract. You may not be sure what the value of each box should be or the number of boxes it should take for a reversal, but, for purposes of illustration, we'll go along with the values established by *Commodity Price Charts*: Each box will have a value of 10 points and it will take three boxes or 30 points for a reversal—a 10 by 3 chart. (See Figure 5.1)

(If you do not want to keep your own charts, several chart services provide point-and-figure charts along with other indicators weekly. Some on-line services and technical analysis software programs also offer point-and-figure charting).

As you start the process for the December Eurodollar, you don't know whether the first column will be Xs for an uptrend or Os for a downtrend. Look at the price range for the day—the spread between the high and the low. If the range covers three or more boxes and the close is above mid-range, you would begin with a column of Xs. If the range covers three or more boxes and the close is below mid-range, you would begin with a column of Os.

FIGURE 5.1

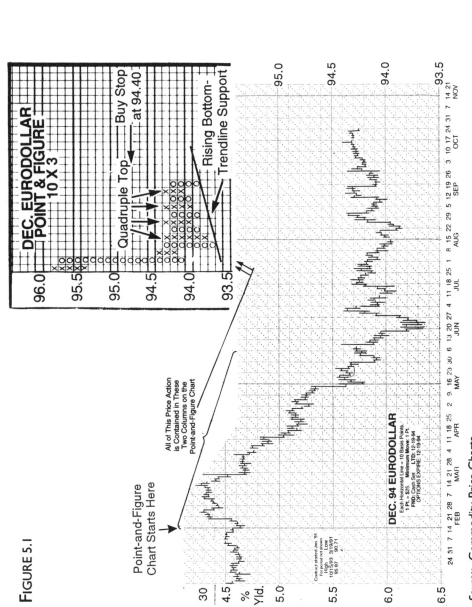

Source: Commodity Price Charts

In the Eurodollar example, the only price box touched initially is 95.40. Because you don't know the direction yet, put a dot in that box on the first day. That's the only mark you have for several days. Then at the end of the first week, you have a wider ranging day that goes through 95.50 and 95.60. Now you have three boxes you can fill in. The close is clearly at the high end of the range so the three boxes for those specific prices should be filled with Xs. If prices had slipped to 95.30 and 95.20, the first column would have started at 95.40 with Os.

Once the first column has been established, the process becomes somewhat simpler. Each day you continue to look at the high and the low. If you are working on a column of Xs, you look at the high first. If the high allows you to fill in at least one box higher than the highest X in the column, you add an X in the appropriate box or boxes. If you can add an X, you ignore the low for that day. As long as your current column is Xs, you will continue to look at the high first and add Xs as long as each new X is one or more boxes higher than the last X in the column.

On many days, of course, the high may not be high enough to require putting an X in a new box. Only then does the low become a factor. If you cannot enter another X on any day, then look at the low. If the low is lower than the highest X by the value of at least three boxes (in our Eurodollar example), then the reversal criteria has been triggered and you begin a column of Os. The first O is placed one column to the right of the X column and one box below the highest X.

Looking at the Eurodollar example, you can see that prices ticked up to 95.70, extending the column of Xs. Then, for a number of days, the highs weren't high enough to add another X, but the lows weren't low enough to cover the value of three boxes either. Your chart remained unchanged for about three weeks. Then, in early February, the market had an unusual wide-range day of 50 points and closed near the low—a bar chartist might have called this a key reversal day. But, because the current column was Xs, you had to look at the high first. The high did hit 95.80, meaning you could add an X to your column of Xs. Therefore, you ignore the low that day, even though it may have suggested a reversal was at hand.

On the next day, however, you obviously did not have a high requiring another X. Turning to the low, you can see that 95.30 is indeed below the highest X by the value of at least three boxes so you begin a column of Os. The first O goes in the 95.70 box, and you also place an O in the boxes for 95.60, 95.50, 95.40 and 95.30.

Now the situation changes. Because you are working on a column of Os, you look at the low first each day. If the low is low enough to require drawing another O, you add an O to the bottom of that column and ignore the high. If the low is not low enough to add another O, you evaluate the high to see if it is at least the value of three boxes above the lowest O, calling for another reversal back to a new column of Xs. You will always be alternating between columns of Xs and columns of Os.

In the case of Eurodollars, you continued the column of Os for more than two months as prices declined to the 94.10 area. That means almost four months of Eurodollar price action, covering perhaps 90 bars on a traditional daily bar chart, was contained in just two columns on a point-and-figure chart. (The December 1994 hog futures chart is even more dramatic: Nearly all of the contract's price history is contained in just three columns on a point-and-figure chart. See Figure 5.2.)

TRADING SIGNALS

By this time, you may have concluded this is a complex way to show price trends, and you may be wondering how these Xs and Os can help you make trading decisions. It is not just a matter of being long when there is a column of Xs and going short when you begin a column of Os, but the basic point-and-figure signals are rather simple:

FIGURE 5.2

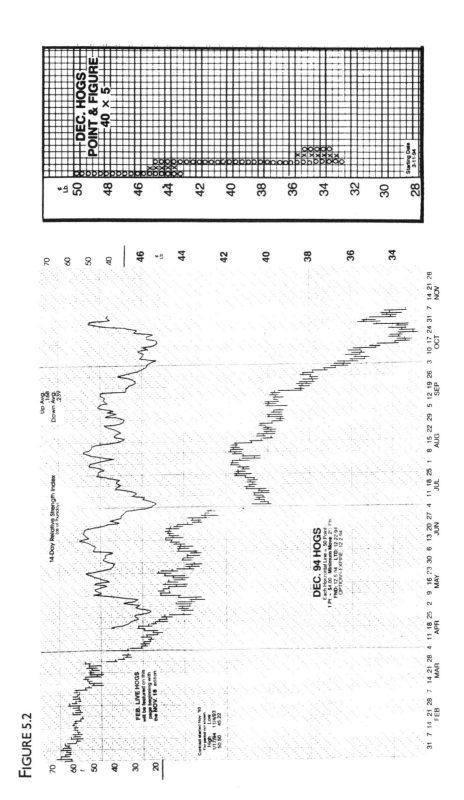

Source: Commodity Price Charts

❑ When the current column of Xs rises one box higher than the previous column of Xs, buy. Many traders use the price of that box as a buy stop.

❑ When the current column of Os drops one box below the lowest O in the previous column of Os, sell. Again, this would be a price for a sell stop.

These rules apply both to entering new positions or getting out of positions. They provide good points for placing stop-loss orders.

Notice the signals on the December wheat chart (Figure 5.3). As with most other methods, not every signal is a winner, and you obviously have to keep sound money management in mind because some of the price swings may be more than your pocketbook can take. But, if you used the box and reversal values from *Commodity Price Charts* and followed the traditional point-and-figure signals, you would have gotten out of short positions or been in a position to go long at $3.36 1/2 per bu. to capitalize on the nice runup in prices.

Because the columns of Xs and Os reflect the battle between bulls and bears, point-and-figure chart formations are rather clear. A column of Xs shows how high the market was willing to go at one point. If the next column of Xs is higher than the previous column, it indicates a stronger market willing to pay more; if the next column of Xs is lower, it suggests a weaker market not interested in paying as much. There are a number of refinements you can apply to point-and-figure charts, but in this basic text, we will look at only four.

One of the most reliable signals point-and-figure analysts look for involves triple (or more) tops and bottoms. When the current column of Xs exceeds two or more previous columns of Xs, the breakout is viewed as a strong buy signal—it means the market is now ready to bid prices higher than it was willing to do previously. If you look at the Eurodollar chart, you'll understand why some analysts were recommending

FIGURE 5.3

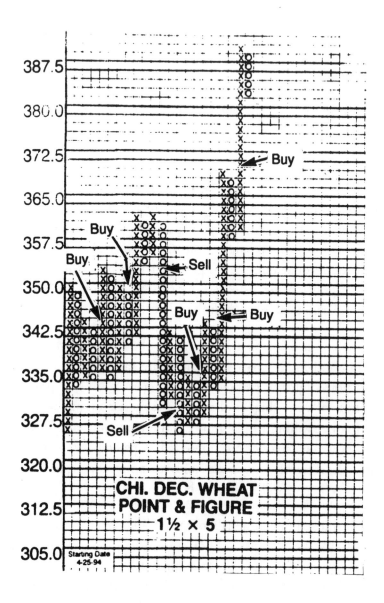

Source: Commodity Price Charts

94.40 as a buy point. A sell signal is similar: Sell at the point where a column of Os drops below the previous two (or more) columns of Os.

A second clue the point-and-figure chart gives for analyzing market strength or weakness is the pattern of the tops and bottoms. The Eurodollar chart provides a good example of a rising bottom, a series of higher lows as each push to a high is turned back. That indicates that on each attempt to go lower, the bearish forces steadily declined. The formation is similar to an ascending triangle on a bar chart but without the time element.

TRENDLINE ANALYSIS

The third useful item in point-and-figure analysis is the trendline, which might be better characterized as bullish and bearish support and resistance lines. Although some analysts use bar chart types of trendlines on point-and-figure charts, the only significant one is the 45-degree angle line.

After you have set up your point-and-figure chart and gotten a buy signal (a column of Xs exceeding the previous column of Xs), go to the empty box below the lowest column of Os on your chart. Draw a line from the lower left corner of the box to the upper right corner of that box—a 45-degree angle—and extend the line across the chart. Note: You are not connecting lows or any prices as you would for a bar chart trendline but are just drawing a 45-degree angle line. That is your bullish support line. You can add other shorter-term bullish support lines at higher levels as you get new buy signals.

You can use the line several ways. As long as prices stay above that line, some analysts advise taking the buy signals but ignoring the sell signals. If prices drop below the bullish support line, they will take the sell signals and ignore buy signals.

The counterpart to the bullish support trendline is the bearish resistance trendline, drawn at a 45-degree down angle (or at 135 degrees) from the empty box above the highest X on your chart once you get a sell signal (column of Os below previous column of Os). As long as prices remain below this bearish resistance line, the overall tone of the market is bearish and should be traded accordingly.

MEASURING MOVES

The fourth element that analysis of a point-and-figure chart can provide is a measurement for price objectives somewhat like measuring gaps or flag formations do on a bar chart. Using the Eurodollar chart as an example again, assume the price hit 94.40 and you wanted an idea how far prices might move. The X in the 94.40 box would be the fourth X in that column. Multiply four by three (the number of boxes for a reversal) by 0.10 (the size of each box). Add that figure—1.20—to the price at the base of the formation—93.70—to get an objective of 94.90.

You can also get a measurement by counting the number of boxes horizontally at the widest point. In this case, that's 10 boxes. Follow the same procedure as above—multiply by three and then by 0.10 and add the result, 3.00, to the lowest price to get an objective of 96.70, which seems to be a somewhat more unlikely goal.

Maybe that's expecting too much from a chart whose forte is providing clear and exact buy and sell signals without the clutter of sideways price action that often occupies much of the space on a bar chart. The key to successful trading with point-and-figure charting, however, remains the size of the box (the price change it represents) and the number of boxes (or total price) the market must move before a reversal is signalled. Getting these numbers right is an ongoing process that will never end and will continue to be a challenge for traders.

Chapter 6

Candlestick charts:
an enlightened view

Japanese candlestick charts have been around for hundreds of years, but they didn't become popular in the western world until the late 1980s. Steve Nison, then a technical analyst for Merrill Lynch Futures in New York, was one of the first analysts to present candlestick techniques to the U.S. market when he introduced candlestick charts to readers of *Futures* magazine in the December 1989 issue. The approach immediately attracted strong trader interest, perhaps because candles offer a better visual glimpse of market action and perhaps because of the colorful names for candle signals. Nison, who moved to Daiwa Securities America Inc. as director of research for its Nikkhah Group, followed with other articles and classes and also has written several books on candlestick charting techniques.

Candlestick charting has become enough of a mainstream approach to technical analysis in just a few years that it is included as one of the chart choices in many electronic quote and analytical services and software packages, and a number of other analysts and services now specialize in candlestick techniques. In addition to Nison, this chapter includes input from Daniel Gramza, president of Gramza Capital Management in Evanston, Ill., and Gary Wagner and Brad Matheny of International Pacific Trading Co., San Clemente, Calif.

While point-and-figure charts focus on the high and low prices of a time period and ignore the opening and closing prices entirely, candlestick charts emphasize the open and close and put less weight on the high and low. Like traditional bar charts, candlesticks use the open, high, low and close, but the open is much more significant for the candlestick chartist.

The difference between the open and close makes up the "body" of a time period's trading range. It actually often looks like a candle with a wick or a tail known as a "shadow" at either end. If the closing price is above the opening price, the body is clear or white; if the price at the close is below the open, the body is solid or black (see Figure 6.1).

FIGURE 6.1

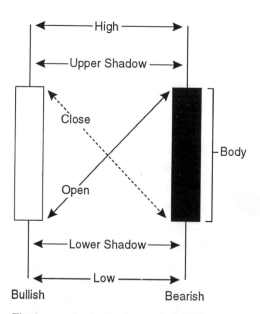

The longer the body, the more bullish
or bearish the implication may be.

Generally, a series of clear or white candles indicates an uptrend or bullish market; the bulls are in control as long as prices continue to close at a higher level than they opened. A series of solid or black candles indicates a downtrend or bearish market; the bears are driving prices down as the closes fall below the opens in a weak pattern. The color and the length of the candlesticks themselves provide a quick visual clue as to whether buying or selling dominates the market.

From there, a number of interpretations can be given for individual candles. While bar charts focus on trendlines and formations, candlestick analysis looks more at the sentiment of traders during a trading period as expressed by the type of candle for that period. However, any candlestick analyst will tell you one candle is not enough to make a trading decision. It is essential to look at the candle before and the candle after the candle being analyzed and to look at the candles in the context of the overall market picture before assessing what an individual candle might be saying.

Although candles provide a fresh new perspective on price action, they also should not be viewed in isolation apart from other technical evidence. Candles are not the Holy Grail. Interpreting candlestick charts, unfortunately, often is as much of an art as figuring out any other type of chart.

Keeping in mind that you need to look at each of these as part of a total picture, here are some of the major candlestick patterns and what they suggest:

Doji

Formed when the opening and closing prices are the same, the doji indicates an uncertain market unsure about the direction it wants to go. The market opens at a given price, then trades higher or lower or both and comes back to the opening price on the close. If the market

FIGURE 6.2 DOJI

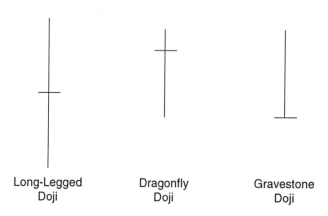

Long-Legged
Doji

Dragonfly
Doji

Gravestone
Doji

has been trending, a doji suggests weakness for carrying on the trend and frequently signals a turning point.

SPINNING TOPS

A spinning top is somewhat like a doji in that it indicates uncertainty or a market losing energy, but it has a small real body—in other words, it reflects a small-range day with some difference between opening and closing prices. If a market is at or near a new high, especially after a steep advance, a spinning top may signal the move is stalling out.

FIGURE 6.3 SPINNING TOPS

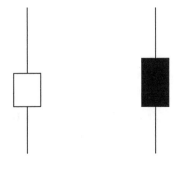

If you add light volume to a spinning top, it suggests demand is fading; heavy volume with a spinning top after a steep advance suggests demand is continuing strong but supply is coming in significantly enough to stall further bullish moves.

HAMMER

A hammer also features fairly tight opening and closing ranges and a small real body, but the lower shadow is at least twice the height of the real body. It indicates a market that has made a push to lower levels but was unable to sustain the move and closes near the high. It occurs at the bottom of a market and suggests a bullish turn.

FIGURE 6.4   HAMMER

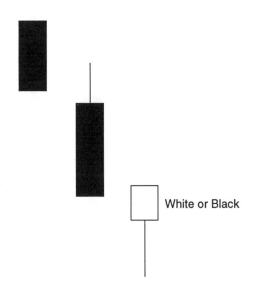

White or Black

HANGING MAN

A hanging man looks much like a hammer, except that it occurs at the top of a market trend. The small body and dangling leg at the top of an uptrend suggests its name and its bearish nature.

FIGURE 6.5   HANGING MAN

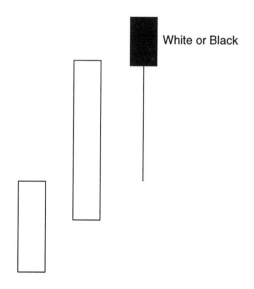

White or Black

STARS

The basic star occurs when a small real body day leaves a gap (candle-stick analysts would call the gap a window) after a much larger real body day. The color of the body on the first day should be the same as the trend prevailing to that point (white body in an uptrend, black body in a downtrend), but the body on the star day can be either white or black. The shadows for the two candles may overlap, but the real bodies do not if it is a star.

There are four major star combinations, all indicating a market that is losing steam and is ready for a reversal, and they all are more signifi-cant if they occur after extended moves.

The "evening star" and "morning star" ideally have gaps before and after the star—a bar chartist would call this formation an island top and island bottom.

FIGURE 6.6

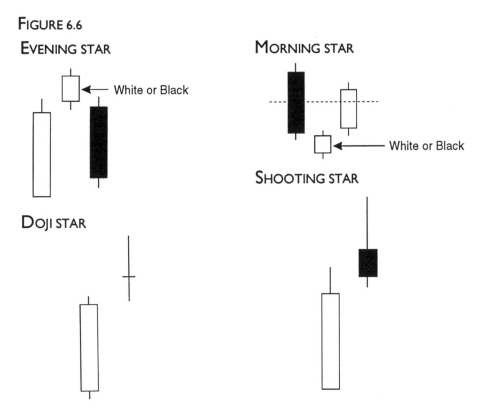

EVENING STAR

White or Black

MORNING STAR

White or Black

SHOOTING STAR

DOJI STAR

The evening star features a small body candle after a larger white body day and is followed by a larger black body candle, confirming a top to the market. A morning star occurs at the bottom of a trend when a large black body is followed by the small body star and a larger white body candle where the top of the body (the close on the third day) extends more than halfway through the black body of the first day. If the body on the third day were black instead of white, more weakness would be expected.

The doji, described above, can also be part of a star formation if it gaps away from the previous day's body. "Doji stars" tend to be more important at market tops, but conservative traders should wait for the next day's trading to confirm a trend change.

A "shooting star" appears at tops. It has a small real body with a long upper shadow representing the high of the day—traders tried to push prices up but the move fizzled at the close. Looking like the opposite of the hammer, a shooting star is usually a minor reversal pattern.

DARK CLOUD COVER

As its name implies, a dark cloud cover puts a bearish damper on an uptrend. It occurs when a wide-ranging day with the close higher than the open (a white candle) is followed by a higher wide-ranging day where the close is lower than the open (black candle). This pattern is more significant if the bottom of the black body (the close) falls below the center of the prior day's white body. At the least, this pattern signals a slowing of the uptrend if not a reversal.

FIGURE 6.7   DARK CLOUD COVER

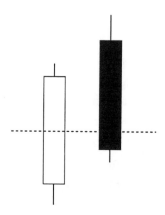

The bullish converse of the dark cloud cover is the piercing line: A long black body candle at the bottom of a downtrend is followed by a white body day that opens lower and then closes higher more than halfway into the prior day's black body.

FIGURE 6.8   PIERCING LINE

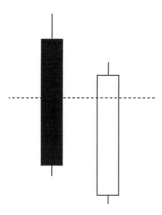

Dark cloud covers seem to occur more frequently than piercing lines.

ENGULFING LINES

There are several types, depending on their color and location. A bearish engulfing pattern is a large black candle that occurs during an uptrend and engulfs the previous day's white candle. The market opens higher than the previous day's close, then closes lower than the previous

FIGURE 6.9   BEARISH ENGULFING PATTERN

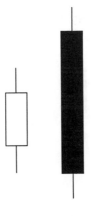

FIGURE 6.10   BULLISH ENGULFING PATTERN

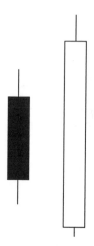

FIGURE 6.11   THE TWO TYPES OF LAST ENGULFING PATTERNS
                 BEARISH ENGULFING PATTERN AFTER DOWNTREND

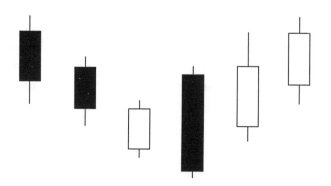

BULLISH ENGULFING PATTERN AFTER UPTREND

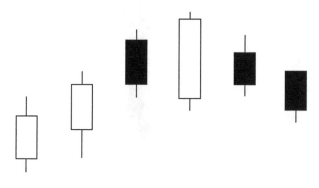

day's open, making its body larger than the previous day's body. A bullish engulfing pattern is a large white candle that appears during a downtrend and engulfs the previous day's real black body.

If a bullish engulfing pattern shows up during an uptrend or a bearish engulfing pattern during a downtrend, they may be last engulfing patterns. At first glance, they may look like continuation patterns, but they may indicate the last gasp to extend a move before a reversal occurs. In an uptrend, a sell signal occurs if the market opens lower than the close of the bullish engulfing pattern (it would leave a gap on a bar chart). Even if the market opens higher and then closes lower after the bullish engulfing pattern in an uptrend, it would produce a dark cloud cover, resulting in a sell signal.

HARAMI

For a bar chartist, an inside day is usually neutral. However, for a candlestick analyst, the same type of formation is known as a "harami" and suggests a trend change may be imminent.

The harami pattern occurs when a small real body forms within the prior day's real body—harami means "pregnant" in English. Like several other candle patterns, it indicates a market that is uncertain. De-

FIGURE 6.12   HARAMI

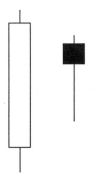

FIGURE 6.13   HARAMI CROSS

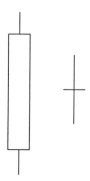

pending on its location on the chart, it suggests the prior move is losing momentum.

If a harami pattern includes a doji, it is called a "harami cross," an important trend change indicator, especially after a strong advance.

BREAKING THE RECORD

You don't necessarily need to use candlesticks to spot a succession of higher highs or lower lows, but a series of white or black bodies makes the task easier. In candle theory when a market has 8 to 10 "record" (higher high or lower low) sessions, not necessarily consecutive, you can expect a correction, especially if a bearish candle signal appears in an uptrend or a bullish candle signal in a downtrend.

Candle strategy suggests that, after eight record highs, you should liquidate half of your longs; after the 10th record high, you should exit all longs. At the least, after this many record highs, you should be watching for bearish candlestick signals more intently. (See Tom DeMark's Sequential program in the next section for a similar tactic).

FIGURE 6.14   TEN RECORD HIGHS

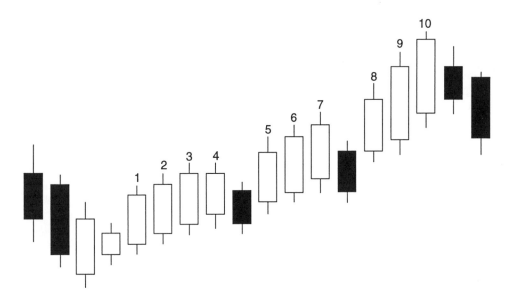

PUTTING PIECES TOGETHER

While candles improve the visual tracking of an active market, remember that candlestick patterns don't stand alone. As Steve Nison admonishes in one of his articles:

"The black candle of a bearish engulfing pattern envelopes the prior white real body, and the black candle of the dark cloud cover only goes partly into the prior white real body. This suggests the bears are more aggressive in the bearish engulfing pattern than with the dark cloud cover. Based on this, you might consider a bearish engulfing pattern more negative than a dark cloud cover.

"However, a dark cloud cover that confirms a resistance area is more threatening than a bearish engulfing pattern that does not confirm resistance. So the overall technical picture at the time a candle pattern forms will have an impact on the importance of that pattern."

CHAPTER 7

MARKET PROFILE

Technical analysis argues that everything that impacts a market—from fundamentals to chart signals to politics—is distilled down into one thing, the price bar for a given period. Some analysts, however, want more precise information out of that price bar. With the advance of the computer and real-time, on-line price quoting services providing tick-by-tick information, day-traders now can break down a daily price bar into smaller and smaller increments, allowing them to apply the waves, chart patterns and all the other familiar technical signals on a micro-cosmic scale within the confines of a day.

One approach to breaking down a day's price action that has attracted technicians since the early 1980s is Market Profile (also known as Market Logic), another way of presenting prices that looks nothing like other chart methods. Market Profile analyzes price, time and volume—how much trading activity takes place at what price and at what time during the trading session. A number of analysts have picked up on this method, but it is most closely associated with its original developer, J. Peter Steidlmayer, and the Chicago Board of Trade (CBOT).

Steidlmayer, a long-time floor trader at the CBOT, became head of the exchange's market information committee in 1980 and helped to develop the liquidity data bank (LDB). The LDB tapped into the huge amount of data generated by the exchange every day to show how much volume occurred at each price and how much volume was done by local or commercial traders. All of the numbers and statistics and data were hard to grasp, but Market Profile helped to visualize it.

Based on his trading experience, Steidlmayer knew that value or price was a result of time plus volume—the more time a market spends at a price and the more volume traded there, the more likely that is its true value. Market Profile breaks the trading day down into half-hour brackets. All the tick prices at which trading takes place during the first half hour are labeled with an A, ticks where trading occurs in the second half hour get a B, ticks in the third half hour a C, etc. As the market action unfolds, the alphabet letters indicating time stack up in horizontal rows at the day's price levels, revealing patterns that those familiar with the intricacies of this approach can recognize (see Figure 7.1).

Steidlmayer's intent in developing Market Profile was to spot value, based on the price at which the most volume occurred. He wanted to buy when prices were undervalued, sell when they were overvalued. His research revealed four trading patterns: normal days, which occurred about 80 percent of the time; two types of trending days, which happened about 15 percent of the time, and nontrend days, which accounted for 5 percent of the days.

On normal days, the trading range is usually established during the first hour or so. Trend days are either elongated, with gradual moves stretching into new highs or lows, or a price change produces a strong reaction (perhaps due to a news event or stops being hit) that results in prices jumping into a higher or lower distribution area. A nontrend day shows trading at relatively few price levels with the market jumping back and forth all day. The goal of all this analysis: Discover the trend days early enough to get onboard the trend.

Over the years, Steidlmayer and others have refined the concepts and defined other profiles and categories of trading days. Not everyone accepts Market Profile's concepts for value or its trading strategies for

FIGURE 7.1

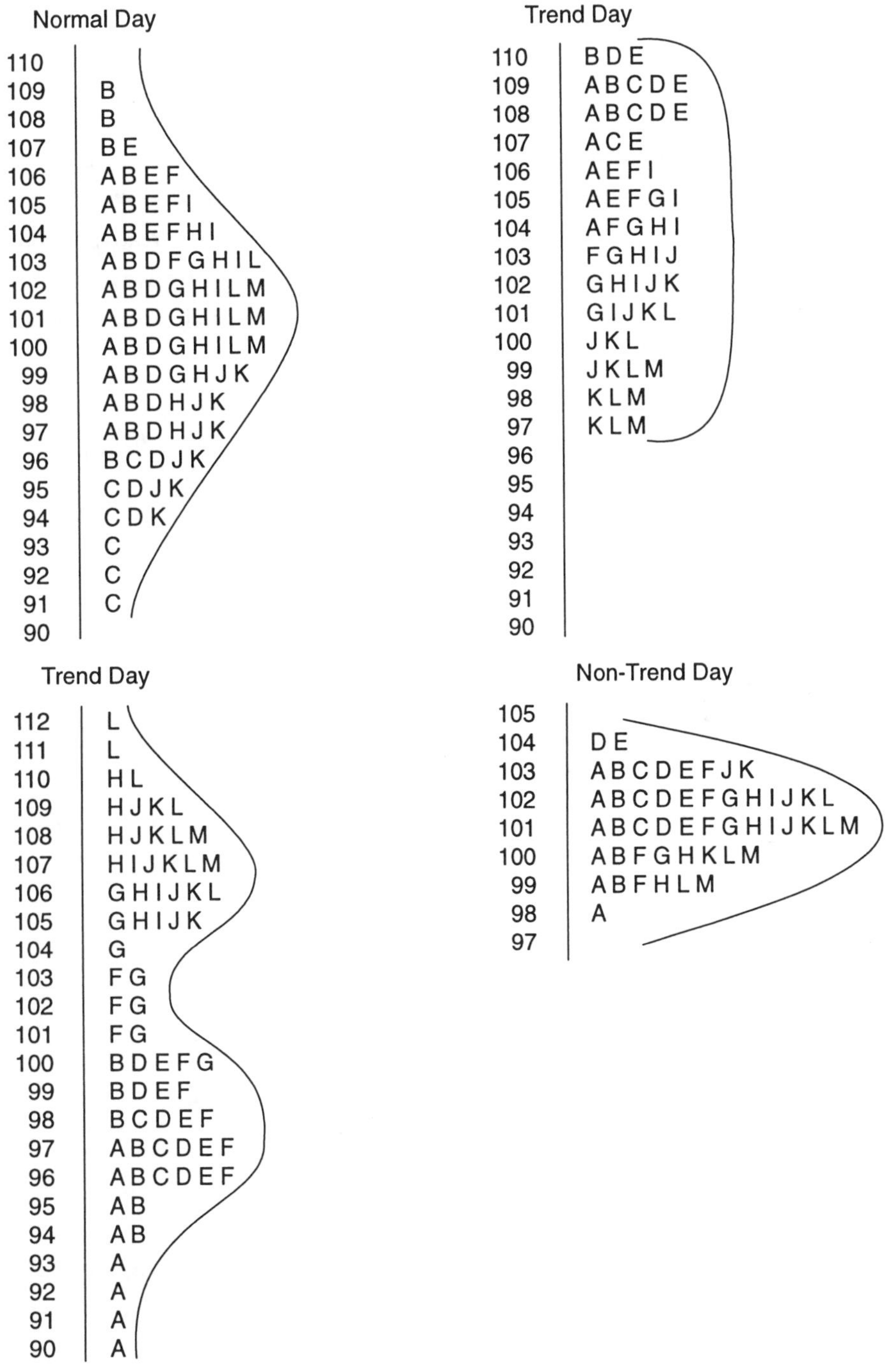

Normal Day

110	
109	B
108	B
107	B E
106	A B E F
105	A B E F I
104	A B E F H I
103	A B D F G H I L
102	A B D G H I L M
101	A B D G H I L M
100	A B D G H I L M
99	A B D G H J K
98	A B D H J K
97	A B D H J K
96	B C D J K
95	C D J K
94	C D K
93	C
92	C
91	C
90	

Trend Day

110	B D E
109	A B C D E
108	A B C D E
107	A C E
106	A E F I
105	A E F G I
104	A F G H I
103	F G H I J
102	G H I J K
101	G I J K L
100	J K L
99	J K L M
98	K L M
97	K L M
96	
95	
94	
93	
92	
91	
90	

Trend Day

112	L
111	L
110	H L
109	H J K L
108	H J K L M
107	H I J K L M
106	G H I J K L
105	G H I J K
104	G
103	F G
102	F G
101	F G
100	B D E F G
99	B D E F
98	B C D E F
97	A B C D E F
96	A B C D E F
95	A B
94	A B
93	A
92	A
91	A
90	A

Non-Trend Day

105	
104	D E
103	A B C D E F J K
102	A B C D E F G H I J K L
101	A B C D E F G H I J K L M
100	A B F G H K L M
99	A B F H L M
98	A
97	

undervalued and overvalued situations, of course, so it, like any other trading style, is not the final word for all traders. Sometimes, the value of an approach such as Market Profile is in the eye of the beholder.

Market Profile's data needs are specific, the trading time frame and opportunities typically are short-lived, and it usually takes a great deal of time and experience to grasp and become comfortable with the system. Consequently, Market Profile may not gain widespread popularity among off-the-floor traders, but it is another interesting way to present and chart prices and is an approach to technical analysis that will appeal to some traders.

SECTION II

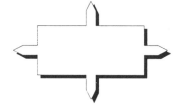

PRICE AND PACE:
INDICATORS

INTRODUCTION

You can probably divide futures and options traders into three broad groups, or you might be able to track the progression of many traders through three similar stages:

1. Those who trade by instinct (seat-of-the-pants or gut feel are other terms that apply). For whatever reason, they have concluded that the price of a commodity is ready to move—they usually seem to be convinced the move will be to the upside—and they want to be in on the action. Maybe they read something in a newspaper or newsletter, maybe a brother-in-law had a hot tip, maybe they've looked at a chart and concluded prices can't go any lower or just look like they have to go higher. In any case, the trading decision is usually the result of a subjective, emotional process.

2. Those trying to make their trading decisions more systematic and less emotional. These traders have gotten a little more serious about the business and want something more reliable than gut feel. They may have tried trading based on fundamentals. They may have used price charts but remain confused and frustrated. They need an "indicator"—something to trigger their trading decision. So they turn to "experts" who have developed indicators to tell them more precisely when they should make a move.

3. Those who do their own research and create their own methods to make their trading decisions. They may have tested and enhanced other people's indicators and ideas. In a more advanced state, they may even have developed their own proprietary trading systems.

There are successful and unsuccessful traders in every category, of course, and this is not to make a case for any category being more correct than any other category. If you are reading this book, however, chances are good you are in Category No. 2: You have enough experience or background to know that emotions and trading do not mix very well, and you may be searching for some help because you have reached the stage where you realize technical analysis is much more than just a casual look at a chart.

The first section of this book showed various ways to present price as a value at different points in time. The next step in technical analysis involves analyzing the movement and quality of price as much as the price itself—in other words, the pace of price movement and who's prompting the movement may provide important signals for prices in the future. How fast are prices changing? What does this say about the strength or weakness of a move? How much momentum does a market have?

In many cases, that is what trading indicators try to decipher. Analyzing charts (see Section I) or market participants (see Section III) or market structure (see Section IV) may reveal much of this information, but the indicators quantify it and can present a clearer picture summary of the forces at work in the marketplace.

In the previous section, traditional bar chart patterns were split into two primary categories: Continuation formations, suggesting the trend in place would remain or would resume after a pause or congestion phase, and reversal formations, indicating that one trend was ending and another beginning. This section is split somewhat similarly, looking first at indicators that deal with trends (Chapter 8) and then at those that analyze price movement mainly to signal changes in price direction. The trend-change indicators are further divided into two chapters, one focusing on the traditional overbought/oversold oscillators whose readings typically are based on a 0-100 index scale (Chapter 9) and the other on a few samples of more proprietary types of indicators that come closer to being trading signals by themselves (Chapter

10). A wrapup chapter shows how several analysts look at various traditional indicators and apply them to trading.

One point must be emphasized here: No indicator is the Holy Grail! I have never heard a successful trader or analyst claim that any indicator, used by itself, is the one and only way to trading profits. At the same time, note that many indicators are price-based and show the same information with different looks. Don't be misled into thinking that using many indicators saying the same thing provides confirmation of a trading signal.

Indicators can provide some invaluable insights but should be considered as just another aid to technical analysis. Those who want to dig more deeply into the mathematics of these and other indicators and systems may want to refer to Perry Kaufman's book, *The New Commodity Trading Systems and Methods*, about as comprehensive a book on this subject as there is for futures traders.

CHAPTER 8

FOLLOWING THE TREND

Even the most experienced trader who has developed a "feel" for what the charts are saying will admit that reading a chart for trend clues can be a very subjective art.

Some trends, trendlines and price formations may be obvious in hindsight, as noted in the previous section on charts. But even when you spot a trend early, chart analysis often is not very precise, whether you are looking at a chart on a screen or using a sharp pencil and a ruler on a printed chart.

What you need is a way to find more specific reference points for a trend: Is it still in place or, perhaps more desirable from a trading perspective, at what point is it not in place?

MOVING AVERAGES

One of the most common and familiar trend-following indicators is a moving average.

You probably already are quite familiar with an average—"the numerical result obtained by dividing the sum of two or more quantities by the number of quantitites," as Webster's dictionary defines it. A moving average is simply an average of prices that "moves" as each new price becomes available.

A moving average provides exact prices for a mechanical trading system to enter or exit a market—no eyeballing a chart for trendlines and no judgments about the message a chart formation may be giving. Consequently, moving averages have been the basis of many trend-following trading systems.

There are several types of moving averages, hundreds of time periods to consider and countless possibilities for combining moving averages or setting up trading strategies based on moving averages. Many traders today naturally will just turn to their computers and analytical software if they are interested in calculating and testing moving averages (or any of the other indicators). If one thing doesn't seem as attractive as another, you just tell the computer to optimize. You can come up with the best results without even knowing how to calculate the moving average or indicator yourself.

However, to gain confidence in using any approach, you should have some understanding of it, and this chapter will cover the basic details of moving averages. (Note: All references to "day" apply to any time period chosen, from a minute to a month; day is used as a convenience.)

WHAT PRICE SHOULD YOU USE?

Before you even get into a moving average system, you have to determine what price you will use. Many moving averages use the closing price at the end of the day (time period). However, the close may not totally represent the tone of the market. You may want to use an average of the open, high, low and close. Or you may want to use a moving average of the highs and another moving average of the lows to produce an envelope or channel on the chart. Or you may use a moving average of a five-day or 10-day average price.

You have many choices, and they are not all limited to price. You can also build moving averages involving volume, technical indicators or other market inputs. Your only limitation is your imagination.

Whatever price you use, keep in mind that your moving average will lag the market because all the numbers you use are from the past. Your choice of prices won't change that.

HOW MANY PRICES SHOULD YOU USE?

The number of days to include in a moving average is another choice subject to testing. The shorter the time period, the more likely the moving average will fluctuate erratically and the more trading signals you will get, especially in futures markets. A longer time frame will give you a smoother moving average but may be too slow getting you into or out of trades.

Much of the choice here depends on how close to the market you want to be. Some traders select time periods related to price cycles and may have different moving average periods for every market. Some go with the popular studies such as the 4-9-18 or 5-10-20 moving averages. The length of the moving average will be one of the most crucial decisions you make in developing any moving average system.

WHAT TYPE OF MOVING AVERAGE SHOULD YOU USE?

A **simple moving average** places equal value on every price for the time span selected. You add all five, 10, 15 or however many prices you want together and divide the sum by the number of prices you used. When you get a new price, you add it into the calculation and drop off the oldest price. In a simple 10-day moving average, the price 10 days ago is as important as the price today (Figure 8.1). With today's computer power, however, not many traders will be satisfied with just a simple moving average.

FIGURE 8.1   SIMPLE MOVING AVERAGE

A simple moving average is simply an average of a selected number of prices.

MA = (P1 + P2 + . . . Pn)/n

where P1 is the price for day 1, P2 the price for day 2, etc., and n is the number of days in the moving average.

The table shows the calculation using closing prices for a simple 10-day moving average at the beginning of the T-bond chart shown. On June 2 add the close for that day and drop the close for May 18, on June 3 add that close and drop May 19, etc., as the average moves through time.

Day	Close			
May 18	105.0625			
May 19	105.625			
May 20	105.625			
May 21	105.15615			
May 24	105.6875			
May 25	105.5			
May 26	1056.3125			
May 27	106.5	Sum		
May 28	105.78125			
June 1	107.25	1058.4999 divide by 10 =	105.84999	**105-27**
June 2	107.25	1060.6874	106.06874	106-2
June 3	107.46875	1062.53115	106.253115	106-8
June 4	106.90625	1063.8124	106.38124	106-12

SIMPLE 10–DAY MOVING AVERAGE   SIMPLE 20–DAY MOVING AVERAGE

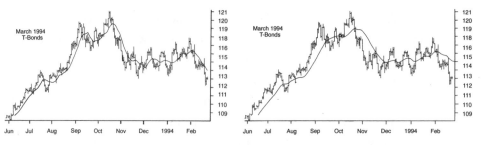

Source: FutureSource

Suppose you think the most recent prices are more important than older prices. A **weighted moving average** puts more emphasis on today's close than the close 10 days ago. The table (Figure 8.2) shows one way to do this, but you can weight a moving average a number of ways to make it more responsive to current market action.

FIGURE 8.2 WEIGHTED MOVING AVERAGE

A weighted moving average gives more value to recent prices—in this case, the June 1 price is multiplied by 10, the previous day's price by 9 and so on back to the May 18 price 10 days ago multiplied by only 1. The sum is divided by 55, the number of weights. The result is a weighted moving average of 106-4 compared to 105-27 for the 10-day simple moving average for the same period.

Day	Close	Weight	Sum	
May 18	105.0625	x 1 =	105.0625	
May 19	105.625	x 2 =	211.25	
May 20	105.625	x 3 =	316.875	
May 21	105.15615	x 4 =	420.6246	
May 24	105.6875	x 5 =	528.4375	
May 25	105.5	x 6 =	633	
May 26	106.3125	x 7 =	744.1875	
May 27	106.5	x 8 =	852	
May 28	105.78125	x 9 =	952.03125	
June 1	107.25	x 10 =	1072.5	5835.96835
		Total: 55	divide by 55 =	
			106.108515	**106-4**

As a new price is added, the oldest price drops out of the time window with both the simple and weighted moving averages. That may eliminate a valuable piece of information. The current value in an **exponential moving average** includes virtually all of the preceding prices for a given futures contract month, even those months before the time period of the moving average, although the impact of the older data naturally diminishes as new points are added.

FIGURE 8.3   TEN-DAY EXPONENTIAL MOVING AVERAGE

Source: FutureSource

An exponential moving average includes all previous prices and features a constant that smoothes the average.

$EMA_t = EMA_{t-1} + (k * (PI - EMA_{t-1}))$

where EMA_t is today's exponential moving average

EMA_{t-1} is yesterday's exponential moving average

PI is today's price

k is the exponential smoothing constant calculated by the formula

$k = 2 / (n + 1)$ with n as the length of the moving average

For a 10-day moving average:

$k = 2 / (10 + 1) = 2 / 11 = 0.1818$

For a 20-day moving average, k would be 0.09523.

Or, starting with a simple 10-day moving average at any point:

$EMA_t = (PI * k) + ((MA_{t-1} * (1 - k))$

where EMA_t = today's exponential moving average

PI = today's closing price

k = constant ($k = 2/n$ where n is the length of the moving average)

MA_{t-1} = previous simple 10-day moving average

Using the figures from the 10-day simple moving average table, the exponential moving average for Day 11 is :

$\qquad$ 107-8 or 107.25 * 0.2 = 21.45

$\quad$ +   105.84999 * 0.8   = 84.679992

$\qquad\qquad\qquad\qquad\qquad$ 106.129992 or **106-4**

The 10-day EMA on this chart hangs closer to price action than the simple 10-day moving average.

An exponential moving average uses a smoothing constant, usually between 0.01 and 0.30, that varies with the length of the moving average. Today's value depends on the value calculated for yesterday.

WHAT PRODUCES A TRADING SIGNAL?

Regardless of the type you choose, the basic principle of any moving average system is that if there is more buying pressure than selling pressure, prices will be above the average and the market will be in an uptrend; if there is more selling pressure, prices will drop below the moving average, indicating a downtrend.

Moving average systems trade these crossovers: Buy when prices move from below the moving average line to above the line; sell when prices go from above the line to below the line. In other words, in its simplest form, when prices are above the moving average line on the chart, you are long; when prices are below the moving average line, you are short.

On the two simple moving average charts (Figure 8.1), note that the 10-day moving average triggers several false signals during the long uptrend. The 20-day moving average is further from the market and has fewer signals but takes longer to get into and out of positions. Neither fares well during the choppy period that began in November.

When the market is moving rapidly in one direction, you want a fast moving average (one with fewer days in it) to catch the trend. When the market is moving sideways or trending erratically, you want a slower moving average (more days) to avoid getting chopped up by numerous signals. Ideally, of course, you would like a moving average that could adapt to changes in market direction and volatility to find the optimum number of days that should be included in the average.

One rule of thumb is that the length of the moving average should be one-half the length of the market's cycle (see Chapter 18 for information on cycles). If a cycle is 28 days (from bottom to bottom), the moving average should be 14 days. Of course, you are now making two assumptions—the length of the cycle and the length of a moving average—so you will want to do some testing before settling on a number of days that your moving average should cover.

To reduce whipsaws, some analysts add wrinkles to moving average systems: The price must move a certain percent or price increment above or below the moving average, for example, before a position is taken or before a stop is activated. Or the system may require any moving average signal to be confirmed by a signal from some other indicator or by a specified volume level or by a seasonal pattern or some other criteria.

IS ONE MOVING AVERAGE ENOUGH?

A simple system might use the relationship of prices to just one moving average to generate its signals. But some incorporate multiple moving averages—short-term, medium-term and long-term—to improve the odds that a signal really does indicate a new trend.

Popular combinations include 4, 9 and 18 days and 5, 10 and 20 days. The late Richard Donchian made moving averages popular with futures traders several decades ago when he developed and successfully traded a system that included 5- and 20-day moving averages (and several other parameters—see page 126).

You can use a combination of moving averages in a variety of ways, especially if you trade multiple contracts. The basic signal comes when a shorter moving average moves above or below a longer moving average.

Ideally, you would like prices and the moving averages to line up—in an uptrend, prices are on top with the short-term, medium-term and long-term moving averages in that order below prices (Figure 8.4). If the short-term average falls below the medium-term average, that can be your signal to get out of some contracts or go flat, for example,

FIGURE 8.4   COMBINING MOVING AVERAGES FOR TRADING SIGNALS

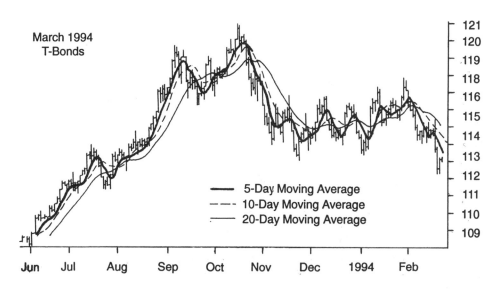

Source: FutureSource

Putting several moving averages together is one attempt to get more reliable signals. This chart uses closing prices for simple 5-, 10- and 20-day moving averages. The uptrend shows a nice alignment of prices and moving averages until July. Then the most sensitive moving average (5 days) falls through both the 10-day and 20-day averages, and the 10-day average drops below the 20-day average briefly. That would normally be a signal to reverse from long to short. However, the 5-day moving average quickly climbs above the other averages again, the signal for another reversal back to long as the uptrend resumes.

instead of reversing your entire position as some always-in-the-market systems would dictate. If the short-term average continues to fall through the long-term average, then you might get out of all long positions and go short.

You can also use several moving averages to make envelopes or channels and then trade the relationship of prices to that channel (see Figure 8.5). You can set up all kinds of other criteria with combinations of moving averages.

FIGURE 8.5   HIGH-LOW MOVING AVERAGES

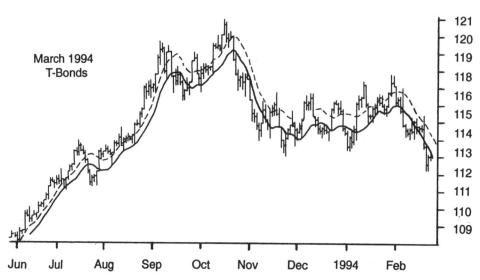

March 1994
T-Bonds

Source: FutureSource

This channel is formed by a simple moving average of the highs for the last 10 days and another simple moving average of the lows for the last 10 days, another possible way to combine moving averages. Typically, you would use the bottom moving average of the lows as the crossover line in an uptrend and the top moving average line of the highs in a downtrend. Prices dip into the channel a number of times during the long uptrend but produce only one bad reversal signal when they drop below the moving average of lows in July.

HOW SHOULD THE AVERAGE RELATE TO CURRENT PRICES?

Sometimes a moving average works best if you shift today's moving average value to some point other than today. For example, a simple moving average for a 10-day period actually reflects price action for the last 10 days. So, to be more representative of the total period, perhaps today's moving average value should be placed halfway through that time at Day 5. The moving average line then would always be five days behind the current day's price.

Or you may want to advance the moving average a few days. As a lagging indicator, typical moving averages don't provide any targets for prices in the future. But shifting today's moving average value ahead does establish another reference point for prices and may reduce the number of false signals (see Figure 8.6). As with other moving average techniques, you have many choices you can test in this area.

FIGURE 8.6   DISPLACING THE MOVING AVERAGES

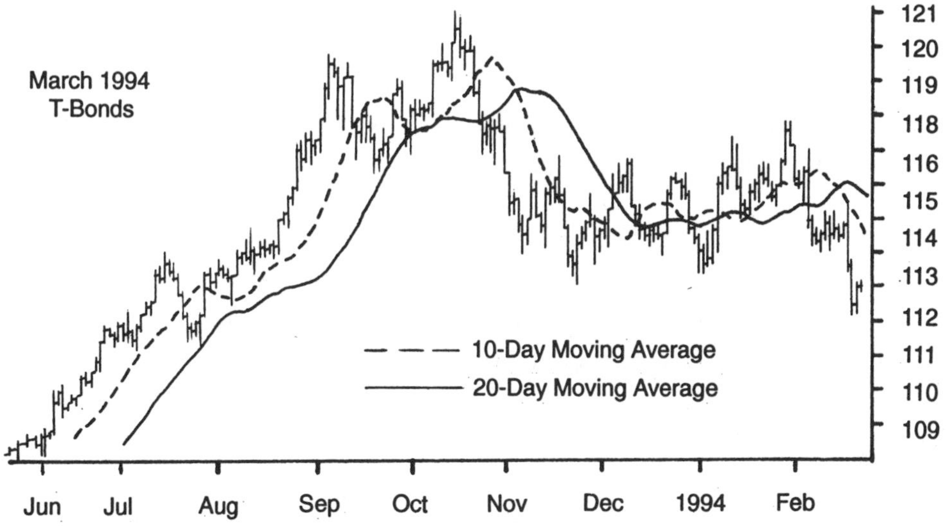

Source: FutureSource

This chart shows simple 10-day and 20-day moving averages displaced half of their length ahead—today's value for the 10-day moving average is plotted five days ahead of today's price and the 20-day moving average is placed 10 days into the future. This approach keeps you in your long positions through the July setback during the long uptrend, but the turns appear to be long and costly—and nothing looks good on the right side of the chart.

MOVING AVERAGE APPLICATIONS

As mentioned, uses of moving averages in a trading system can be very simple or quite complicated. Dennis Dunn, president of Dunn & Hargitt in Lafayette, Ind., once reported that one of the easiest to understand and profitable methods at the same time was a seven-week moving average technique: Buy on a Thursday close over the moving average line and sell on a Thursday close below the moving average. If the market is closed on Thursday, use Wednesday's close.

The seven-week moving average line was NOT plotted in coincidence with the close but was plotted two weeks in advance to make a market decision earlier. After a Thursday close, all you had to do was enter your order for the coming Thursday (or Friday morning). You were always in the market.

Whether that particular technique would work in all times in all markets would have to be tested, of course. But it illustrates how simple a moving average system can be.

On the other hand, Richard Donchian had a number of conditions in his well-known 5- and 20-day moving average method in the 1970s. Donchian, a pioneer in technical analysis and trend-following systems in the futures industry, even broke the 5- and 20-day method rules down into general and supplemental. Here is a condensed version:

General rules

1. The extent of penetration of the moving average is broken down into units, depending on price level. For commodities selling over 400 (wheat, soybeans, silver), for example, a penetration of 40¢ was required (Donchian had six price classes in the days before interest rate and stock index futures).

2. No closing penetration of the moving averages counts as a penetration at all unless it amounts to at least one full unit (39¢ in rule 1 was not enough for a penetration—it had to be 40¢ to count).

Basic Rule A: Act on all closes that cross the 20-day moving average by an amount exceeding by one full unit the maximum penetration in the same direction on any one day on the preceding occasion (no matter how long ago) when the close was on the same side of the moving average. For example, if the last time the closing price of cotton was above the moving average it stayed above for one or more days, and the maximum amount above on any one of the days was 64 points, then when the closing price of cotton moves above the moving average, after having been lower in the interim, a buy signal is given only if it closes above the average by more than 64 points (the unit in cotton is 0.10). This principle—the requirement that a penetration of the moving average exceed one or more previous penetrations—is a feature of the 5- and 20-day method that distinguishes it from other moving average methods.

Basic Rule B: Act on all closes that cross the 20-day moving average and close one full unit beyond (above or below, in the direction of the crossing) the previous 25 daily closes.

Basic Rule C: Within the first 20 days after the first day of a crossing that leads to an action signal, reverse on any close that crosses the 20-day moving average and closes one full unit beyond (above or below) the previous 15 daily closes.

Basic Rule D: Sensitive 5-day moving average rules for closing out positions and for reinstating positions in the direction of the basic 20-day moving average trend are:

1. Close out positions when the commodity closes below the 5-day moving average for long positions or above the 5-day moving average for short positions by at least one full unit more than the greater of (a) the previous penetration on the same side of the 5-day moving average, or (b) the maximum point of any previous penetration within the preceding 25 trading sessions. If the distance between the closing price and the 20-day moving average in the opposite direction to the Rule D close-out signal has been greater within the prior 15 days than the distance from the 20-day

moving average in either direction within 60 previous sessions, do not act on Rule D close-out signals unless the penetration of the 5-day average also exceeds by one unit the maximum distance both above and below the 5-day average during the preceding 25 sessions.

2. After positions have been closed out by Rule D, reinstate positions in the direction of the basic trend (a) when the conditions in paragraph 1 above are fulfilled, (b) if a new Rule A basic trend signal is given or (c) if new Rule B or Rule C signals in the direction of the basic trend are given by closing in new low or new high ground.

3. Penetrations of two units or less do not count as points to be exceeded by Rule D unless at least two consecutive closes were on the side of the penetration when the point to be exceeded was set up.

Supplemental rules

1. Action on all rules is deferred for one day except on Thursday and Friday. For example, if a basic buy signal is given for wheat at the close on Tuesday, action is taken at the opening on Thursday morning. The same one-day delay applies to Rule D close-out and reinstate signals.

2. For signals given at the close on Friday, action is taken at the opening on Monday.

3. For signals given at the close on Thursday (or the next to last trading day of the week), action is taken at the Friday (or weekend) close.

4. When there is a holiday in the middle of the week or a long weekend, signals given at the close of the sessions prior to the holiday are treated as follows: (1) for sell signals, use weekend rules; (2) for

buy signals, defer action for one day, as is done on regular consecutive trading sessions.

It worked for Donchian over a number of years, but yesterday's system may not work today and today's system may not work tomorrow. Whether all of those rules can be programmed to work today would be a subject for testing. This example is cited only to show how rules can be added to moving averages to produce a more complex trading system.

VARIATIONS ON A THEME

You can modify moving averages to use them in many other ways:

❑ Instead of the close, use an average of the open, high, low and close as the number for your moving average. Of course, the moving average could be simple, weighted, exponential . . .

❑ Use a moving average of the highs and a moving average of the lows to build a channel. They don't even have to have the same number of days. A moving average channel might use 10 days for the highs and eight days for the lows, for example.

❑ The top and bottom of the channel could be based on some percentage of a moving average of the closes. The top band could be 105 percent of a 10-day moving average of the close and the bottom band could be 95 percent, for example.

❑ The top of the channel might be some percentage of a moving average of the lows and the bottom of the channel some percentage of a moving average of the highs.

❑ The moving average doesn't necessarily have to be price. It could be volume, open interest or some other factor.

❑ You can incorporate volatility or some other element into a moving average indicator. Bollinger Bands, for example, adjust in distance from a moving average based on volatility, using standard deviations above and below the moving average rather than percentages.

MOVING AVERAGE TRUTHS

No matter which moving averages you try or how many twists you give them, you will discover that moving averages:

❑ are not perfect indicators.

❑ work great in markets with long-lasting trends. But so do most other trend-following methods.

❑ can be simple to calculate and easy to follow—or quite complex.

❑ will never get you in at the bottom or out at the top or vice versa. You may give up a lot of profit potential compared to some other methods. The best you can ever do is capture part of a move—and just hope that part is enough to be profitable.

❑ offer a mechanical, nonemotional means to get aboard the big move.

❑ also can generate many false signals if too short. That can chew you up in whipsaw city if a market turns from a trend into a trading range. You cannot avoid this unless you abandon your moving average system. This can become a big test of your trading discipline.

The T-bond charts used with the explanations of the various moving averages provide a good example. If you have tested any moving average system based on daily closes that did well during the long uptrend and also performed well from mid-November to mid-February, you have discovered a gem.

MACD

The market makes its judgment of value every day with a closing price, and a moving average of these closing price values provides a good view of the general mood of traders in that market. Typically, when a market gets into a groove or trend, that trend tends to persist, sometimes well past its expected target level, until something tells the market otherwise. Along the way, a trend may strengthen or weaken, providing clues for market direction before prices confirm the fact.

One indicator for trend continuation or reversal is known as moving average convergence-divergence (MACD). Generally credited to Gerald Appel as a stock market indicator originally, MACD involves three exponential moving averages and has become widely used in futures markets. It is particularly effective on weekly charts as a direction indicator (you trade only in the direction of MACD, using indicators from your daily charts as entry and exit techniques).

As mentioned earlier, an exponential moving average incorporates virtually all previous prices for a futures contract and reduces the impact that an unusual price might have on a trading signal based on a simple moving average. The important factors with MACD are not just the prices but the crossovers of the averages, the direction in which they are going and their direction compared to prices.

Start your MACD study by calculating two exponential moving averages of closing prices—12-day and 26-day EMAs are often used but the number of days is a variable that you may want to test for yourself. Subtract the longer (26-day) EMA from the shorter one (12-day). The difference is plotted as a solid line. Then calculate another EMA of the difference between the two EMAs—9 days is often used for this EMA. This EMA is plotted as a dashed line (see Figure 8.7).

The trading signals are generated similarly to other moving average crossover systems. You buy when the solid line—the difference between

FIGURE 8.7

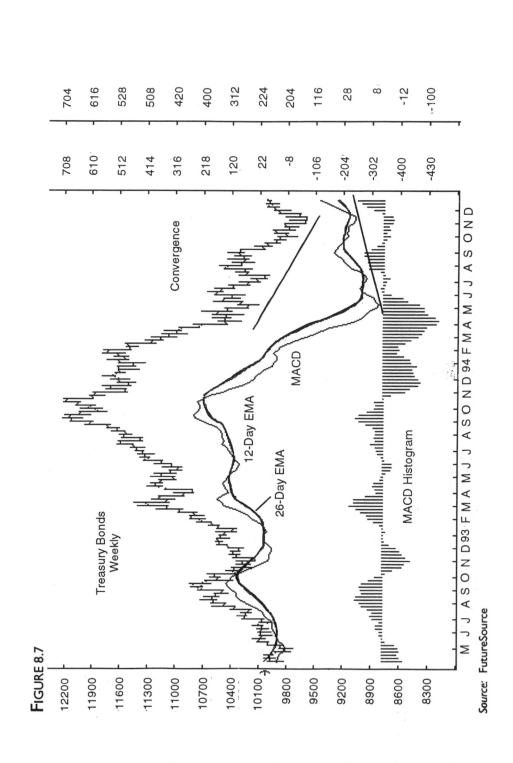

Source: FutureSource

the 26-day and 12-day EMAs representing shorter-term changes—crosses above the slower dashed line—9-day EMA of the difference between the other two EMAs; you sell when the solid line crosses below the dashed line.

You can also plot MACD as a histogram, each bar representing the distance between the two lines and giving a more precise picture of the enthusiasm of the crowd. Instead of waiting for lines to cross, you can act on changes in the direction of the histogram as the bars shrink or grow when the moving averages begin to converge or diverge.

If the fast line is above the slow line, the MACD histogram is above the zero line and points up; if the fast line is below the slow line, the histogram bars are below the zero line and MACD points down. The greater the distance between the two lines, the longer the MACD histogram bars. If the histogram bar is rising (growing longer above the zero line or getting shorter below the zero line), it indicates buying pressure is increasing.

Perhaps the most useful aspect of the MACD histogram is when it diverges from the price pattern. Sometimes prices and the histogram move up together to a top, drop back together and then the price drives on to an even higher top while the histogram rallies but does not make a new high. As prices moved to the new high, the histogram indicated the crowd enthusiasm just wasn't there, hinting the market was setting up for a price decline. You should either close out long positions or go short. The same effect in reverse also applies to bottoms.

DMI

Another indicator that measures trends and their direction is the Directional Movement Index (DMI). J. Welles Wilder Jr. introduced the DMI along with Relative Strength Index (see next chapter) in his book, *New Concepts in Technical Trading Systems*, in 1978. Any serious technical analyst will want to study that book although I suspect that most traders who use DMI or other technical indicators will simply crank up their analytical software and start optimizing numbers without bothering to understand the calculations involved.

DMI has three components: +DI measures upward price movement, -DI measures downward price movement, and ADX uses the difference between +DI and -DI to show trendiness or lack of it without regard to the direction of the trend. It is a quick way to see whether the market is bullish or bearish on an index from 0 to 100.

The computations to arrive at DMI are not difficult but are a bit cumbersome and need to be taken in steps.

1. The first is understanding directional movement (DM). It is defined as the largest part of the current period's trading range that is outside of the previous period's trading range. You compare today's high minus yesterday's high with today's low minus yesterday's low to get a DM value. (For inside days or when the values are equal, DM is zero.)

2. Use only the larger value. When the difference between the highs is the greatest, you put it in the +DM column; when the difference between the lows is the greatest, you put the value in the -DM column. (Both DM values are positive numbers; the minus sign just indicates its downward movement.)

3. Compute the true range (TR). TR is the largest of today's high minus today's low or today's high minus yesterday's close or to-

day's low minus yesterday's close. Only the largest of those values is used.

4. Determine how many days (periods) to use in your calculations. Wilder used 14 days, half the length of a typical price cycle. That figure continues to be most popular although others have been tested.

5. Add up all the +DM figures and compute the average value for the time period you've chosen (14 days?). Do the same for -DM and TR to get an average value for each of the three columns. After you've done this once, you can save time on future calculations by using this formula: Today's average = (yesterday's average - (today's average/number of days)) + today's value.

6. Now, you are ready to calculate the directional indicator, which can be either up or down, depending on directional movement.

   If DM is up: $+DI = (+DM/TR) * 100$.
   If DM is down: $-DI = (-DM/TR) * 100$.

7. Compute the difference between +DI and -DI (remember, both are positive numbers): $DI_{diff} = ((+DI) - (-DI))$.

8. Then, add up all the DI values: $DI_{sum} = ((+DI) + (-DI))$.

9. Calculate DX or the directional movement index: $DX = (DI_{diff} / DI_{sum}) * 100$. This will be a percentage figure between 0 and 100. If the market is moving strongly up or down, the reading will be high, indicating the bulls or the bears are firmly in control; if price action is choppy or sideways, the reading will be low, indicating bulls and bears are battling it out on more even terms with neither side in control of the market.

10. To allow for volatile, extreme periods, Wilder added the average directional movement index (ADX) calculation to smooth the DX:

$$ADX_t = ((ADX_{t-1} * (n - 1)) + DX_t) / n$$

If you use 14 for your time period, this makes ADX a 14-day average of a 14-day average, making reaction to market changes somewhat slower than some traders like.

Looking at the figures for the components themselves can be useful as indicators. ADX, by itself, tells you whether prices are trending or wandering around aimlessly. High DM readings suggest a market that should be traded with a trend-following system. If your trading system is designed for nontrending or trading range markets, you would look for markets at the lower end of the DM scale. If the ADX line drops below both DI lines, do not use a trend-following system.

Another component of DM you can use as an indicator is called the average directional movement index rating (ADXR). To get ADXR, you add today's ADX to the ADX reading from a specified number of days ago and divide by two. It's like another moving average of ADX. When ADX crosses above ADXR, the market usually is trending. When ADX is lower than ADXR, the market is chopping around.

The DMI can go beyond being an indicator to become a trend-following trading system. The basic strategy for using DMI is relatively simple: When +DI crosses above -DI, you buy; when -DI crosses over +DI, you sell. The system also involves an extreme point rule: On the day of the crossover, the extreme price that day is a reverse point for a stop. If long, it is the low of the crossover day; if short, it is the high.

Some require ADX to be above both +DI and -DI lines, using a turn lower by ADX as a signal the market is reversing the current trend. Some require ADX to be rising before making a trade on a crossover. However, because ADX will only begin to rise after a crossover when

FIGURE 8.8   DAILY PERPETUAL COTTON WITH DMI

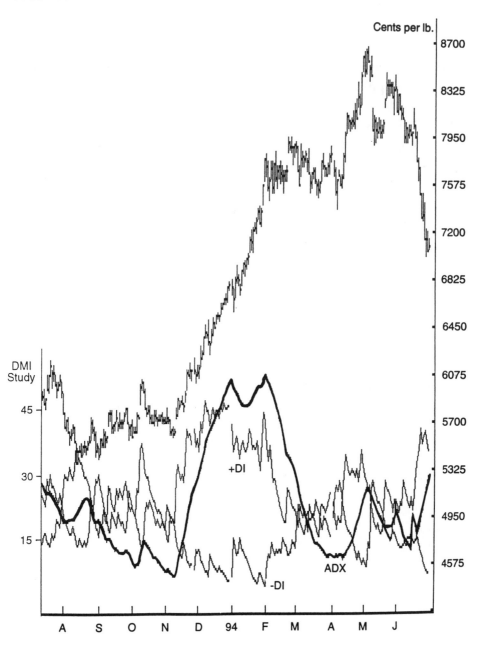

Source: FutureSource

137

+DI and -DI are moving wider apart or have already made a strong move, the lagging effect may produce a trending signal just when you don't want one.

Figure 8.8 provides an illustration of DMI and ADX—for an explanation of its application, see page 215.

Perhaps the best use for ADX and DMI is as a filter for other systems or simply as a signal for market conditions in which a trending or nontrending trading system would work best.

CHAPTER 9

SIGNALING THE TURNS: OSCILLATORS

A great deal of emphasis in technical analysis is placed on identifying the trend or knowing when a market is trending. For many futures and options traders, of course, this is where most of the money is made. However, many markets spend less than 20 percent of the time in tradable trends, and some may gyrate within a trading range without ever exhibiting any real trends for extended periods of time. So, for successful trading, it is essential to spot these trend opportunities when they do occur.

Naturally, that implies it is equally important to recognize when there isn't a trend, when a trend is ending or when a market may be setting up to begin a trend. The trend-following indicators in the previous chapter not only track trends in place and the likelihood they will continue but also give clues that a trend is ending or beginning when their readings weaken or reverse. In fact, they could be used not for measuring trends at all but only for finding potential trend reversals, if that is your style.

Another set of indicators evaluates market action with an eye more to discovering market turns. Often, these indicators consider the pace of price as it progresses and assess the momentum of a move or the rate at which prices are changing or some other factor to determine whether a market might be overbought or oversold. These overbought/oversold indicators also can be categorized as oscillators because they usually move up and down on an index scale ranging from 0 to 100. They are more effective in trading range markets, especially for shorter-term traders.

A number of these price-based indicators use similar inputs and produce similar signals. Aside from the crossovers and their high or low overbought/oversold readings, perhaps their biggest value as a group is the divergence/convergence signals they give—prices do one thing and the indicator does another.

You may be one of those traders who just turn to your analytical software to run the numbers and the indicators for you. However, it is important that you understand the basis for the numbers. Sometimes, to get away from the misinterpretations and misuses that are likely to accumulate over time, you may want to go back to study the original material on the subject. You might be able to add a twist here or a new component there and who knows? You could produce the next great trading system yourself if you have learned the concepts incorporated in these indicators by the masters.

RELATIVE STRENGTH INDEX

By J. Welles Wilder Jr.

Few books have introduced as many innovative concepts to technical analysis in futures trading as New Concepts in Technical Trading Systems *by J. Welles Wilder Jr. in 1978. In addition to the Directional Movement Index (see Chapter 8), the book included the Parabolic System, the Volatility System and others, but perhaps the best known and most tested has been the Relative Strength Index (RSI). Wilder, president of Trend Research Ltd. in McLeansville (Greensboro), N.C., moved on to other technical analysis concepts, but RSI, DMI, ADX and several other indicators in that book have become standards of technical analysis for futures traders everywhere.*

The following is from the article that explained basic oscillator concepts and introduced RSI to traders in the June 1978 issue of Commodities *magazine. Reprinted here with permission.*

One of the most useful tools employed by many technical commodity traders is a momentum oscillator that measures the velocity of directional price movement.

When prices move up very rapidly, at some point the commodity is considered to be overbought; when they move down very rapidly, the commodity is considered oversold at some point. In either case, a reaction or reversal is imminent. The slope of the momentum oscillator is directly proportional to the velocity of the move, and the distance traveled up or down by this oscillator is proportional to the magnitude of the move.

The momentum oscillator is usually characterized by a line on a chart drawn in two dimensions. The 'Y' axis (vertical) represents magnitude or distance the indicator moves; the 'X' axis (horizontal) represents time. Such a momentum oscillator moves very rapidly at market turning points and then tends to slow down as the market continues the directional move.

Suppose we are using closing prices to calculate the oscillator, and the price is moving up daily by exactly the same increment from close to close. At some point, the oscillator begins to flatten out and eventually becomes a horizontal line. When this occurs, if the price begins to level out, the oscillator will begin to descend.

PLOTTING THE OSCILLATOR

Let's look at this concept using a simple oscillator expressed in terms of the price today minus the price X number of days ago—let's say 10 days ago, for example. The oscillator is measured from a zero line. If the price 10 days ago is higher than the price today, then the oscillator value is minus; conversely, if today's price is higher than the price 10 days ago, then the oscillator value is plus.

The easiest way to illustrate the interaction between price movement and oscillator movement is to take a straight-line price relationship and plot the oscillator points based on this relationship (see Figure 9.1). In our illustration, we begin on Day 10 when the closing price is 48.50. The price 10 days ago on Day 1 is 50.75. So, with a 10-day oscillator, we take today's price of 48.50, subtract the price 10 days ago, 50.75, and the result, -2.25, is the oscillator value. This oscillator value of -2.25 is plotted below the zero line. By following this procedure each day, we develop an oscillator curve.

The oscillator curve developed by using this hypothetical situation is very interesting. As the price moves down by the same increment each day between Days 10 and 14, the oscillator curve is a horizontal line. On Day 15, the price turns up by 25 points, yet the oscillator turns up by 50 points. The oscillator is going up twice as fast as the price. The oscillator continues this rate of movement until Day 23 when its value

Figure 9.1

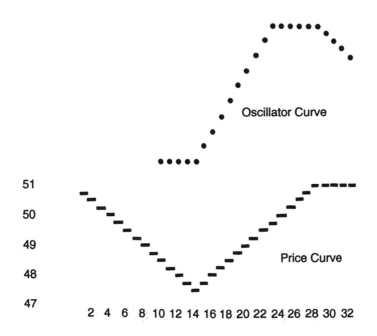

becomes a constant although the price continues to move up at the same rate.

On Day 29, another very interesting thing happens. The price levels out at 51.00, yet the oscillator begins to go down. If the price continues to move horizontally, the oscillator will continue to descend until the 10th day at which time both the oscillator and the price will be moving horizontally.

Note the interaction of the oscillator curve and the price curve. The oscillator appears to be one step ahead of the price. That's because the oscillator, in effect, is measuring the rate of change of price movement. Between Days 14 and 23, the oscillator shows that the price rate of change is very fast because the direction of the price is changing from down to up. Once the price has bottomed out and started up, then the rate of change slows down because the increments of change are measured in one direction only.

THREE PROBLEMS

The oscillator can be an excellent technical tool for the trader who understands its inherent characteristics. However, there are three problems encountered in developing a meaningful oscillator:

1. Erratic movement within the general oscillator configuration. Suppose that 10 days ago the price moved limit down from the previous day. Now, suppose that today the price closed the same as yesterday. When you subtract the price 10 days ago from the price today, you will get an erroneously high value for the oscillator today. To overcome this problem, there must be some way to dampen or smooth out the extreme points used to calculate the oscillator.

2. The scale to use for the 'Y' axis—in other words, how high is high and how low is low? The scale will also change with each commodity being charted. To overcome this problem, there must be some common denominator to apply to all commodities so the amplitude of the oscillator is relative and meaningful.

3. The necessity of having to keep up with enormous amounts of data. This is the least of the three problems; however, it can become burdensome to the trader who is following several commodities with an oscillator technique.

ONE SOLUTION

A solution to these three problems is incorporated in the type of indicator which we will call the Relative Strength Index (RSI):

RSI = 100 - (100 / (1 + RS))

$$RS = \frac{\text{Average of 14 days' closes UP}}{\text{Average of 14 days' closes DOWN}}$$

For the first calculation of the RSI, we need closing prices for the previous 14 days. From then on, we need only the previous day's data. The initial RSI is calculated as follows:

1. Obtain the sum of the UP closes for the previous 14 days and divide this sum by 14. This is the average UP close.

2. Obtain the sum of the DOWN closes for the previous 14 days and divide this sum by 14. This is the average DOWN close.

3. Divide the average UP close by the average DOWN close. This is the Relative Strength (RS).

4. Add 1.00 to the RS.

5. Divide the result obtained in Step 4 into 100.

6. Subtract the result obtained in Step 5 from 100. This is the first RSI.

SMOOTHING EFFECT

From this point on, it is necessary to use only the previous average UP close and the previous average DOWN close in calculating the next RSI. This procedure incorporates the dampening or smoothing factor into the equation:

1. To obtain the next average UP close: Multiply the previous average UP close by 13, add to this amount today's UP close (if any) and divide the total by 14.

2. To obtain the next average DOWN close: Multiply the previous average DOWN close by 13, add to this amount today's DOWN close (if any) and divide the total by 14.

Steps 3 to 6 are the same as for the initial RSI.

An easy way to keep up with the RSI on a daily basis is to use a 10-column worksheet (see Figure 9.2). On Day 16 and thereafter, you are no longer concerned with data for the previous 14 days. The RSI is calculated using only the previous day's average up close and average down close.

To illustrate the procedure for updating the average up and down closes:

On Day 16, take the previous up close in Column 5 (0.84) and multiply it by 13. Add the up close for the day (from Column 3) and divide the total by 14.

$$0.84 \times 13 = 10.92$$
$$\underline{+0.07}$$
$$10.99 / 14 = 0.79$$

The result, 0.79, is the new average up close and is placed in Column 5.

Because the price on Day 16 closed up, the value of the average down close must naturally decrease relative to the 14-day average. However, the procedure is the same. Take the average down close in Column 6 (0.29) and multiply by 13. Because the down close on Day 16 was zero, there is nothing to add back. Now divide the total by 14.

$$0.29 \times 13 = 3.77$$
$$\underline{+\ \ 0}$$
$$3.77 / 14 = 0.27$$

FIGURE 9.2

DAILY WORK SHEET
RELATIVE STRENGTH INDEX

COMMODITY_____

CONTRACT MONTH_____

(1) DATE	(2) CLOSE	(3) UP	(4) DOWN	(5) UP AVG	(6) DOWN AVG	(7) (5) ÷ (6)	(8) 1 + (7)	(9) 100 ÷ (8)	(10) 100 − (9)
1	54.80								
2	56.80	2.00							
3	57.85	1.05							
4	59.85	2.00							
5	60.57	.72							
6	61.10	.53							
7	62.17	1.07							
8	60.60		1.57						
9	62.35	1.75							
10	62.15		.20						
11	62.35	.20							
12	61.45		.90						
13	62.80	1.35							
14	61.37		1.43						
15	62.50	1.13/11.80	4/4.10	.84	.29	2.90	3.90	25.64	74.36
16	62.57	.07		.79	.27	2.93	3.93	25.45	74.55
17	60.80		1.77	.73	.38	1.92	2.92	34.25	65.75
18	59.37		1.43	.68	.46	1.48	2.48	40.32	59.68
19	60.35	.98		.70	.43	1.63	2.63	38.02	61.98
20	62.35	2.00		.79	.40	1.98	2.98	33.56	66.44
21	62.17		.18	.73	.38	1.92	2.92	34.25	65.75
22	62.55	.38		.71	.35	2.03	3.03	33.00	67.00
23	64.55	2.00		.80	.32	2.50	3.50	28.57	71.43
24	64.37		.18	.74	.31	2.39	3.39	29.50	70.50
25	65.30	.93		.75	.29	2.59	3.59	27.86	72.14
26	64.42		.88	.70	.33	2.12	3.12	32.05	67.95
27	62.90		1.52	.65	.42	1.55	2.55	39.22	60.78
28	61.60		1.30	.60	.48	1.25	2.25	44.44	55.56
29	62.05	.45		.59	.45	1.31	2.31	43.29	56.71
30	60.05		2.00	.55	.56	.98	1.98	50.51	49.49
31	59.70		.35	.51	.55	.93	1.93	51.81	48.19
32	60.90	1.20		.56	.51	1.10	2.10	47.62	52.38
33	60.25		.65	.52	.52	1.00	2.00	50.00	50.00
34	58.27		1.98	.48	.62	.77	1.77	56.50	43.50
35	58.70	.43		.48	.58	.83	1.83	54.64	45.36
36	57.72		.98	.45	.61	.74	1.74	57.47	42.53
37	58.10	.38		.45	.57	.79	1.79	55.87	44.13
38	58.20	.10		.43	.53	.81	1.81	55.25	44.75

Column 1: Date.

Column 2: Closing price for the day.

Column 3: Amount the price closed UP from the previous day. (Note: Entry is made in this column only if the price closed up from the previous day. For example, on Day 2, the price closed up 2.00 from Day 1.)

Column 4: Amount the price closed DOWN from the previous day. (Note: Entry is made in this column only if the price closed down from the previous day. For example, on Day 8, the price closed down 1.57 from the close on Day 7.)

Column 5: Value of the average UP close. (On Day 15, you have the necessary information to begin calculating a 14-day RSI. Add all the values in Column 3. The sum in this example is 11.80. Divide this sum by 14 to obtain the average UP close for the 14-day period. This value of .84 is put in Column 5.)

Column 6: Value of the average DOWN close. (Add the down closes in Column 4—a sum of 4.10 in this example. Divide this figure by 14 for the average down close. Put this value of .29 in Column 6.)

Column 7: Result of dividing the number in Column 6 by the number in Column 5— .84 / .29 = 2.90.

Column 8: Result of adding 1.00 to the number in Column 7—2.90 + 1.00 = 3.90.

Column 9: Result of dividing 100 by the number in Column 8—100 / 3.90 = 25.64.

Column 10: Value of the Relative Strength Index derived by subtracting the number in Column 9 from 100—100 - 25.64 = 74.36.

RESOLVING OSCILLATOR PROBLEMS

The RSI approach surmounts three basic problems of oscillators:

1. Erroneous erratic movement is eliminated by the averaging technique. However, the RSI is amply responsive to price movement because an increase of the average close up is automatically coordinated with a decrease in the average close down and vice versa.

2. The question, "How high is high and how low is low?" is answered because the RSI value must always fall between 0 and 100. Therefore, the daily momentum of any number of commodities can be measured on the same scale and compared to each other and to previous highs and lows within the same commodity. The most active commodities are those in which the RSI is showing the greatest vertical movement, either up or down.

3. The problem of having to keep up with mountains of previous data is also solved. After calculating the initial RSI, only the previous day's data is required for the next calculation.

USING THE INDEX

Learning to use this index is a lot like learning to read a chart. The more you study the interaction between chart movement and the Relative Strength Index, the more revealing the RSI will become. If used properly, the RSI can be a very valuable tool in interpreting chart movement.

RSI points are plotted daily on a bar chart and, when connected, form the RSI line. Here are some things the index itself indicates:

Tops and bottoms—These are indicated when the index goes above 70 or below 30. The index will usually top out or bottom out before the actual market top or bottom, giving an indication that a reversal or at least a significant reaction is imminent.

Chart formations—The index will display graphic chart formations which may not be obvious on a corresponding bar chart. For instance, head-and-shoulders tops or bottoms, pennants or triangles often show up on the index to indicate breakouts and buy and sell points.

Failure swings—Failure swings above 70 or below 30 (see Figure 9.3) are very strong indications of a market reversal.

FIGURE 9.3

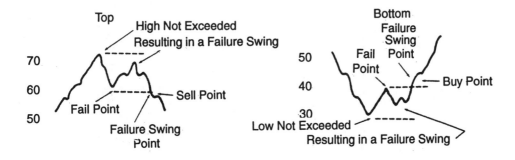

FIGURE 9.4

Here is an example of what several indicators look like on a major print chart service, Commodity Price Charts. Many of the popular indicators are also available on real-time analytical services or with technical analysis software packages such as SuperCharts, Trading Recipes, MetaStock, and others. Looking at the boundaries of overbought/oversold here, note what happens to prices when the Relative Strength Index tops 70 in late January and late August and when RSI sinks below 30 in late March, June, and (almost) at the end of September. Note also how much time the Stochastic indicators spent in overbought territory while prices rallied in July–August.

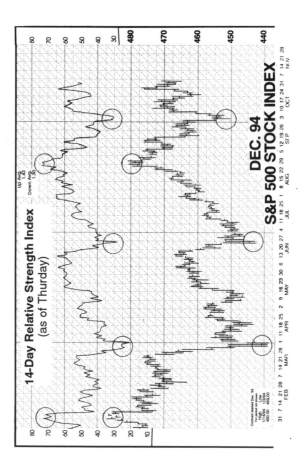

Source: Commodity Price Charts

FIGURE 9.5

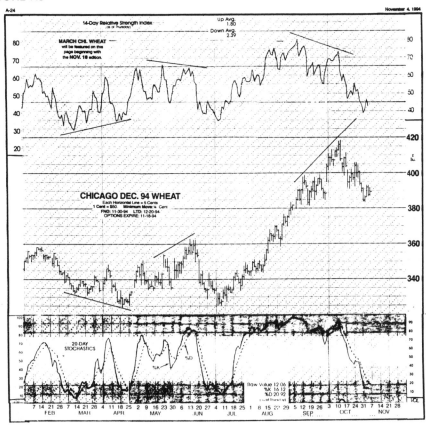

Perhaps even more important than the absolute levels of indicator readings are signs of divergence—prices drop to a new low or reach a new high, but the indicator doesn't. Note how prices dropped to a new low in April but neither RSI nor the Stochastic indicators did. In June, prices appeared to be headed higher, but RSI showed divergence (Stochastics didn't) before prices set back 35¢. The clearest divergence signal came in October when prices exceeded the previous high by 20¢ but RSI fell well short of its previous peak and Stochastics also diverged. The price suggested strength, but the indicators showed the market was weaker than it looked at the time. Note also how the Stochastic indicators provided some good signals but then got tangled up during an extended stay of nearly three months in the overbought zone while prices trended upward in one of the better bull moves of 1994.

Source: Commodity Price Charts

In conjunction with a bar chart, the index helps to define these inter-actions:

Support and resistance—Areas of support and resistance often show up clearly on the index before becoming apparent on the bar chart.

Divergence—Divergence between price action and the RSI is a very strong indicator of a market turning point. Divergence occurs when the RSI is increasing and price movement is either flat or decreasing. Conversely, divergence occurs when the RSI is decreasing and price movement is either flat or increasing.

The Relative Strength Index, used in conjunction with a bar chart, can provide a new dimension of interpretation for the chart reader. No single tool, method or system is going to produce the right answers 100 percent of the time. However, the Relative Strength Index can be a valuable input into this decision-making process.

STOCHASTICS

By George C. Lane and Caire Lane

Few indicators are as widely known in the futures industry as "Stochastics," yet few seem to be as confusing to traders. Frequently misunderstood, misinterpreted and misapplied, it still is a popular technique, and no volume on technical analysis in futures trading would be complete without a discussion of Stochastics.

Generally acknowledged as the originator of and foremost authority on Stochastics is George Lane, professional trader and teacher of thousands of brokers, analysts, arbitrageurs and other traders. Lane was a floor broker for 10 years, wrote a daily market letter for 16 years, was a member of three exchanges and on the board of one of them, owned a regional brokerage office with 41 branch offices and served as economist/director of research for two other regional brokerage firms.

Caire, his wife and a former teacher, joined Lane in his business in 1979, becoming a broker and commodity trading advisor and taking over all of Lane's endeavors when he is on the road teaching classes. Together, they operate Investment Educators in Watseka, Ill., and continue to train traders. "Wasting time and money trying to learn everything about trading by yourself as you go is like trying to teach yourself to be a brain surgeon," they contend.

The following includes some material from Lane's original work in the 1950s, but most of it is brand new and presented to traders for the first time.

Markets offer only a few sources of information on which to base indicators:

❑ **Price**—First and most important, the price action on any given day—open, high, low and close—tells you the true value of a commodity on that day. This information can be dissected internally or compared to information from other days, weeks or months. That is the premise of the bar chart.

❑ **Time**—Price changes over time can happen quickly or slowly. They also tend to repeat patterns over a given time. Therefore, a bar chart, which contains time information, is more beneficial to a trader than an old-fashioned point-and-figure chart.

❑ **Volume**—Knowing how much trading accompanies a price change can tip you off as to changes in the direction of the market when price data is inconclusive. Most charting systems require volume to be drawn as a histogram, or as a line on a graph, below the price bars.

❑ **Open interest**—Unlike stock transactions, commodity trades can remain open for a long period of time; those trades not offset in the same day are known as open interest. Open interest fluctuations are another source of information to commodity traders, but there is no open interest in the stock market, so any indicator based on it is unavailable to the stock trader.

All of the indicators used in the markets are based on some combination of these four items or on changes in the direction/rate of change of these four factors. These data are either number-crunched, graphed or both.

The short formula for Stochastics is:

%K = ((Close - X-day low) / (X-day high - X-day low)) * 100

The sum of the last three %K divided by three equals %D.

The sum of the last three %D equals %D - S.

This is how it works. In an up market, closes will tend to crowd the top of the range until, just before the top, the closes lose their momentum and do not reach the top of the range. Stochastics looks first at the relationship of the close to the low of a specified number of time periods. This information is then compared with the range of a specified number of periods to see what the deviation from the norm is and to reduce it to a percentage. That data is smoothed by a specified number of time periods to create %D. Averaging it a second time, into %D and %D-S, gives a smooth sine wave that looks like a snake undulating between the walls of a cage.

The S&P 500 Index five-minute bar chart shows a heavily trending market (Figure 9.6). Beneath the bar chart of prices are examples of an 11-bar fast Stochastics and a 13-bar slow Stochastics. The fast Stochastics is jerkier looking, with many craggy hills and deep valleys. The more pointed hills are %K. The lighter dotted line is %D. The slow Stochastics is much smoother.

At the first selloff at 45200 (left side of chart), %K in the fast Stochastics had tapered off its rate of ascent, although the commodity continued to make new highs. A minor reaction occurred. Then the trend resumed.

At the next selloff just below 45300, fast %K turned down two days before the break and %D went flat the day *before*. In the slow, both %K and %D went flat and turned down, with %K crossing %D the day *before* the break.

The market returned to the trend and had a double top with the right leg higher. But slow Stochastics went flat and turned down the day *before*, giving divergence. Fast Stochastics had shown marked divergence between the first and second highs.

The next selloff pushed the indicator to the 50 percent level. We could now expect a final high and we got it at 45570. Again, we got divergence but only a small selloff in price. There were probably many who thought it was the perfect time to buy, especially when they saw fast Stochastics at the 25 percent level. But NO! The fast chart is saying the

FIGURE 9.6

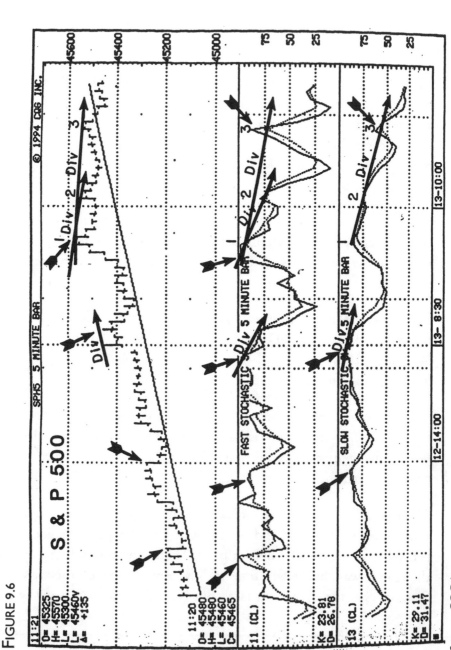

Source: CQG Inc.

reaction to the downside has greater momentum than the ones preceding it. This is confirmed at the last high, when Stochastics gives us a sharp spike, returned us to the trend—the new trend, which is down!

Because of the way it is structured, Stochastics can identify an overbought or oversold market. But it can't tell you precisely how much farther the price will go once the market becomes overbought or oversold. Stochastics can tell you whether a high or low is made on as much momentum as a previous high or low. Stochastics can tell you when the market is about to correct. But it cannot give you an exact price at which to buy or sell.

Stochastics is a tool. It cannot be used alone but must be used in conjunction with the price chart. The data provided by these must be evaluated by that marvelous computer between your ears—and you must be the one to decide whether or not to act!

The question asked most often by beginners is, "What parameters shall I enter into my computer program?" The answer to this varies, depending on the computer program you are using. There are too many variations of the formula, and different programs massage the data differently.

Generally, the first parameter is the number of time periods you want to use as an envelope for comparison. The second and third parameters are used for internal operations and probably should be three and three. Other parameters may be requested for exponential smoothing and other uses, depending on the program used. Consult the manual for your software for an explanation of these. When all else fails, experiment.

Charting services tend to use either 9 or 14 bars for Stochastics out of hand. This is not "right" or "wrong," only convenient for them. But, as a professional trader, you'll want to be more precise. You will want to select the number of periods that will give you a finer edge.

As a general principle, Stochastics confirms the bottom of a cycle; therefore, the number of periods to use for your Stochastics is based on the cycle you are trading.

To select the correct periodicity:

1. Study each of the charts you could possibly trade, be it 3-minute, 5-minute, 15-minute, daily, weekly or monthly charts of the commodity of your choice. Decide which you are going to use, based on your own gut level feel and trading style. Pick the charts where you see the most opportunity for profit, commensurate with the amount of risk you can stand money-wise and psychologically. This is a personal decision; no one can make it for you.

    If you aren't sure, start small. Pick a commodity with smaller daily risk limits and start with longer-term charts. You can always move to bigger and faster games after you've learned how to play.

2. Determine the cycles in the charts you select as previously discussed. Count the days (time periods) from the low to the crest to the low. Do this for several cycles. Then, add them together and divide by the number of cycles you used to get the average number of periods per cycle.

3. Use a periodicity (number of periods) that is 50 percent of the cycle you choose to trade as a starting point. Then, refine it based on whether you are using fast or slow Stochastics and according to the volatility of the market.

4. Use the smaller number of periods only when you are at the point of decision as a way to confirm an anticipated signal. Immediately, revert back to your optimal Stochastic. This will keep you with the trend and in a profitable trade as long as possible.

Stochastics should be adjusted as needed. Remember, it is a tool. If you are using a wrench, you pick the one appropriate for the job. If you pick one that doesn't work for you, you select another that will do the job better. It's the same way with your Stochastics.

RULES FOR STOCHASTICS

I. Divergence/convergence

When a stock or commodity has made a high, then reacts and subsequently goes to a higher high while the corresponding peaks on %D make a high and then a *lower* high, a bearish divergence is indicated. Conversely, when a stock or commodity has made a low, then rallies and subsequently moves down to a lower low while the corresponding low points of %D have made a low and then a *higher* low, you have a bullish convergence (see Figure 9.7).

The weekly T-bond chart (Figure 9.8) and the monthly wheat chart (Figure 9.9) both show examples of divergence at major tops. The wheat chart also shows convergence at the bottom. The bond chart does not show a completed pattern of convergence, and price has gained momentum to the downside, according to the steeper trendline.

Please note that, in the case of a bottom, the downtrending arrow off the commodity and uptrending arrow off the oscillator will, if extended, converge, while at a top, the two arrows will never converge. Therefore, tops diverge while bottoms converge.

The signal to act on this divergence or convergence comes when %K crosses on the right-hand side of the peak of %D in the case of a top or on the right-hand side of the low point of %D in the case of a bottom.

Divergence/convergence is a signal that will cause you to buy or sell, but it may be against the major trend of the market. "A right-hand

FIGURE 9.7

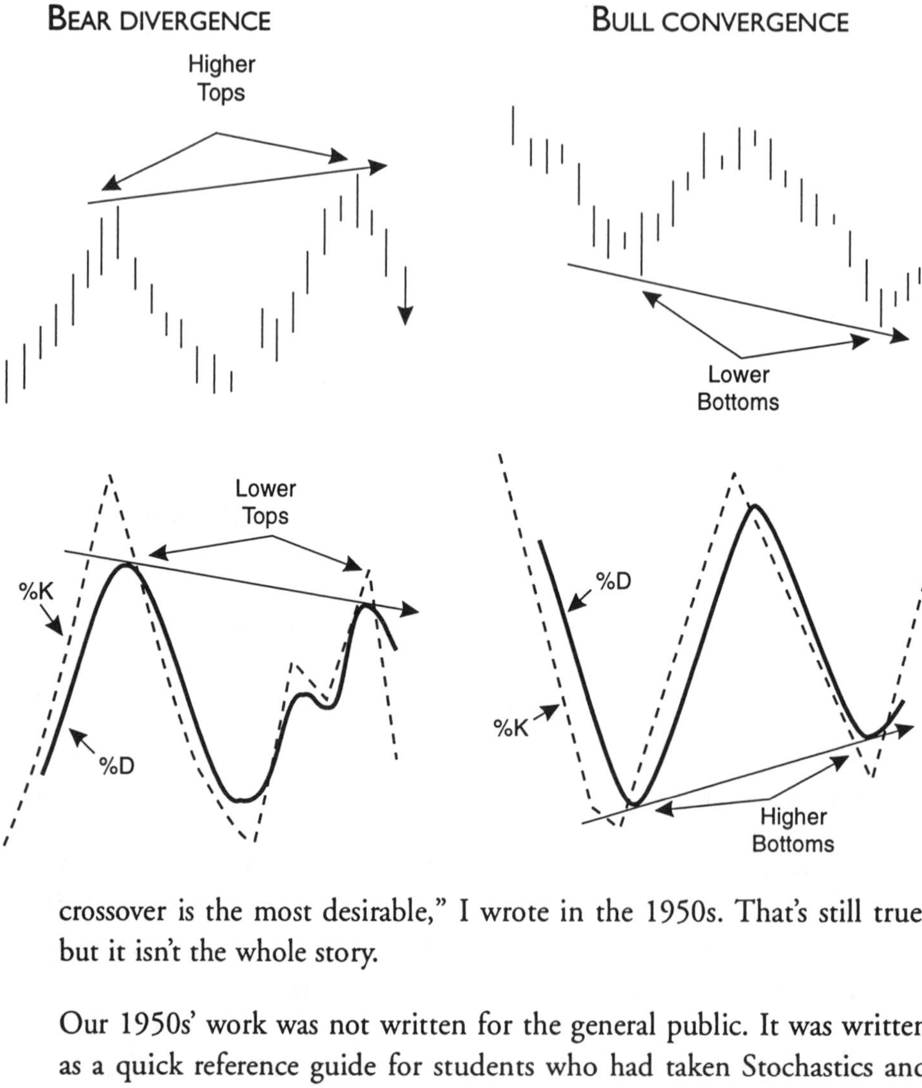

BEAR DIVERGENCE

Higher
Tops

BULL CONVERGENCE

Lower
Bottoms

Lower
Tops

%K

%D

%D

%K

Higher
Bottoms

crossover is the most desirable," I wrote in the 1950s. That's still true, but it isn't the whole story.

Our 1950s' work was not written for the general public. It was written as a quick reference guide for students who had taken Stochastics and Elliott Wave courses from us and who were thoroughly familiar with certain ideas that were not contained in the syllabus, among them the classic and secondary divergence signals.

In the classic divergence signal, the corresponding top in the oscillator follows the classic pattern: The second high is lower than the first high,

FIGURE 9.8

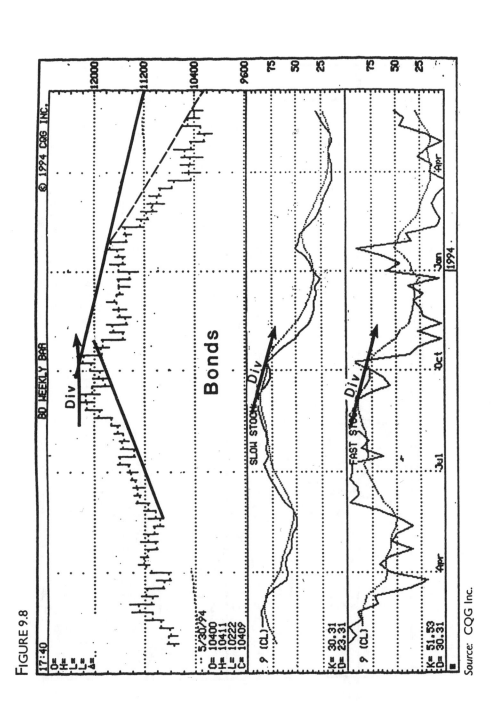

Source: CQG Inc.

FIGURE 9.9

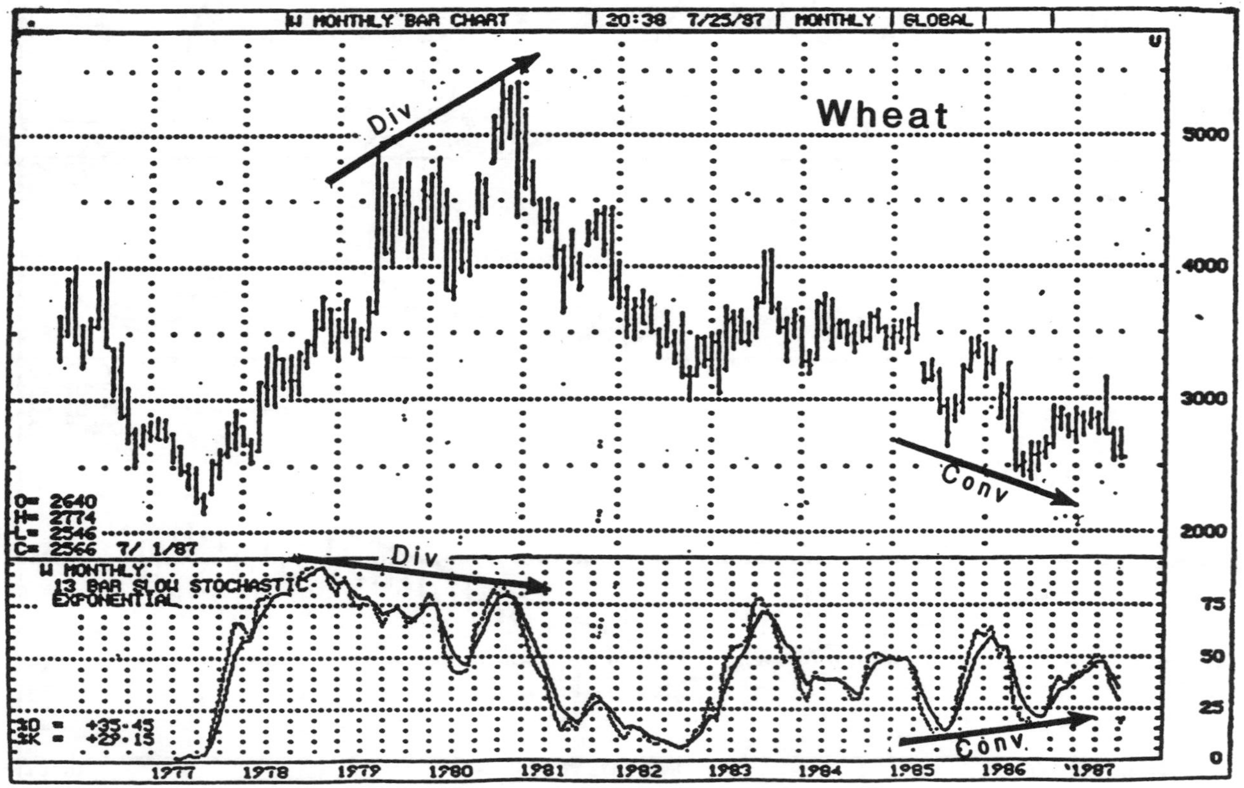

Source: CQG Inc.

showing divergence. However, the third high is lower than the first high, but it is higher than the second high (see Figure 9.10). The Value Line chart shows both classic divergence and classic convergence signals (see Figure 9.11). In each, the third corresponding hill on the oscillator falls within the range created by the first and second.

FIGURE 9.10   CLASSIC DIVERGENCE SIGNAL

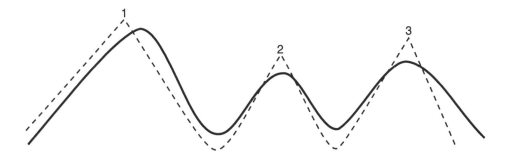

We all know the market does not always behave like a lady, so we can readily accept the secondary pattern signaling divergence (see Figure 9.12). In this pattern, the commodity makes three rallies to a top, while the oscillator shows a second high lower than the first high and the third high lower than the second high, giving a divergence signal.

To further complicate matters, I have seen a few instances of *four* rallies to a top. In this case, the oscillator shows four divergent highs. But I have never seen five rallies to a top. That doesn't mean it can't happen or hasn't happened—but, in 33 years of making a living trading commodities, I just haven't seen one.

II. Types of crossover

When a change in trend returns the commodity to the major trend, a *spike* or "V" bottom (or top) will occur. When returning to the major trend at such a bottom (or top), a left-hand crossover is acceptable.

FIGURE 9.11

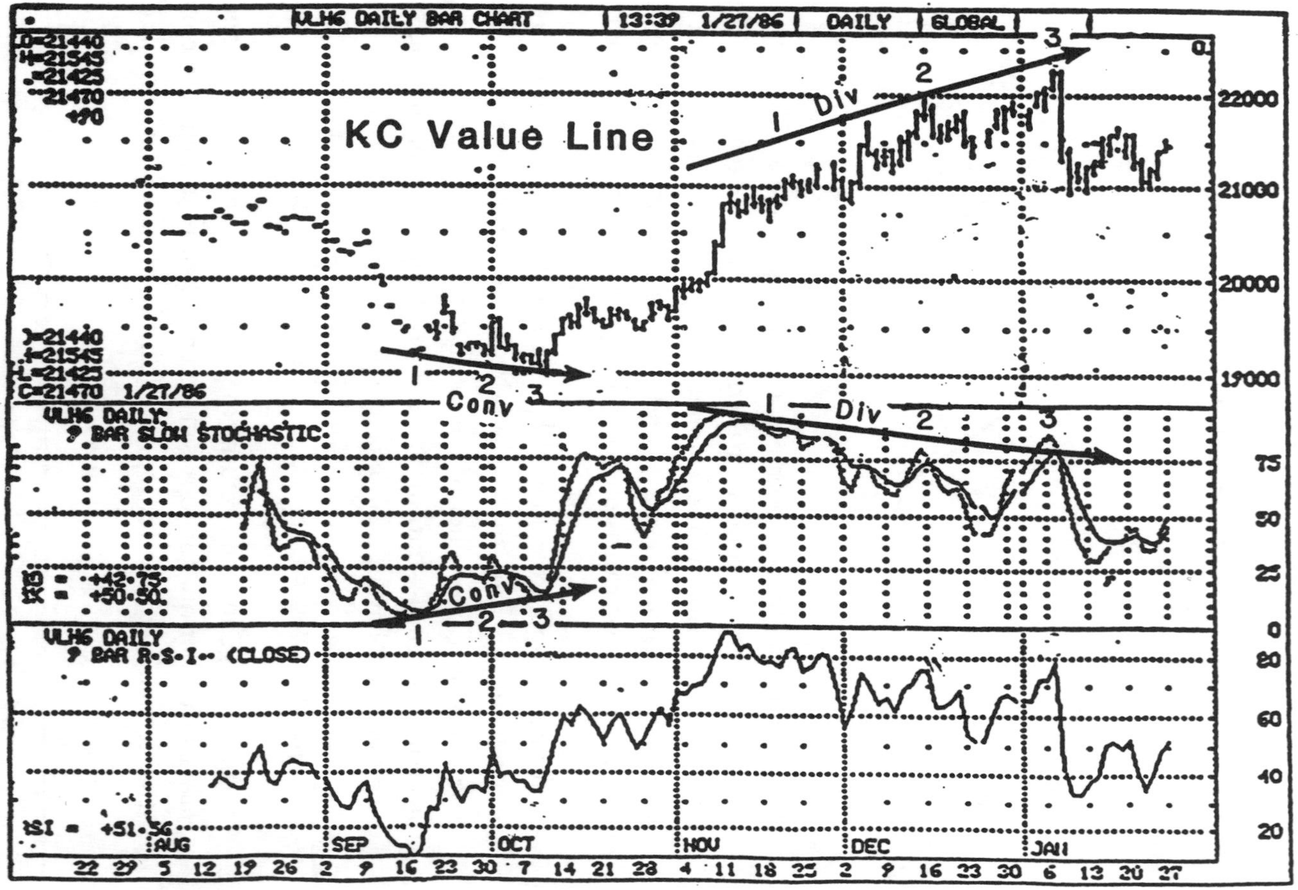

Source: CQG Inc.

FIGURE 9.12   SECONDARY DIVERGENCE PATTERN

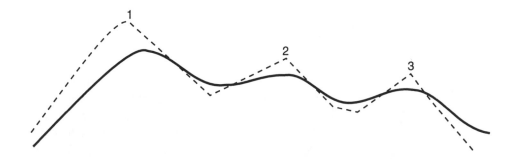

The same does not hold true in the case of *garbage* bottoms, which are basically congestion changes in trend (see Figures 9.13 and 9.14). This

FIGURE 9.13   CROSSOVERS

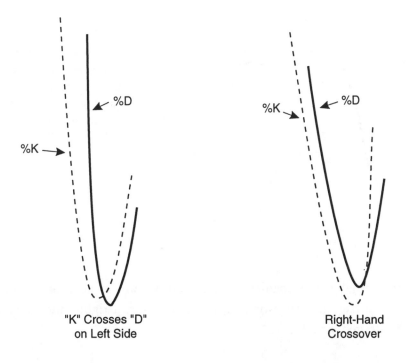

"K" Crosses "D"
on Left Side

Right-Hand
Crossover

FIGURE 9.14

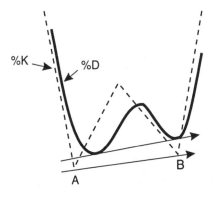

This illustration shows a less-than-desirable change in trend at Bottom A (a left-hand cross-over) but an acceptable right-hand crossover at B, with convergence in both %K and %D.

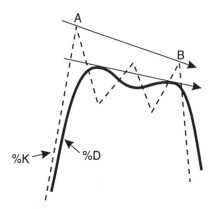

On this illustration of a top, note that Top A has a less desirable left-hand crossover while Top B has a good, clean right-hand crossover, with divergence in %K and %D.

pattern usually accompanies a double bottom in the stock or commodity. In garbage or congestion tops and bottoms, a right-hand crossover is the desired signal.

III. Hinge

A reduction in the velocity of movement in either %K or %D usually indicates a reversal of trend for the next period (see Figure 9.15).

FIGURE 9.15

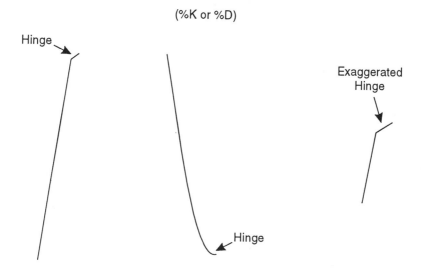

(%K or %D)

Hinge

Exaggerated
Hinge

Hinge

IV. Warning

When %K has been declining each period and then one period reverses sharply (2 percent-12 percent), this is a warning that you may have only a few more time periods before a reversal (see Figure 9.16).

V. %K reaching the extremes (0 percent or 100 percent)

When %K declines to a value of 0, this does *not* denote an absolute bottom in the stock or commodity. On the contrary, it signifies extreme weakness.

Important: After %K initially reaches 0, it will rebound, usually to about 20 percent-25 percent, and then come back toward 0. It may

FIGURE 9.16

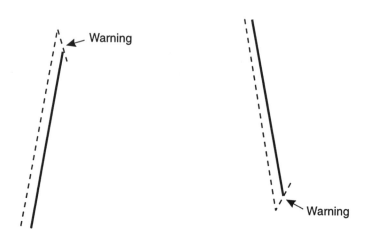

not always reach 0 the second time, but it should at least come close. (Your experience and observation will indicate what close means.) Normally, it will take from two to five time periods for %K to come back this second time, depending on the velocity of the commodity or stock.

The importance of it all is that you can depend upon its coming back toward 0. On the second run against 0, you can expect at least a minor rally to start.

The reverse of these rules apply at tops, using 100 percent. As in the case of the low, expect a selloff, or correction, after the second attempt at 100 by %K.

You must remember that 100 percent does not mean the price of the stock or commodity is as high as it can go nor does 0 percent mean it has reached the culmination of the downward move. In fact, they may mean just the opposite. You will have a reaction, or hesitation, at that level, then a resumption—of that degree—of the major trend, which is still in force.

"Stochastics Pop"

It is in this statement that we find the basis of the "Stochastics Pop," named and popularized by Jake Bernstein.

In a market returning to the major trend: The short-term trend is up, the intermediate-term trend is up, and the long-term trend is up. When %K reaches the 75 percent overbought level, the commodity is frequently only halfway to its price high.

So your plan of action is as follows:

A. Plan to take profits (or move a stop-loss up close) when the stock or commodity has moved up to a price that is twice the price it had at the 75 percent level, its 100 percent price objective.

B. Or take profits when %K falls below 60 percent.

C. Or take profits when %K crosses below %D.

D. Expect a garbage (or congestion) top; therefore, take profits when you complete a pattern of divergence.

"Stochastics Poop"

The "Stochastics Poop," which I so named because of its close relationship with the down or "diarrhea" phase of the market, is a "Pop" in reverse. In a downmove, note the price of the commodity when %K reaches the 25 percent level, double the size of the decline and use that to compute a price objective (see Figure 9.17). Take profits when %K rises above 40 percent or when %K crosses above %D or when a pattern of divergence is complete.

FIGURE 9.17

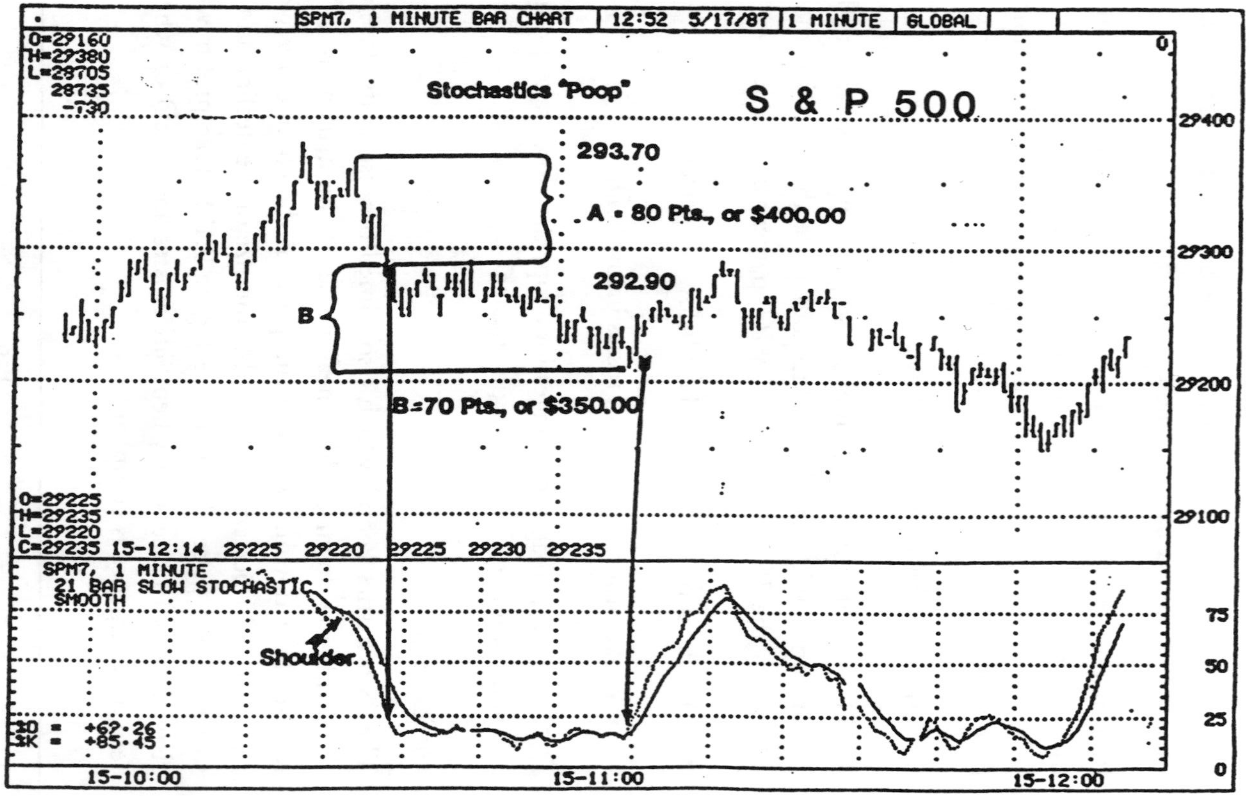

Source: CQG Inc.

VI. Knees and shoulders (originally labeled "failure")

When %K has crossed up through %D and then pulls back a few percentage points the next period but fails to repenetrate %D on the downside before turning up again, we call this a "knee" (see Figure 9.18). It denotes strength or a continuation of upward progression.

FIGURE 9.18

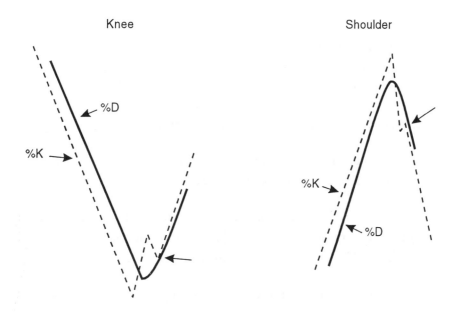

Knee

Shoulder

The same holds true on the downside, only we call that a "shoulder."

This signal is used mostly at a spike change in trend where the crossover is the less desirable left-hand version. %K rectifies its earlier left-hand crossover by reacting to and kissing (or almost kissing) %D, after which they both waltz off together in the direction of the major trend.

Note that %K gives divergence at the spike top or convergence at the spike bottom, even though %D cannot. This is a good signal in %K.

VII. Divergence in %K only

In a garbage top or bottom, many times we observe divergence in %K only. These divergences are necessarily a few periods apart. The significance of this signal in this circumstance is not as great, for it merely suggests a minor reaction. However, if you happen to get this signal in conjunction with a major divergence or convergence in %D, you will have an additional aid in timing.

VIII. Setup

This is another form of divergence or convergence. The primary function of this signal is to forewarn you of a coming *important* top or bottom (Figure 9.19).

Here is what signifies a bear divergence setup:

A corresponding low is made on the stock or commodity and on %D and then a swing to the upside occurs.

On the selloff from the upswing, the correction in the price of the stock or commodity is normal (in proportion, making a higher bottom) but %D falls to new lows, exceeding its prior low.

This means the next swing up will probably provide an important top.

The reverse of this holds true for tops.

Be prepared to study and learn the above, as it is not logical. In fact, the illogical signal, as juxtaposed to a normal signal, is at an advantage.

USING STOCHASTICS

Here are ways Stochastics should be used:

FIGURE 9.19

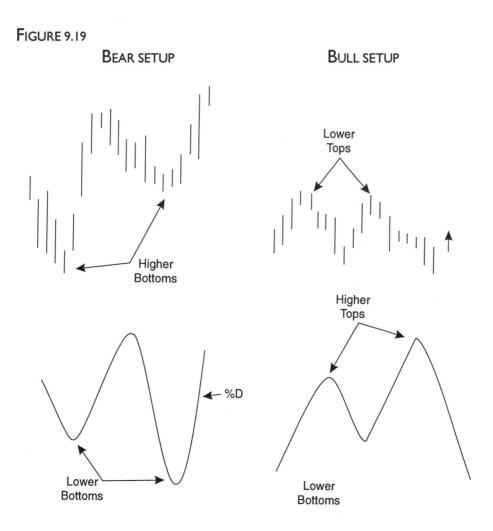

BEAR SETUP   BULL SETUP

Always know and refer to a chart of the next larger degree complete with Stochastics. This will contain the next larger cycle than the one you are trading. Keep the big picture in mind. With this chart, you can anticipate the type and speed of the next change in trend. When in doubt, trade in the direction of the longer-term Stochastic.

While everyone accepts that Stochastics can be used when the market is in a trading range, some people believe that Stochastics is of little help in a heavily trending market. I do not find this to be true. However, Stochastics should be used differently in different types of markets.

Where price is working up and down in a sideways channel, or trading range, Stochastics will notify you of selloffs through crossovers or divergence. You take the signal *if* the point values on the price chart will permit you enough of a gain to justify the risk and *if* you can place your stop-loss advantageously. If the potential reward is too small, or the risk too great, pass the trade.

In a trending market, Stochastics will notify you of changes in trend by divergence. But divergence may take a long time to develop. During the uptrend, you will see garbage tops and spike bottoms in price and in Stochastics. You can expect garbage tops in the Stochastics at countertrend moves while price will give you only small selloffs or will move sideways.

At these points, knowing that countertrend moves are short-lived and not always productive, you have to decide whether or not to:

1. Sell against the longer trend.

2. Take profits and re-enter in the direction of the trend on the low of the reaction.

3. Ride out the reaction.

At such times, you need to be looking at the price chart with trendlines, top and bottom patterns, Dow theory and Elliott Wave in mind. Look at the Stochastics the same way, with all of the above in mind.

In a heavily trending market, if you enter a position on a 14-period Stochastic, you may get what appear to be false signals as the indicator flutters along the top band (80 percent-100 percent). This is a Stochastic Pop. The answer is to lengthen your Stochastics, probably to 28 periods or perhaps even longer. This will give you a smoother indicator as it continues to flutter along the top band. As long as the fluttering continues, you can be assured that the trend is intact.

During a Stochastic Pop, toward the end of the move, the indicator will usually break below the upper band, perhaps down as low as 50 percent-60 percent, then go back up to it. On the next break, you can expect a good signal and a true change of trend.

Another way to handle it is to return to the 14-period Stochastic, after the major break of the top band on the indicator. You may even wish to go to a 9-bar Stochastic. The rationale for this is that the diarrhea phase of the market will be quick and dirty. In a volatile market, you need to get your signals more quickly.

Stochastics is the most popular indicator of technicians worldwide. Its success is due to its reliability and its adaptability. Trading range markets normally present traders with their greatest challenges. Year after year, in market after market, Stochastics reliably calls the turns. While using Stochastics in a trending market is trickier, it is the adaptability of this indicator that allows it to be useful in these market conditions, too.

TAKING PROFITS

After getting into a trade with the help of Stochastics, the last step is getting out profitably. As a chartist, I get out of the market at the first sign of weakness!

One such signal is a closing price reversal of trend (CPR). As the market goes up, the closes crowd the top of the daily range. But, one day, the market no longer has enough strength to stay even or go higher, and the close is at the bottom of the range, effectively reversing the trend. That is weakness! It also is the anatomy of a spike top.

A double top is another reason to get out. If the market has made a high, reacted and, on the second try, cannot go higher, it's weak. Get out! If that second high has lower volume, take the money and run!

Dow theory gives three signals for the end of a market. Dow wrote that a market moves up with higher highs and higher lows. At some point, it makes a high but, on the retracement, breaks the trendline. This is signal No. 1. Then, the market makes a high at or near the previous high but this high is below the trendline. This is signal No. 2. Then, the market makes a new low that takes out the previous, intervening low. This is signal No. 3. The new trend is established—and it's down. This gives you three more signals and a darn good reason to get out!

ON THE ROAD

Now you have enough information to trade with Stochastics and to protect yourself as you do it. But don't get too cocky. You also have enough information to be dangerous to your own financial well-being—and not enough experience to know the difference!

What you need is mileage. You need to get the feel of the road while sitting next to an experienced driver. Then, you take to the track. Whether you have the heart and the guts to stay the course and to become a winner will be proven through the years.

WILLIAMS' %R

Williams' %R is another variation on Stochastics. The indicator generally is associated with Larry Williams because of his research and writing on it, but it was originally conceived by Investor Educators and has been used by a number of other analysts.

While %K in Stochastics compares the closing price with the lowest low for n periods, %R (the name comes from percent of range) compares the close with the highest high. Instead of reading from 0 percent at the bottom to 100 percent at the top, the index scale for %R is flipped upside down so an overbought condition occurs when the indicator is less than 20 percent or 30 percent and the oversold area is above 70 percent or 80 percent. (You can derive %R quickly by taking 100 minus %K. Or you can find %K by taking 100 minus %R.)

In addition, the time period for %R traditionally is 10 periods vs. 5 for %K, and %R usually does not show the three-day moving average (%D).

These cosmetic differences may sound significant, but essentially the %K line from Stochastics and the %R line are the same.

RATE OF CHANGE, MOMENTUM

These are two similar types of indicators that measure the velocity of a price move. Essentially, they tell you how the current price compares with a price n periods ago. Momentum is expressed as price, Rate of Change (ROC) as a percentage.

If you want to measure how fast a market's price is moving, you would just divide today's close by the close 10 days ago (a popular number to start with but it could be any period over which you want to make a comparison). Multiply by 100 if you want to avoid decimal points. The ROC reading will oscillate above and below a 100 (or zero) line.

When the ROC is above the 100 line and rising, it indicates prices are accelerating to the upside. When the ROC is above the 100 line and falling, it indicates a market that is still advancing but more slowly than before. When the ROC is below the 100 line, of course, the same type of movement is occurring to the downside.

A momentum study can use a specific number of points as the zero or 100 line against which the price changes are compared to determine overbought or oversold conditions.

Momentum and ROC, unlike moving averages that lag prices, tend to be leading indicators because as markets move, they tend to run out of steam or momentum as they approach a top or bottom. The direction and slope of the indicator line can tip you off when that is occurring several days before the market actually reverses. The 100 line (or zero or center line, as you may want to call it) also plays an important role as a crossover point that could signal a reversal.

You could spend days or even years testing the parameters for just these indicators alone. First, the number of periods to include is wide open: 10 is common, but it could be any length you choose. Then, you don't have to use closing prices. You can use any of the moving averages, you could average the open-high-low-close each day and compare them, you could use one price for today and a moving average for n days ago, you could do moving averages of averages—your only limitation is your imagination.

COMMODITY CHANNEL INDEX

The Commodity Channel Index (CCI), introduced by Donald Lambert of Los Angeles in the October 1980 issue of *Commodities* magazine, is a timing tool that works best with seasonal or cyclical markets. It compares the current price with a moving average of past prices and tries to adjust for both trading range and trending market conditions.

The first two steps are easy. First, you compute the day's "typical" price by averaging the high-low-close, then you compute a moving average of n days' typical prices. The tough step is computing the mean deviation for the number of days desired from the new moving average each day. Once you have that, the formula for CCI is:

CCI = (1.5 * (Today's Typical Price - Average Typical Price)) / Mean Deviation

The use of the 1.5 constant in the CCI formula scales the resulting CCI value so 70 percent to 80 percent of the random fluctuations fall within a +100 percent to -100 percent channel. If the CCI goes above the +100 line, it's a signal to establish a long position. When the CCI drops below the +100 line, the long position is closed out. When the CCI drops below -100, you sell; when it comes back up above -100, you close out the short position. You can modify these criteria to suit your trading style.

It should also be noted that some traders have been successful doing just the opposite. They treat CCI as an overbought/oversold indicator, using +100 and -100 (or other parameters of their choice) like the top and bottom of a trading channel. When the CCI exceeds +100, they consider the market overbought and a signal to sell; a -100 indicates oversold and a signal to buy.

The key to CCI, as for a number of other indicators, is the length of the data base. Too short produces whipsaws, too long slows response time too much to capture profitable moves. A 20-day CCI has been the standard, but here is another opportunity for you to experiment with technical analysis.

CHAPTER 10

SIGNALING THE TURN II

The indicators in Chapter 8 generally evaluate trends and the oscillators in Chapter 9 primarily determine overbought/oversold conditions. Other indicators also assess the strength or weakness of a move or the quality of the buying or selling but are not as widely known. As a result, they may seem like "new" indicators to you, but they actually have been around for many years, in most cases.

The indicators in this chapter come closer to being trading signals, depending on the circumstances, but like other indicators, they do not suggest a trading position by themselves. They are still indicators, not trading systems.

Analysts and system developers mentioned in this volume have produced many indicators; I have selected only a few examples that seemed most interesting and useful. While you may be able to conclude quickly what indicators in the previous chapters are saying—based on one line crossing another line or an index reading of 70, for example—odds are good you'll have to work with the following indicators for a while to get a good feel for what they are telling you and to become comfortable with them.

SEQUENTIAL

Sequential is a relatively new indicator as far as the trading public is concerned, but its origin actually goes back to 1977. Its creator is Tom DeMark, one of the most remarkable innovators in technical analysis in this generation but virtually unknown until the 1990s because most of his work was backstage while those he worked with and for—Larry Williams, Paul Tudor Jones, Charles "Charlie-D" DiFrancesca, George Soros, Michael Steinhardt, plus a number of major firms—were in the spotlight.

He's almost like the title character in the *Forrest Gump* movie: If anything important happened in the history of technical analysis since 1970, DeMark was there. Unlike the slow *Forrest Gump*, however, DeMark is brilliant in his market insights and his ability to develop ways to trade them profitably.

DeMark is not a trend-follower like most analysts and trading system developers. Much of his work is based on his conviction that there are no smart buyers at the bottom and no smart sellers at the top. If a market turns, he is convinced it's because the last seller has sold or the last buyer has bought—the selling pressure has been exhausted at a bottom and the buying pressure has been exhausted at a top. No genius is at work selling the exact top or buying the exact bottom. His indicators try to identify and buy or sell this exhaustion in anticipation of price turns.

DeMark also likes to eliminate all subjectivity in his methods. He favors precise counts and exact, mechanical methods that leave no room for interpretation. He likes Fibonacci numbers, for example, but not conventional Elliott Wave analysis, which he considers too subjective and useful only in hindsight.

DeMark has summarized more than 20 years of his research and ideas in a book, *The New Science of Technical Analysis*, published in the fall of

1994, and in a videotape series that any serious technical analyst of the 1990s should check out. One of the most interesting indicators he presents is Sequential, the result of his frustration with typical market cycles that also was featured in the September 1993 issue of *Futures* magazine.

As the ultimate technician, DeMark is likely to continue to study and analyze this indicator further, and others also may massage it as happened to RSI and other Wilder indicators. Whether today's Sequential will stand up 20 years from now is unknown, but its approach provides a unique new look at trend analysis that is worth exploring. There is more to Sequential than what follows and obviously much, much more to DeMark and his work with indicators, systems and technical analysis. But this gives you a taste of his style.

SEQUENTIAL STEPS

The Sequential indicator has three distinctive phases: The setup, the countdown and market entry action.

Setup: Compare today's close with the close four trading days ago. When a market closes lower than the close four days ago nine days in a row, the buy setup is complete. If today's close is higher than the close four days ago for nine consecutive days, you are set up to sell. "Having a nine" is significant because it indicates the market is oversold or overbought and has almost exhausted the potential to continue the trend.

The number of days in the setup must be nine, and they must be consecutive. A close equal to the close four days ago does not count; you have to start over. There are other qualifiers such as the low on Day 9 should be less than the low on Day 8 and especially below the low of Day 6 in a buy setup, for example, but this illustrates the basic concept of a Sequential setup.

Countdown: Once the "nine" package is in place, you move into the countdown period to the ultimate low or high. Before the countdown begins, you must be sure there is "intersection"—that is, in a buy setup, the Day 8 or 9 high has to be greater than the low three trading days earlier or any day before that in the setup period. Lack of an intersection may indicate a breakaway situation, and you don't want to be in the way of a freight train that isn't ready to turn around yet.

If you don't have intersection, you continue to look for it on Day 10 and following days until you get it. Then the countdown can begin.

In the countdown phase, you compare the close on Day 9 with the low two days earlier. You have a Sequential buy signal when you have 13 days—these do not have to be consecutive and you can use equals in the countdown—where the day's close is lower than the low two days ago. The 13th day often is the low day on a buy situation and the high on a sell setup when the move is exhausted and ready to turn.

Again, there are other qualifying factors to consider such as comparing the current setup to the previous setup and being aware of a "recycle" possibility, but this illustrates the basic idea.

Action: After you complete the setup and reach Day 13 in the countdown, you are ready to take your position. You can wait for a signal confirmation from another indicator, place a stop and wait for the price to come to you or use some other entry technique. In a buy situation, DeMark looks at the low day and measures the distance between the day's low and the day's close. He places a buy stop that distance below the low day's low.

DRAWBACKS

Sequential has produced some excellent signals, but it isn't perfect. Some markets obviously turn without ever making a "nine."

While it has exact guidelines, you have to keep in mind a number of requirements that could sidetrack the Sequential pattern. Until you have some practice with this method, it may be a challenge to be sure everything conforms to the Sequential rules.

As you might imagine after reading the description above, a Sequential trading signal does not come along very often. It may not produce enough trades for you. Sequential is not for the impatient, impulsive trader.

Sequential produces only entry signals. As an indicator, it is not a trading system so you will have to rely on other methods for exit rules.

When a Sequential signal fails, it may really fail. Although it provides low-risk entry points, what seems like an exhaustion top may not be the top in a runaway market. See the reference to freight train above.

ACCUMULATION-DISTRIBUTION

Larry Williams has already been mentioned in association with the %R or, as it is sometimes called, Williams %R indicator in the previous chapter. Williams has developed, tested, worked with hundreds of indicators, patterns, signal methods, etc. in nearly 30 years of trading and has written a number of books himself explaining his techniques. Some of his ideas require an exact set of circumstances to occur; some are as simple as sell on a Friday and buy on a specific Monday.

One indicator that he uses is particularly interesting for identifying the beginning of bullish or bearish moves. Accumulation-distribution analyzes the relationship of closes and opens, building on the concept that this relationship reveals a good deal about market sentiment.

To determine how a market is doing, the public usually looks at today's price vs. yesterday's close—to the public, saying corn is up 2¢ at noon, for example, means the price at noon is 2¢ higher than the close yesterday. To the professional trader, the more important question is, "How did the market do after the open?" Quite often, Williams points out, the open is near the high or the low of the day because of public buying or selling. His conclusion:

Public activity = yesterday's close - today's open

Professional activity = today's close - today's open

Sometimes both are buying, driving prices up to close at the top of the day's range. Or both are selling, pushing the day's close to the bottom of the day's trading range. That could be a sign the market is running out of buyers at a top or sellers at a bottom and could be setting up for a turn. The public isn't always wrong, of course, so a market could continue its move for several days. But, given a choice between going with the public and going with the professionals and commercials, odds are good you would prefer to be on the side of professional.

To measure the sentiment of the professionals, you need to compare today's close with today's open to tabulate the number of units of buying power. Williams' formula:

If today is an up day (today's close is higher than yesterday's close), then take today's close minus today's true low. That represents buying accumulated by the professionals.

If today is a down day (today's close is lower than yesterday's close), then take today's true high minus today's low. Again, that represents long positions accumulated by professionals.

Each day you add this number to the previous day's total to get a cumulative total. There is no 0-100 scale; the number could be small or large. The important thing is not the number itself, but the direction of the accumulation-distribution line and, even more important, the divergence between that line and prices. If prices are hitting a new high but accumulation-distribution is not, it indicates a sell signal; if prices hit a new low but accumulation-distribution stays above its low, a buy signal is indicated.

A market could be collapsing into new lows and appearing hopelessly bearish but underneath the surface professionals could be accumulating positions, indicated by an accumulation-distribution line that is refusing to follow price down. The point is, when price diverges from A/D, A/D is pointing the way price will go. That could be an important tip-off to a bullish turn or at least the end of the down move.

MARKET FACILITATION INDEX (MFI)

By Bill M. Williams

Another approach that attempts to evaluate the quality of the price action is the Market Facilitation Index (MFI). Developed by Bill Williams, president of Profitunity Trading Group in Mobile, Ala., it is a simple but effective method for determining the "efficiency" of the market.

Williams has been trading and teaching trading for about 35 years and, after five years of research, first introduced what he called the "mud factor" in 1983—when markets were in a bracket or range-bound, trading was like slogging through mud; when they were trending, it was as if they were running on concrete. In 1986 he changed the name to "tick mileage" because what it was actually measuring was the effective price change attributed to each new tick coming into the market.

"Finally," Williams says, "we decided to sound more sophisticated and now refer to it as the MFI or Market Facilitation Index."

The following goes beyond the MFI indicator itself but serves as an example of how a specific indicator can lead to trading signals. You will find more about volume aspects of trading and the impact of volume on price in Chapter 13.

Before a trend can start, there must be more volume coming to the floor—trends are created by outside paper and not on the floor.

The first thing that changes in a market then are decisions in traders' minds off the floor. This is then reflected in changes in tick volume. After that comes a change in momentum, followed by a price change and then, finally, a change in trend. Our goal is to get in on the first 10 percent of any change in trend and get out on the final 10 percent of that same trend. If you can do this, you will be rich.

Again, for emphasis, the first key is a change in tick volume. A practical rule in intraday trading is a difference of one tick is enough. You are interested in whether there is more or less volume than the previous time period. If you are trading on a daily chart, use +/- 10 percent to count as a significant difference in volume. Today's volume must be 110 percent of yesterday's volume to count as a "+". Volume that is 90 percent or less would count as a "-". Anything between 91 percent and 109 percent of the previous volume would count as the same volume.

The only language the market speaks is price, volume and time. Whenever the tick volume goes up, you know more outside paper is coming in; whenever it goes down, you know less outside paper is coming to the floor. Your next task is to assess accurately the effect this change in volume has on the market.

It is not enough to know how much; it is much more important to know how the market reacts to this change in volume. Heavier volume does not always mean the market will move. Remember, the market's main task is to find its balance point, and it will do it in a fraction of a second. That balance point will only move when there is a bias of incoming orders. So you need a bias finder that works in both trending and bracketed markets. It is relatively easy to make profits in a trend; the problem is keeping those profits when there is not a trend.

The Market Facilitation Index is very simple. You determine the range of whatever time period you are observing by subtracting the low from the high and divide that number by the volume: MFI = Range/Volume.

Breaking this formula down, you can see it is measuring the change in price per tick:

Range/Volume = D Price/Tick

Comparing this to Einstein's $E = mc^2$, you can solve for the constant c^2 by transposing the m (mass) with the following results:

$$c^2 = E/m = Range/Volume$$

In trading, the mass would correspond to volume while the energy would correspond to the price movement. Whether or not Einstein would agree, I have no idea. It is fun to speculate, however (both in trading and thinking).

What you are measuring is the effective change in price per tick. This number has no absolute value. Its value lies in comparing this number with a previous MFI. For example, if the current bar's MFI is 0.541, that is not comparable in any way with a bar from yesterday's chart that might have a value of 0.541. You are interested in the MFI in relation to the immediate previous market action. You want to know if there is more or less market facilitation of price movement. The MFI is a measure of the market's willingness to move the price.

The MFI's measurement of how many points the market traveled per tick is an extremely accurate description of the efficiency of the market during this particular bar. If the current MFI is greater than the previous MFI, we observe more price movement per tick, greater facilitation of price movement through time. Again, we are comparing only the current bar's MFI with the immediately preceding bar's MFI. This allows you to determine whether the present time period is providing more or less trading opportunities.

When you combine two factors—volume and MFI—you can get what I call profitunities, which are more than windows of opportunity because your odds are so much better. I have given names to each of the four possible combinations of volume and MFI to describe exactly what is happening in both the broad market and the reaction in the pits.

FIGURE 10.1   CALCULATING FOR MFI

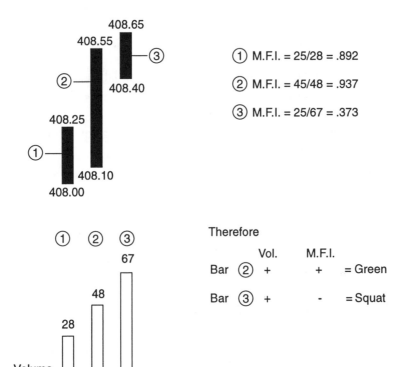

① M.F.I. = 25/28 = .892

② M.F.I. = 45/48 = .937

③ M.F.I. = 25/67 = .373

Therefore

		Vol.	M.F.I.	
Bar	②	+	+	= Green
Bar	③	+	-	= Squat

Using the simple formula, MFI = Range/Volume, here is the calculation for three bars. Bar 1 has a range of 25 and a tick volume of 28 – 25/28 = an MFI of 0.892. This means each tick of volume accounted for a 0.892 point move in the price. Bar 2 has a range of 45 with a tick volume of 48 – 45/48 = 0.937 for the MFI reading. Like Bar 1, Bar 3 also has a range of 25 points but the tick volume has jumped to 67 – 25/67 = 0.373 for MFI. The number itself means nothing but in comparison to the immediately preceding bar's MFI, it does. In these three bars it is obvious that traders are moving the price through time most efficiently on Bar 2 because its MFI is higher than the other two. This bar is more "trending" than either of the other two bars whereas Bar 3 (+ volume, - MFI) is a "squat" produced by the bias of the incoming new participants in the direction opposite the way the market is moving. The squat suggests the trend may be changing.

Tick volume/MFI combinations			Indicator
1.	+ Tick volume	+ MFI	Green (+ +)
2.	− Tick volume	− MFI	Fade (− −)
3.	− Tick volume	+ MFI	Fake (− +)
4.	+ Tick volume	− MFI	Squat (+ −)

Green (+ tick volume, + MFI)—This bar is labeled "green" because it is a green light for market movement. Movement is already happening.

Pretend you are a hobo in a freight yard looking for a train going west. You could adopt two different approaches to finding the right train: (1) Wander around the freight yard, and if you find a train whose way-bills were all for western states, you would surmise that this train will be going west eventually. Then you could find a nice box car, make yourself comfortable and wait for the engine to hook up and go. (2) Stand on the western edge of the freight yard and jump on the first train coming out of the yard going west.

The second choice would be a "green." It is a train already on the move. It may, as a moving train coming out of the yard, be dangerous to tag onto. You certainly would not want to stand in front of it, which is exactly what you would be doing if you tried to fade a green bar.

A green is a breakout signal, and your best immediate strategy is to go with whatever direction it is going. It signifies three things:

❑ More players are entering the market (+ volume).

❑ They are biased in the direction the bar is moving.

❑ The price movement is picking up speed as it goes (+ MFI).

Fade (- tick volume, - MFI)—A "fade" occurs when the market is taking a breath or just losing interest. It is the opposite of a green because there are both less volume and less MFI (price movement).

Because the markets are an auction market, the bidders are losing interest.

If I were auctioning this computer on which I am writing, I am sure many people would give me $100 for it instantly. With that kind of response, I, of course, would raise the price. Considerably fewer traders would offer me $1,000 for it, and I am sure no one would offer $5,000. As the price goes up, more and more bidders lose interest.

This is what a fade indicates. Often, the top of the first wave in an Elliott Wave sequence has a fade top—not a lot of action and the excitement of the market is dwindling. Now it is very important to point out that fade areas (which may be more than two bars) are the start of big moves. So the very time the market is most boring is exactly the time when a good trader must be on guard for any sign that momentum is building.

Fake (- tick volume, + MFI)—Here we have a situation where the MFI is increasing, which means the market is facilitating itself by moving price through time, but it is not supported by increasing volume from outside the pit. Therefore, the facilitation is less robust as indicated by the decrease in raw volume.

For whatever reasons, the market is attracting less volume than during the previous period. It sometimes indicates a pause in the market action before the market "takes off." Unless this situation is followed shortly by increasing volume, this is a picture of a fakeout generally manipulated by locals in the pit. The locals are in temporary control simply because there is no significant volume of outside paper coming into the pit. The fake is a trademark of pit manipulation and should be viewed with a high degree of skepticism.

The locals have sensed that a move is imminent during the lull in the pit action. This is the only time the locals have enough power to "run your stops." They will, if possible, take the market in the opposite direction of the anticipated move to acquire inventory to take the other side of the anticipated paper coming into the pit. They are building their inventory so they can sell the next rally or buy the next decline.

Squat (+ tick volume, - MFI)—This is the strongest potential money-maker of these four profitunity windows. Virtually all moves end with a squat as the high/low bar plus or minus one bar of the same time period. Another way of saying this is that all significant trends end with a squat on one of the three top or bottom bars. This provides a potentially very effective way to get in on the beginning of a trend.

While all trends end in a squat, not all squats are the end of a trend. Squats appear quite often in the middle of Elliott Wave 3 and at Fibonacci retracements and Gann line intersections (see Section IV for all these topics). If it does not end the immediate trend, it tends to become a "measuring squat" (similar to a measuring gap) predicting how far the current move will continue. This measuring squat gives you a target zone to look for another squat that may end the current trend.

Squats are characterized by a greater tick volume and a lower MFI and, usually but not always, a smaller range that the previous bar. If you are trading short-term charts (intraday), a visual shorthand for a squat would be the same or smaller range with a higher tick volume (compared to the previous bar).

The squat is the last battle of the bears and bulls, with lots of buying and selling but little price movement. There is an almost equal division between the number and enthusiasm of both bears and bulls. A real war is taking place; you are watching the equivalent of hand-to-hand combat in the pits.

I labeled this a squat because it appears the market is squatting, getting ready to leap one way or the other (often a reversal of the current trend). The market has moved up or down on substantial volume, and now a flood of sellers or buyers enters the market. Volume increases, the trend stalls, and price movement virtually stops. The key is that the price movement stops on higher volume. One of the two opposing forces (buyers or sellers) will win. Usually the breakout of the squat will let you know whether this squat is a trend continuation or trend reversal squat.

Like all volume indicators, this works better with larger volume. Our research indicates you may use these indicators confidently on any time frame that has an average tick volume of 20 or more ticks per bar. If you are trading a certain time period and notice the average volume drops below 20 ticks per bar, all you do is tab up to the next higher time frame that does average 20 or more ticks per bar and keep trading.

After using MFI for a short while, you will recognize visually whether the MFI is greater or less. Don't get bogged down thinking you have to use the calculator on every bar. You can also obtain several computer programs to color the bars depending on changes in the MFI.

Remember, we are uncomplicating the market action for easy, accurate and quick decisions. You don't need to find an index or zero point from which to work. You work only with what is happening in the market now. What formerly took me 5-9 hours per day to analyze now takes me less than 20 minutes of analysis time per day for 30 markets, using the procedures outlined on the last few pages.

CHAPTER 11

INDICATOR APPLICATIONS

One message that has been repeated over and over in this section is that you should never look at one indicator in isolation to make a trading decision. Perhaps you know chart patterns well but you need some kind of indicator to provide the trigger point for a trade. Or perhaps you have found an indicator that looks promising but you would like some confirmation of its signals.

How do you combine technical indicators with charts and other input to read markets? How do you apply to actual trading what looks good in theory in your analysis?

Obviously, a number of systems traders have put together techniques that work well for them. This chapter will give you just a couple of examples of how traders have incorporated technical indicators into their trading programs. This process of practical application of technical analysis to real markets in real time is the challenge that faces you.

THE TRIPLE SCREEN APPROACH

By Alexander Elder

One of the people who has put his trading act together is Alexander Elder, whose escape from a Soviet ship and entry into trading is an amazing story in itself. As an eager student of the markets, he seems to have read and studied about everything there is to know about technical analysis and has a knack for digesting complex ideas and making them understandable. His unique text-workbook combination, Trading for a Living, *is high on the recommended reading list for anyone who wants practical, real-world trading help.*

A professional trader and practicing psychiatrist in New York, Elder also is director of Financial Trading Seminars Inc. A prolific writer and teacher, he has written a number of articles and reviews for Futures *magazine over the years. Several were on the triple screen method, a very useful overall approach to trading. This is taken from the April 1986 issue of* Futures. *Reproduced here with permission.*

Those positive features in many trading techniques can also lead to dangerous losses when market conditions change.

Even the most widely accepted techniques—"The trend is your friend," "Buy (or sell) breakouts" and "Buy low, sell high"—can be costly. It's like running an obstacle course, where being 6 feet tall may be an advantage in running on a straightaway but won't help when you have to crawl through a 10-inch tube.

So how can you resolve the contradictory advice provided by normally sound trading techniques? In discussing trading approaches, you first need to be clear which trends and breakouts you are trying to catch. Trading weekly, daily or hourly trends calls for different techniques.

To be successful, you have to combine several trading techniques, selected so their negative features can cancel out each other while their positive features stay undisturbed. The secret is to apply each technique to a different time frame of market events.

Robert Rhea, the great market technician of the 1930s, compared the three market trends—major, intermediate and minor—to a tide, a wave and a ripple. Most traders, especially those who cannot follow intraday moves, can benefit from intermediate trends, which last from two weeks to two months. You want to ride the wave (intermediate move) while taking advantage of the tide and letting even the ripple run in your favor.

That is the goal of the triple screen system, which uses three consecutive screens, or tests, before entering any trade. Each test uses a different trading approach. Many trades that seem attractive at first are rejected by one or another screen. Those potential trades that pass the triple screen tests have a high degree of profitability.

SCREEN 1: CATCHING THE TIDE

Your first goal is to identify the major trend, the market's tide. Start by examining weekly charts. The longer-term perspective puts you a jump ahead of those who watch only daily charts—with everybody looking at the same few months of data.

You can use several techniques to find the weekly trend. Trendlines and channels are useful. So are moving averages, which smooth week-to-week fluctuations.

My favorite indicator of the major trend on weekly charts is moving average convergence divergence (MACD), originally developed by Gerald Appel. It is a sophisticated system of three exponential moving averages on closing prices.

The weekly chart of Treasury bond futures has MACD plotted underneath the prices, both as exponential moving average lines and as a histogram (Figure 11.1). The lines show crossovers between faster and

FIGURE 11.1   MACD LINES AND HISTOGRAM

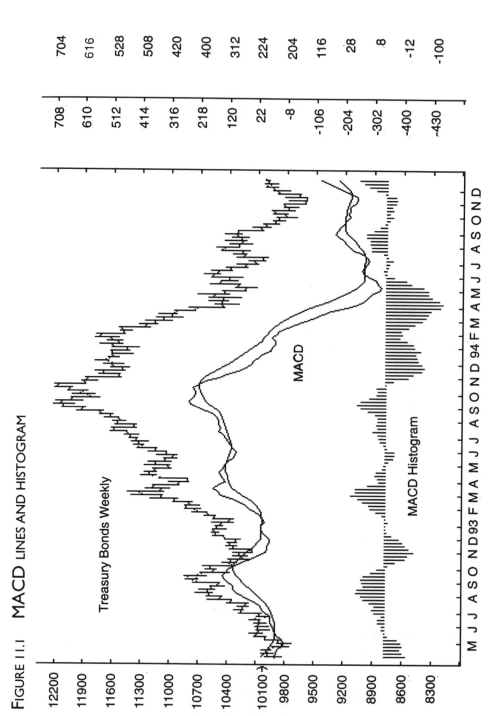

Source: FutureSource

slower exponential moving averages while the histogram tracks the difference between the two lines.

The histogram that keeps growing in either a positive or negative direction indicates growing bullish or bearish sentiment and forecasts a turn in market direction, frequently in advance of the price reversal. MACD line crossovers come later and issue decisive buy and sell signals.

The first "screen" (market test) before entering a trade involves finding the direction of the weekly MACD histogram. If it is rising (bullish), take only long positions. If it is falling (bearish), only trade short. Always trade in the direction of the market tide.

SCREEN 2: RIDING THE WAVE

After finding the weekly trend, switch to daily charts and indicators for the second screen to identify the intermediate trend. Look for daily moves against the weekly trend.

For this screen, use oscillators with daily charts instead of trend indicators. Their rapid fluctuations between positive and negative extremes help you locate temporarily overbought or oversold conditions (that means the market has moved too far up or too far down and is likely to snap back).

While the first screen put you in a trend-following mode, you now want to go countertrend—"buy low, sell high." That can be dangerous, but now you can use it with confidence because buy and sell signals from daily oscillators make logical sense. When the market tide is coming in (weekly MACD rises), every pause and wave that goes against the tide—shorter countertrend moves—offers an opportunity to get aboard the trend. It is probable that the weekly trend will reassert itself, leading to profits.

It would be dangerous to rely on oscillators alone. In major down-trends, they can go into an oversold mode and stay there for weeks at a time, hurting a premature buyer. But, when the weekly trend is up-ward, you can use negative readings of a daily oscillator to get ready to buy. When the weekly trend is down, use positive readings of a daily oscillator to get ready to sell short.

One daily indicator that does a good job of identifying intermediate daily reactions against weekly trends is the Stochastic indicator, devel-oped by George Lane (see Chapter 9). Stochastics track the positioning of daily closing prices within the daily range (Figure 11.2).

Closing prices tend to accumulate toward the tops of the ranges in advance of upside reversals of downtrends and toward the bottoms in advance of downside reversals of uptrends. The raw data is smoothed and represented by two lines, one faster, the other slower. You derive buy-sell signals when the faster line crosses above or below the slower line.

There are other methods for interpreting Stochastics, but this one serves our purpose. The chart shows how crossovers by the faster line of the five-day Stochastic above the slower line have given good buy signals while the weekly MACD was in an uptrend.

SCREEN 3: READING THE RIPPLE

The third screen uses intraday trends to help you enter positions. When the weekly trend is up, you want to buy each time the daily countertrend pushes prices down. But you also want to protect yourself from the danger that the countertrends may continue even lower.

The third screen helps you benefit from the buying opportunities while protecting you from the risk that the brief downtrend may turn into a major one. In major downtrends, it helps you benefit from shorting

FIGURE 11.2   STOCHASTICS AND T-BONDS

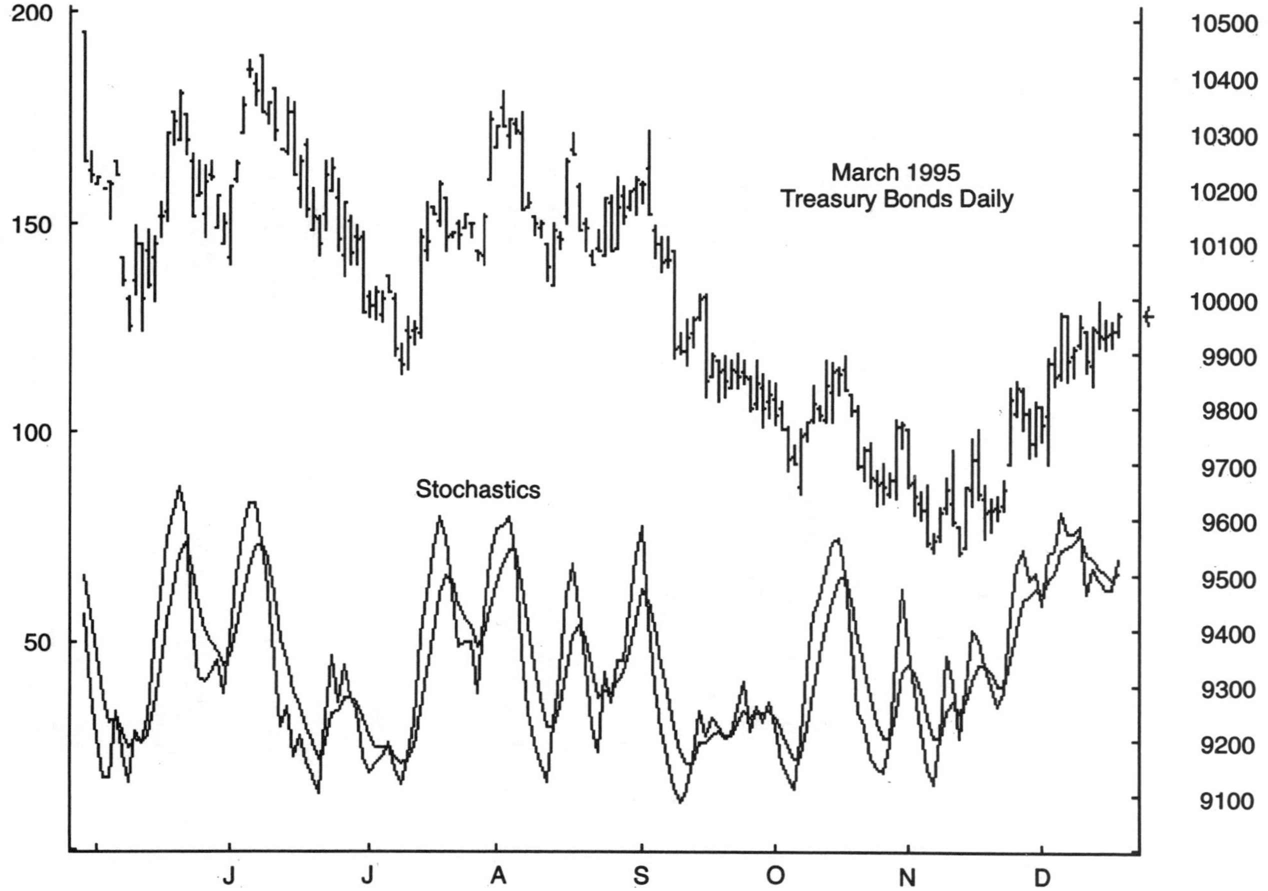

March 1995
Treasury Bonds Daily

Stochastics

Source: FutureSource

into the countertrend rallies while protecting you from the risk that those rallies will become bullish reversals.

This screen consists of using trailing stop techniques (not to be confused with stop-loss orders). A trailing buy-stop order trails above the previous day's range on the way down, angling for the upside reversal. A trailing sell-stop order trails below the previous day's range on the way up to catch a renewed downturn.

If the daily oscillator goes negative on Tuesday while the weekly trend is up, then place a buy order, good for Wednesday only, above Tuesday's high. If the weekly trend pushes back up, as you expect, you will be "stopped in," automatically buying a short-term breakout from the intermediate downtrend.

If prices continue lower on Wednesday, you remain out of the market. You lose nothing, but the buy signal remains in effect as long as the oscillator remains in negative territory. Then, on Thursday you place a buy order, good for one day only, above the Wednesday high. You continue this procedure until you are either "stopped in" on an upside reversal or a bearish trend is signaled by the weekly MACD, canceling the buy signal.

This buy-stop technique is reversed to a sell-stop technique for shorting when the weekly trend is down but the daily oscillators rally into positive territory.

THREE SCREEN SUMMARY

Thus, the triple screen system consists of three consecutive screens or tests, each applied before entering any market position:

1. Identify the major trend, using a MACD histogram on weekly charts.

2. Identify the intermediate daily trend running counter to the major trend. Use short-term oscillators, such as force index, Stochastic or Williams' %R. When the weekly MACD is bullish, watch for daily oscillator declines. When the weekly MACD is bearish, watch for daily oscillator rallies.

3. When the weekly trend is up and the daily oscillator is negative, use a trailing buy-stop technique to enter or add long positions. When the weekly trend is down and the daily oscillator is positive, use a trailing sell-stop technique to enter or add short positions.

MAINTAINING A STOP

Using stop-loss and protect-profit orders is essential in trading futures. After the triple screen system gives you a buy signal and you go long using the trailing buy-stop technique, your new stop-loss level becomes the low of the day you went long or the low of the previous day, whichever is lower. That low will rarely be violated because you are trading in the direction of the market tide. Reverse the procedure in downtrends. This gives you tight protection with relatively low dollar risk.

Conservative traders should buy or sell on the first signal from the triple screen system and stay with those positions until the weekly trend reverses or until stopped out. Aggressive traders can use renewed buy or sell signals from the triple screen system for pyramiding or adding to the original positions.

COMBINING INDICATORS

By Ken Seehusen

Ken Seehusen, editor of Chart Insight, *an Oster Communications Inc. newsletter based in Cedar Falls, Iowa, has been through the process of analyzing markets and setting up a trading program that works for him. He explains how he looks at indicators, charts, etc. and combines them in his trading strategies.*

In developing a trading system, you need to determine when to enter a market, when to exit the market with a loss and when to exit with a gain.

To be a true trading system, the rules for your decisions must be objective. "Buy cotton when I think it's going up and sell it if I lose a little or make a lot" is not a trading system. It's a guessing game, and in the futures markets guessing games cost money.

Then how do system traders decide when to get in and when to get out of a market? One of the most popular methods is to use technical indicators. Technical indicators are mathematical formulas based on the elements of price, volume or open interest. Some indicators combine the elements, but most are based solely on price. There isn't enough space in a single book to discuss all the ins and outs of every technical indicator, so I'll cover only some of the better-known ones I use. You'll need to study them further yourself. But, remember, never use an indicator you don't understand.

Technical indicators tend to fall into two groups: trend-following or overbought/oversold studies.

Trend-following indicators, such as moving averages, DMI (Directional Movement Index, which indicates how much of a trend is there) and, to some extent the MACD (moving average convergence-divergence, which indicates a directional change), are ideally suited for markets that have established well-defined trends but tend to get chopped up in range-bound markets.

On the other hand, overbought/oversold indicators, such as Stochastics, RSI (Relative Strength Index, which smoothes price movement and compares strength of move to trend), rate of change, momentum, line oscillators and %R (compares the close with the highest high) are well-suited for markets that are locked in sideways trading ranges or markets locked in up or down channels. They tend to be less reliable when markets enter strong trends either up or down. To combine any or all of these indicators into a successful trading system, you must determine the market stage you're in to know which indicators to use.

To begin, always determine the trend of a market one degree above the level being traded. For example, if you're day-trading using intraday charts, knowing the direction of the daily trend will help market analysis and eliminate trades that are likely to be unprofitable because they are against the prevailing trend. Likewise, if you are trading based on daily charts, knowing the direction of the intermediate trend from weekly charts will help eliminate trades against the weekly trend.

More comfortable as a position trader, I base the majority of my entry and exit decisions on daily charts. But first I determine the direction of the weekly or intermediate trend by using a combination of weekly Stochastics and RSI and the DMI studies. I use the normal 14-period Stochastics but change the time frame for the weekly RSI to five periods. I also use a nine-period DMI instead of the normal 14 periods. Through back-testing over a 10-year period, I've found a five-period RSI tends to spot bullish and bearish divergence much earlier than a nine- or 14-period time frame. I shortened the time frame measured by the DMI study because I've found it identifies weekly trend changes earlier.

The cotton charts offer a good example of a combination of sideways trading and strong trends. Before the 1994 bull market, cotton had been locked in a broad sideways trading range that was well defined on the weekly chart. The upside breakout of that trading range during the fall of 1993 was confirmed by an upturn in both weekly Stochastics and the RSI. Further confirming the uptrend or bull market was the weekly DMI study that also turned positive to confirm the birth of the uptrend (see Figure 11.3).

By the time cotton broke out above the upper boundary of its weekly trading range, both the weekly Stochastics and five-period RSI were already in a positive mode. The weekly DMI study was below 15 and had turned up as added confirmation of the weekly upside breakout and birth of cotton's bull market.

Once these three technical indicators confirmed the intermediate trend in cotton had turned up, I turned to the daily charts to look for buying opportunities that fit my predefined risk parameters. By having determined the intermediate trend of the market, I had prequalified the trades based on the daily chart. Once market analysis was complete one degree above the level I normally trade, I was ready to move to the time frame I use to make and place entry and exit decisions—in this case, the daily charts.

Look at the daily perpetual cotton chart with Stochastics (an overbought/oversold indicator that tends to work well when a market is in a trading range but which is of little use during most of a trending move). To its credit, Stochastics turned positive and confirmed the upside breakaway gap that launched cotton's rally. However, once the sustained uptrend was underway, Stochastics became overbought (Figure 11.4).

This is where many traders and analysts misuse overbought/oversold indicators. They look for a top and try to sell any minor correction against the major trend. Overbought/oversold indicators have their place when a market is in a strong trend, but their value usually comes near the end of a trending move. As cotton neared its initial high,

FIGURE 11.3 WEEKLY COTTON

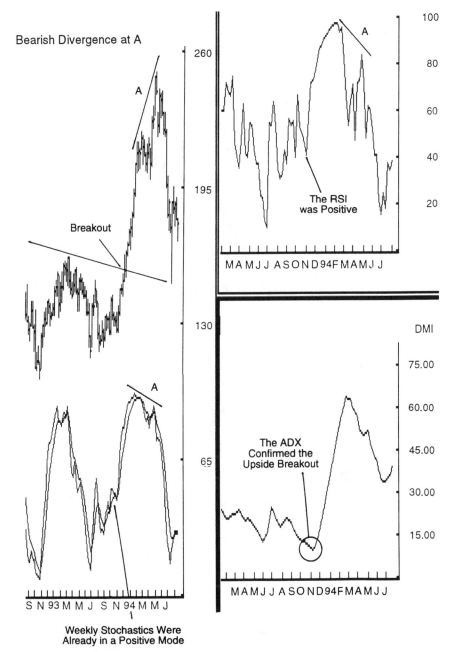

Source: FutureSource

FIGURE 11.4   DAILY PERPETUAL COTTON WITH STOCHASTICS

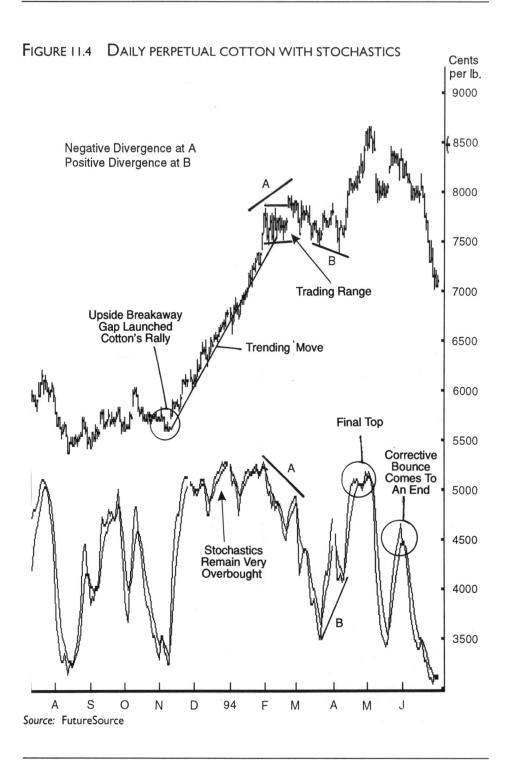

Cents
per lb.

Negative Divergence at A
Positive Divergence at B

Source: FutureSource

Stochastics picked up the weakness in the uptrend, displaying it in the form of bearish divergence. (A on Figure 11.4, daily perpetual cotton chart with Stochastics.)

After posting a minor exhaustion gap, cotton rallied for a brief period of time, marking the upper boundary of a small trading range. As you can see, Stochastics, through positive divergence (B), again signaled a minor trend change was approaching. Once the upper boundary of the trading range was broken, it signaled cotton had resumed the larger-degree uptrend, and I could reenter a long position on the breakout of the trading range.

Once the prevailing trend has ended—in this case, an uptrend—Stochastics, RSI and the line oscillator begin to take over the leadership role from the trend-following indicators. After the trend ends, the overbought/oversold indicators can help determine the extent of the initial correction in the opposite direction of the recent move.

By combining retracement levels with Stochastics and RSI, you can estimate the length of the correction. After the initial correction has ended, these overbought/oversold indicators begin to rebound along with the market. However, the rebound or decline following the initial correction after a trending move is the market's way of relieving an overbought or oversold situation and not the birth of another trending move. Knowing this, you can again use the retracement levels and these indicators to determine the extent of the rebound.

In 90 percent of these market corrections, Stochastics and the RSI will only test their overbought or oversold zones. For example, on the daily perpetual cotton chart with RSI, after the final top was in and cotton had completed its initial decline (1), the corrective rally following it (2) saw Stochastics barely reach the bottom of its overbought zone (see Figure 11.5). This was again the case after the next decline had completed (not shown).

FIGURE 11.5   DAILY PERPETUAL COTTON WITH RSI

Source: FutureSource

I also use a 14-period RSI on the daily charts. Again, because the RSI also is an overbought/oversold indicator, it tends to work better when a market is in a trading range but becomes either overbought or oversold when a market is trending. As with Stochastics, the RSI is useful when it is near the end of a trending move when divergence begins to show up. Divergence is a warning sign that a trend change is nearing, and you should increase your vigilance in this market as profits can erode just as quickly as they were made (and probably faster).

The DMI study is a trend-following indicator, meaning it tends to give false signals when a market is in a trading range but does well when a market is in a trend. When cotton was locked in a sideways range during much of the fall of 1993, the +DI and -DI crossed over each other many times, giving false signals (see Figure 11.6).

In the meantime, the ADX continued to decline to a position at or below 15 on the DMI scale. This is an ideal position for the ADX to be in to confirm a trend change and birth of a trending move. As you can see, in November, when cotton gapped higher, both the +DI and -DI crossed over with the +DI rising. This was the first legitimate technical signal given by the DMI study indicating a trend change was underway.

After this crossover and cotton's breakout above the trading range, the ADX also turned positive to confirm the upside breakout and the start of an uptrend. As cotton continued to rally, the ADX corresponded by rising higher to indicate the trend was increasing in strength. However, near the end of the year (1) cotton posted a minor correction that turned the ADX down.

Many traders make the mistake of taking a downturn by the ADX as a signal a top or bottom has been posted. That's wrong. A downturn by the ADX simply means up movement or down movement, depending upon the direction of the trend, has come to an end. Trendline support

FIGURE 11.6 DAILY PERPETUAL COTTON WITH DMI

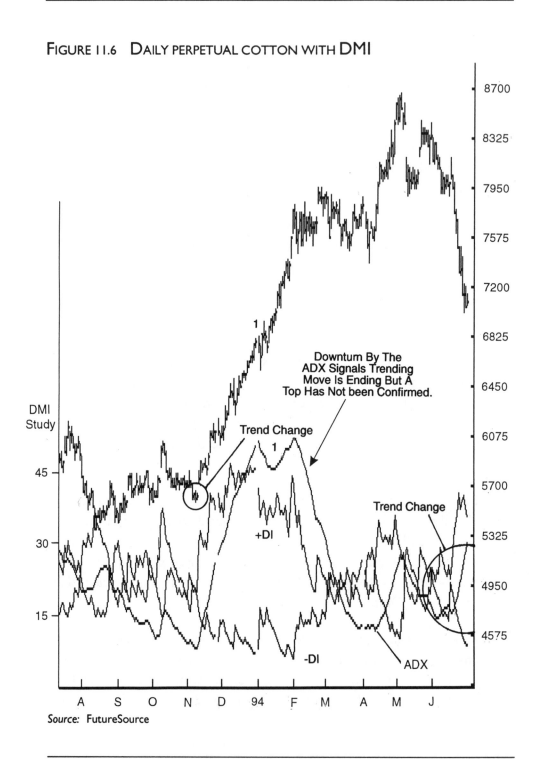

Source: FutureSource

or resistance must be broken along with a downturn by weekly technical indicators to confirm a major top or bottom is in place.

After a brief pause in the uptrend, cotton resumed its advance into late-January/early-February before the ADX once again turned down. As you can see, the ADX was above 40 and outside the range of the +DI. Most of the time when the ADX is at these high levels and turns down for the second time, an important top or bottom is in place.

Cotton then spent over two months trading in a sideways trading range before the +DI and -DI once again crossed over. Meanwhile, the ADX had retreated back down to 15 on the DMI scale. The upturn by the ADX confirmed the breakout of the trading range and signaled the larger-degree uptrend had resumed. With the gap down in May, the ADX, which had been in a bullish trend mode, turned down, signaling up movement had ended.

Note the level at which the ADX was compared to the January and February levels when it turned down. This strong bearish divergence from the previous high, along with a downturn for the second time by key weekly technical indicators, confirmed a major top had been posted.

If a technical indicator gives a buy or sell signal, wait for confirmation on the chart before acting. See whether the market has broken out above or below key support areas on the chart. This will give you a higher probability of profit.

Remember always to determine the direction of the major trend. For example, as a day-trader, it is important for me to know the direction of the weekly trend. Once I've determined the weekly trend, I know what positions to take based on the daily charts.

Next, decide what stage the market is in. If it is trading sideways, emphasis should be geared toward overbought/oversold indicators like Stochastics, RSI, line oscillator, rate of change and momentum indicators. At the same time, keep an eye on either moving averages or the DMI study as they move into position to confirm a breakout of a trading range and the beginning of a trending move.

If a market is in a well-defined trend, focus on moving averages or the DMI study. At the same time, however, remain aware of the over-bought/oversold studies so you can spot divergences that are often a precursor to a trend change. Once you become familiar with these technical studies and when they should be used, it will be easy to shift your emphasis among trend-following and overbought/oversold indicators, depending on which stage the market is in.

THE WELL-CHOSEN EXAMPLE

By Jack Schwager

Indicators can be invaluable tools to traders in their technical analysis, but we would be remiss if we didn't end this section on a bit of a cautionary note. That's because traders tend to get very excited about hot new indicators and systems and often seem to get carried away by the promises, worrying they'll be the one who misses out on the Holy Grail when it finally is discovered. But any indicator and any trading system must be kept in perspective.

Jack Schwager is director of futures research for Prudential Securities and has held similar positions at several of the largest U.S. brokerage firms in New York. He is also a coprincipal of his own trading firm, Wizard Trading Inc. in Indianapolis, and is the author of some of the best books ever written on futures trading including the two Market Wizards *volumes and* The Complete Guide to Futures Trading, *which is being expanded into a series of* Schwager on Futures *books. Although a 100 percent systems trader himself, he is one of the biggest skeptics when it comes to trading systems, software, etc. and their promotion packages. In his writing, he has dispelled a number of myths about fundamentals, trading systems and other futures "truths."*

The following is from his article that appeared in Futures *magazine in September 1984 and may be more valid today than it was then. It should be read every time you think you have discovered THE magic indicator or THE Holy Grail trading system.*

You've plunked down your $495 to attend the 10th annual "Secret of the Millionaires" futures trading seminar. At that price, you figure the speakers will be revealing some very valuable information.

The current speaker is explaining the Super-Razzle-Dazzle (SRD) commodity trading system. The slide on the huge screen reveals a price chart with "B" and "S" symbols representing buy and sell points. The slide is impressive: All of the buys seem to be lower than the sells.

This point is brought home even more dramatically in the next slide, which reveals the equity stream that would have been realized trading this system—a near-perfect uptrend. Not only that but the system also is very easy to keep up.

As the speaker says, "All it takes is 10 minutes a day and a knowledge of simple arithmetic."

You never realized making money in futures could be so simple. You could kick yourself for not having attended the first through the ninth annual seminars.

Once you get home, you select 10 diversified markets and begin trading the SRD system. As the months go by, you notice a strange development. Although the equity in your account exhibits a very steady trend, just as the seminar example did, there is one small difference: The trend on your chart is down. What went wrong?

The fact is you can find a favorable illustration for almost any trading system. The mistake is in extrapolating probable future performance on the basis of an isolated and well-chosen example from the past.

A specific example might be helpful. Consider a system with the following trading rules:

1. If the six-day moving average is higher than the previous day's corresponding value, cover short and go long.

2. If the six-day moving average is lower than the previous day's corresponding value, cover long and go short.

A couple of years ago, a published article presented a similar system and used the Swiss franc during 1980 as an illustration. We won't go through the details but suffice it to say that applying the above system to the Swiss franc in 1980 would have resulted in a profit of $17,235 per contract (assuming an average round-turn transaction cost of $80).

Even allowing for a conservative fund allocation of $6,000 per contract, this would imply an annual gain of 287 percent! Not bad for a system that can be summarized in two sentences. It is easy to see how traders, presented with such an example, might eagerly abandon their other trading approaches for this apparent money machine.

Now let's see what happens when we examine results beyond the narrow scope of this carefully chosen example. First, we expand the survey period from 1980 to the years from 1976 through 1983 (the choice of the survey period's ending date merely reflects the date on which I tested this particular system).

Beginning with the Swiss franc, we find that the total profit during this period was $20,473. In other words, excluding 1980, the system made only $3,238 during the remaining 6 1/2 years. Thus, assuming you allocated $6,000 to trade this approach, the average annual percent return for those years was a meager 8 percent—quite a comedown from 287 percent in 1980.

But wait. It gets worse. Much worse.

Applying the system to a group of 25 markets from 1976 through mid-1983, the system lost money in 19 of the 25 markets. In 13 of the markets—more than half of the total survey—the loss exceeded $22,500 or $3,000 per year per contract! In five markets, the loss exceeded $45,000 and $6,000 per year per contract!

Also, it should be noted that, even in the markets where the system was profitable, its performance was well below gains exhibited for these markets during the same period by most other trend-following systems.

There is no question about it. This is truly a bad system. Yet, if you looked only at the well-chosen example, you might think you had stumbled upon the trading system Jesse Livermore used in his good years. Talk about a gap between perception and reality.

This system witnessed such large, broadly based losses that you may well wonder why fading the signals of such a system might not provide an attractive trading strategy. The reason is that most of the losses are the result of the system's being so sensitive that it generates large commission costs. This sensitivity of the system occasionally is beneficial, as was the case for the Swiss franc in 1980. However, on balance, it is the system's major weakness.

Losses due to commission costs would not be realized as gains by fading the system. Moreover, doing the opposite of all signals would generate equivalent commission costs. Thus, once commission costs are incorporated, the apparent attractiveness of a contrarian approach to using the system evaporates.

The kind of market in which a system is traded may, in fact, be a dominant factor in the system's performance. Sometimes poor results do not suggest inadequacies in the system. Rather, they are an unavoidable consequence of a particular sequence of price movements.

The moral is simple: Don't draw any conclusions about a system (or indicator) on the basis of isolated examples. The only way you can determine if a system has any value is by testing it (without benefit of hindsight) over an extended time period for a broad range of markets.

SECTION III

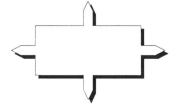

PRICE AND
PARTICIPANTS:
SENTIMENT

INTRODUCTION

The way price is presented (charts) and the pace at which it moves (indicators), described in the previous sections, are major elements of technical analysis. But, of course, those things are only tracks left by people—the thousands of market participants who search for information, sort through all the data, filter it through their trading biases and systems and finally pull the trigger to buy or sell. The marketplace, in the end, is really only a massive psychological contest between people pitting their judgment against one another.

Analyzing the people behind the prices and the actions they take to implement their market opinions is another important facet of technical analysis. The challenge is finding out who these people are, what they are thinking and how much influence they have on price. Charts and indicators reveal their actions, reflecting the collective psychological thinking of all those who have made a commitment to the market. But another large group, the uncommitted on the sidelines, may be the most powerful market force. Until they commit to a position, they won't show up on a price chart or in an indicator.

You know where you stand, but who are these other people and what do they think? Who is with you and who is against you if you are long or short at a specific price? Who is trading what size at what price level? How many people are trading at each price level? How many are interested in trading as prices increase or decrease? Are those on the sidelines predominantly bullish or bearish?

Studying the makeup of market participants and what they may be thinking can give you some early insight into market direction. At times the market may take its cue momentarily from just one or two traders—a Richard Dennis stepping into the soybean pit in the 1970s, for example, or the Hunts in their forays into the sugar, soybean and silver markets in the 1970s and early 1980 or George Soros or Paul Tudor Jones in more recent financial markets—but its movements are usually the result of an elusive and even mysterious mass psychology.

This section will look at various ways to read and gauge market sentiment by analyzing the people factor in the marketplace from four angles:

Psychology of price movement—We have indicated the market is a massive psychological game, and charts are a way to watch it unfold. This chapter analyzes the thought processes of traders as a chart pattern develops.

Volume and open interest—Information on these two items is the most readily available and most often used to assess the strength or weakness of a market. In conjunction with price, they are vital components for many areas of technical analysis.

In addition to revealing details about market participation, volume and open interest also are important gauges of liquidity. To avoid large gaps between prices and poor fills, you generally do not want to trade a market unless it has a daily volume of at least 1,000 contracts and an open interest of at least 5,000, preferably more.

Commitments of traders—This information, also readily available for U.S. markets in a government report, tells you the size of positions held by various types of traders. It's wise to know where the commercials stand.

Bullish consensus—Everyone would like to know the extent of bullish or bearish feelings about the market. Although it is harder to discern, analysts have developed various ways to "read" the prevailing mood of those uncommitted people on the sidelines.

CHAPTER 12

THE PSYCHOLOGY OF COMMODITY PRICE MOVEMENT

By Robert Joel Taylor

The psychology of trading and money management are two aspects of trading that deserve much more attention than this volume can give. Books and videotapes and seminars have been produced on these subjects, but the scope of this book is limited to how they fit into technical analysis.

One of the best articles summarizing the basics of the psychology of the marketplace at various stages of a chart pattern and the role of analyzing people in the process was written by Robert Joel Taylor, a broker at E.F. Hutton and Co. in Dallas when it appeared in the May 1972 issue of Commodities *magazine. Some of the observations here will be very familiar when you read the chapter on Elliott Wave later.*

Contracts may change, price levels may change, the names of companies and traders may change, but people basically do not. The concepts below apply as much to today's markets as those more than two decades ago. Reproduced with permission.

The price of a commodity at any given instant is the result of a decision on the part of both a buyer and a seller—a decision that, broadly speaking, represents a conclusion on the part of the buyer that prices are going higher and a conclusion by the seller that prices will decline.

Those decisions are tangibly represented by a trade at an exact price. And this price is a function of previous decisions because, in most cases, it was partially the result of conclusions drawn from those previous decisions and prices.

Once the buyer and seller make their trade, their influence in the market is spent—except for the opposite reaction that they will ultimately have. That is, once a trader buys a contract, he must later sell. And, likewise, after a trader has sold short, he must later buy to close out the position. Thus, we have two vital aspects of every trade: (1) the fact that each must ultimately have an opposite reaction on the market and (2) the influence that their decision will have on other traders.

If several hundred trades take place within a narrow trading range and then a single trade is made below that range, everyone who bought futures contracts within that range has lost money based on the last trade, and all who sold within that range are ahead. As prices move progressively higher or lower, one group becomes increasingly better off while the other group's losses grow greater.

Each commodity trader's reaction to market price movement can be generalized into the reactions of the three basic groups that are always present in every market situation: (1) the traders who have long positions in the market, (2) those who hold short positions and (3) those who have not taken a position in the market but who are possibly about to enter the market on either the long or the short side. At all times these three basic groups of traders are responding to changing market prices but each in a basically different manner.

The first group is made up of traders who have bought and who are hoping for prices to advance.

The second group is exactly equal to the first group, at least in number of contracts, but they have sold short and are eager for prices to decline. It is essential to keep in mind that there is a long position for every short position, although the actual numbers of traders on each side of the market would probably be unequal. One large-position trader may carry the same number of contracts as many small traders. But the number of contracts on each side of the market is exactly even, just as the market expectations of the long and short position traders are exactly opposite.

The third group is made up of traders who are considering entering the market but who, up to the current time, have neither bought nor sold. Of course, this group also includes those who have previously liquidated an earlier market position and who might be considering getting back into the market.

Traders in this third group have mixed views on the market's probable direction. Some are bullish while others are bearish, but a lack of positive conviction has kept them out of the market. Therefore, they also have no vested interest in the market's direction. It is this group which probably wields the greatest power because their market impact is still in "reserve." They neither fret nor rejoice as the market moves. But, as it moves, their particular market bias is either strengthened or diminished.

A bullishly inclined trader with no position in the market may decide to take a position if the market responds as he thinks it should. He may be prepared to buy a breakout or perhaps a reaction. Likewise, the bearishly inclined trader with no position in the market becomes more convinced of his bearish posture as the market declines. Seeing the price decline, as he expected, may motivate him to go short "before the market gets away."

But the most important aspect of the psychology of this group is that they want to go with the market, whichever the direction. They are awaiting a confirmation of their market views.

A basic understanding of the general attitude of the three groups of traders is fundamental to a useful appreciation of the psychology of commodity price movement as well as the underlying reasons for major chart formations. Standard chart formations, whether they be classified as bottom, top, reversal or continuation formations, generally result in predictable market action because of the predictable psychology of the traders in that market pattern.

The impact of human nature on commodity price movement can perhaps best be seen by examining changing market psychology as a typical market moves through a complete cycle, starting with a period of sideways price movement, an advance that develops into a full-fledged bull market, the top out and the decline in prices to the level where the bull market began.

Assume first that prices trade within a relatively narrow trading range for a period of time (between A and B in Figure 12.1). Recognizing the sideways price movement, traders who have bought contracts might be considering adding additional contracts if the price would advance above the recent trading range. They may even enter stop orders to buy at point B to add to their position if they should get some confirmation that the trend is actually higher. But, by the same token, recognizing that prices might decline below the recent trading range and begin to move lower, they might also be expected to enter stop-loss orders below the market at point A to limit their loss.

The group of traders who have sold in this trading range—exactly the same size in number of contracts as the first group—has exactly the opposite reaction to the market. If the price should begin to advance above the recent trading range, many of them might be inclined to enter stop loss orders to buy above point B to limit their loss. But they,

FIGURE 12.1

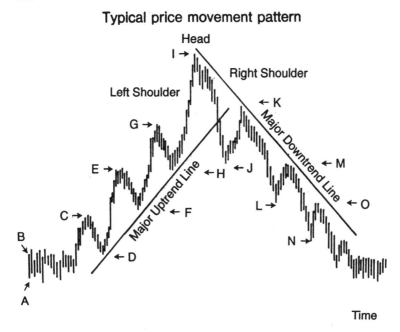

too, may be willing to add to their position if the price should decline below point A. Also, some traders with short positions would enter orders to sell additional contracts on stops below point A.

The third group is not in the market, but they are watching it for a signal either to go long or short. This group may have stop orders to buy above point B because, presumably, the price trend would begin to indicate an upward bias if point B were penetrated. They may also have standing orders to sell below point A for converse reasons.

Assume now that the market does advance to point C for some reason. If the trading range between points A and B has been relatively narrow and the time period of the lateral move relatively long, the accumulated buy stops above the market could be quite numerous. Also, as the market breaks above point B, brokers contact their clients with the news, and this results in a stream of market orders—to add to present long positions with additional buy orders, to cover previous short positions (again with buy orders) or just to go long because of the apparent uptrend (with still more buy orders).

As this flurry of buyers becomes satisfied and profit-taking from previous long positions causes the market to begin to dip from the high point of C to point D, another distinct psychological attitude begins working in the market. Part of the first group that went long within points A and B did not buy additional contracts as the market rallied to point C. Now they may be willing to add to their position "on a dip." Consequently, buy orders begin trickling in from these traders as the market drifts down.

The second group of traders with short positions established in the original trading range have now seen prices advance to point C, then decline to move back closer to the price at which they originally sold.

Digressing for a moment, it is important to remember that whenever a trader's position moves into the losing column, the natural reaction is one of apprehension that increases as the loss grows. The second group of short position traders all have been carrying a loss and, psychologically speaking, experiencing some degree of discomfort. Therefore, if these traders did not cover their short positions on a buy stop above point B, they may be more than willing to "cover on any further dip" to minimize the loss.

The third group of traders—those not yet in the market—who did not enter the long side with a buy stop above point B but who are impressed with the market's recent bullish behavior will place price orders just below the market with the idea of "getting in on a dip."

On balance, then, the net effect of the rally from A to C would be a beginning psychological change in all three groups. The result of the change would be a different tone to the market, where some support could be expected from all three groups on dips. As this support is strengthened by an increase in market orders and a raising of limit buy orders, the market begins once again to advance toward the high point of the previous rally at point C. Then, as the market gathers momentum and rallies above point C toward point E, the psychology again changes subtly.

The first group of long traders may now have enough profit to begin pyramiding additional contracts with their profits. In any case, as the market advances, their enthusiasm grows and they begin to set their sights on higher price objectives. Psychologically, they have the market advantage.

The original group who sold short between A and B and who have not yet covered are all carrying increasing losses. Their general attitude is negative because they are all losing money and confidence. Their hopes fade as their losses mount. Some of this group begins to say "Uncle" by liquidating their short positions either with stops or market orders. Perhaps some even reverse their position and go long.

The group that has still not entered the market—either because their orders to buy the market were never reached or because they had hesitated to see whether the market was actually moving higher—begins to "buy at the market."

It is important to understand that, even if a number of traders have not entered the market because of too-low bids or hesitation, their attitude is still bullish. And perhaps they are even kicking themselves for not getting in earlier. As for those who sold out previously established long positions at a profit, only to see the market move still higher, their attitude still favors the long side. They may also be among those who are looking to buy on any further dip.

So, generally speaking, with each dip the market should find the support of (1) the group of traders with long positions who are adding to their positions; (2) traders who are short the market, much to their chagrin, and are attempting to buy back their shorts "if the market will only back down some," and (3) new traders without a position in the market who are attempting to get aboard what they now consider a full-fledged bull market.

This rationale causes the price action to be generally one where each prominent high is higher than the previous high, and each prominent reactionary low progressively higher than the last reactionary low. In a broad sense, it should appear as an upward series of waves of successively higher highs and higher lows.

But, at some point, the psychology again begins to change subtly. Those in the first group with long positions and fat profits are no longer willing to add to their positions. In fact, they are looking for a place to "take profits."

The second group of battered traders with short positions has finally been worn down to a nub of diehard shorts who absolutely refuse to cover their short positions. They feel that their loss is "too big to take." The important point is that they are no longer a supporting element, eagerly waiting to buy the market on dips.

The third group of those who never quite got aboard the upmove become, at some point, unwilling to buy because they feel they missed out on the greatest part of the upside move. They consider the risk on the downside too great when compared to the now limited upside potential. In fact, they may be looking for a place to "short the market and ride it back down."

The first signal that this reversal psychology is beginning to overtake the market is when it demonstrates a noticeable lack of support on a dip that "carries too far to be bullish." The decline from point I to point J on the chart would be the classic example of a dip that carried "too far." This decline would signal a new tone to the market. The support on dips would become resistance on rallies, and a more two-sided market action could be expected.

To use a slightly different example, let's assume you bought a stock for $50 a share and then happily watched it advance to $100 per share. At that point you are telling your spouse and associates at work what a smart investor you are. Perhaps you are already counting your profits and planning to buy something extravagant.

But now assume that, before you cash in, the stock declines to $65. You have already realized that you were too greedy and should have sold out long ago. With the bulk of your profits dissipated, your only hope now is that the stock will rally again, say perhaps to $85, so that you can get out with your well-deserved but fleeting profits. After a decline to $65, you are no longer optimistically waiting for the stock to reach $150. Salvaging a $35 profit per share after having a $50 profit slip through your fingers is your current objective. You are planning to "sell on the next rally."

This basic psychology is exactly the same for a commodity trader who bought low and witnessed a handsome profit grow as the market advanced. After the first reaction or dip that carries prices down considerably lower than before, the commodity trader, like the stock trader above, is also looking for the next rally to "take profits." In fact, even he may be a little nervous about the likelihood of the next rally. His psychology is no longer one of a confident bull with a smile from ear to ear but rather of a nervous trader with a long position who is trying to decide when to sell.

The traders without a position in the market also notice the rather precipitous decline from an otherwise bullish price pattern. Recognizing that the market may be in the process of "topping out," they are also prepared to sell the next rally, perhaps with a buy stop above the contract highs.

Actually, the earliest indication of a change in market psychology to one with bearish overtones may be an advance that is markedly greater than the other previous advances (for example, from point H to I). This can signal a final short-covering rally of near panic proportions. Also, if the volume at the top of the advance is near the highest for the entire move, it may be a harbinger of an impending buying climax.

But the dead giveaway is the subsequent decline (to point J) that carries back to the approximate level of the previous decline (point H) so this latest reactionary low is not really prominently higher than the previous reactionary low.

Now the picture has changed. As the market begins to advance again from point J to point K, traders with previously established long postions are taking profits by selling out. Most of the hard-nosed traders with short positions have covered their shorts, so they add no significant new buying impetus to the market. In fact, having witnessed the recent long decline, they may be adding to their short positions ("averaging up," some call it, but "suicide" is more like it).

If the rally back toward the contract highs fails to establish new recovery highs, this failure is quickly noticed by the more professional traders as a possible signal that the bull market has indeed run its course. This would be even more true if the rally carried only up to the approximate level of the rally top at point G. If the open interest also declines during the rally from J to K, it is another sign it was not new buying that caused the rally but short covering.

As profit-taking and new short-selling forces the market to decline from point K, the next critical point is the reactionary low point at J. A major failure or bear signal is flashed if the market penetrates this prominent low following an abortive attempt to establish new contract highs.

In the vernacular of chartists, a head-and-shoulders reversal pattern has been completed. But rather than simply explaining away price patterns with names, it is important to understand how the psychology of the market action at different points causes the market to respond as it does. It also explains why certain points are quite significant.

In a bear market, the attitudes of the traders would be reversed. Each decline would find the bears more confident and prosperous and the bulls more depressed and threadbare. With the psychology diametrically opposite, the pattern completely reverses itself to form a series of lower highs and lower lows.

But, at some point, the bears would be unwilling to add to their previously established short positions. Those who were already long the market and had refused to sell higher would eventually be reduced to a hard core of traders who had their jaw set and refused to sell out. Traders not in the market who were perhaps unsuccessfully attempting to short the market at higher levels will begin to find the long side of the market more attractive. The first rally that "carries too high to be bearish" would signal another possible trend reversal.

With this basic understanding of market psychology through three phases of a market, a trader is better equipped to appreciate the significance of all technical price patterns. No one expects to establish short positions at the high or long positions at the low, but development of a feel for market psychology is the beginning of the quest for trades on which even hindsight could not improve.

CHAPTER 13

VOLUME AND OPEN INTEREST: OLD STANDBYS

Many trading systems and approaches to technical analysis incorporate volume and open interest in one form or another. In the eyes of some analysts, even basic bar chart patterns are not "real" patterns unless accompanied by appropriate volume figures. Momentum indicators often are driven by volume.

In futures trading, volume is the number of contracts traded in a given period; every transaction involves a buyer and a matching seller. Open interest is the total number of contracts outstanding at any given time—that is, a purchase that has not been offset by a sale or vice versa.

In the stock market, a company has a fixed number and type of shares available, and demand determines their price. An investor who wants a position buys shares from someone getting out of a position. In futures and options, there is no set number of contracts and no limit on how many can be outstanding, and you do not know whether the person on the other side of the trade is taking a new position or exiting an existing position.

The traditional, simplified view of the relationship among price, volume and open interest is that if volume and open interest are high and rising, the trend in place is strong; if volume and open interest are low and declining, the move is weak. Stated another way, if price, volume and open interest are all up, the market is bullish; if price is down and volume and open interest are up, it's bearish. When prices are up or down and volume and open interest are down, the market may be ready to make a turn.

Of course, as we have already suggested a number of times, nothing in technical analysis is quite that easy, and you won't be surprised to learn that this area of analysis also has its subjective elements requiring a good deal of market sense.

A useful algorithm to determine the number of new positions (and the possible strengthening of a trend) vs. the number of positions being covered (evidence of a possible tiring trend) was created by Don Iglehart of Stanford University a few years ago. The formula is:

$$\text{PN (percent of volume representing new positions)} =$$
$$100 \times [0.5 + (COI/(2 \times V))]$$

Where: COI = change in open interest (+ or -)
        V = daily volume

The formula produces a reading of 0 to 100. If all the volume represents new positions, the reading is 100; if none of the volume is new positions but represents only long or short covering, the reading is 0; if half of the volume represents new positions and half is from closing out old positions, open interest does not change and the reading is 50. Anything less than 50 percent new positions indicates contract liquidation. The degree of expansion or contraction in open interest, connected to the current chart picture, suggests the strength or weakness of the current move.

Many analysts have worked with volume and open interest over the years and could be quoted here. This chapter, however, draws primarily on material written by Philip Gotthelf, president of Equidex Inc. in Guttenberg, N.J. Phil is the son of the late Edward B. Gotthelf, a trading master who, long before the era of computers, developed the proprietary and copyrighted COMMODEX® system based on price, volume and open interest. Introduced in 1959, it was one of the first futures trading systems and is still active in the 1990s. A look at the role of volume and open interest in technical analysis of futures markets would not be complete without input from Gotthelf.

MAKING A SYSTEM THAT MEASURES MARKET PSYCHOLOGY

By Philip Gotthelf

The following, taken from a series Phil Gotthelf wrote for Futures *magazine in the December 1986 and early 1987 issues, not only explains the basics of price/volume/open interest analysis but also illustrates their role in accumulation-distribution studies and how they can be incorporated into a trading system.*

If you are to duplicate the skills of great traders, you must try to develop a more complete understanding of how markets function by asking basic questions as simple as, "What makes prices move higher?"

Prices increase when new buyers are willing to bid at ever higher prices. Buyers are confident prices will continue to move up. In addition, sellers are only willing to sell if greater price incentives are given.

Prices decrease when sellers continue to ask for ever decreasing prices. Sellers believe prices will move lower while buyers can only be tempted by falling prices.

The imbalance between the willingness of sellers and buyers is reflected by price movements.

Most financial markets represent giant open auctions, which is nothing more than a public negotiation forum. Each time a buyer bids or a seller offers, a test is made. When the auctioneer cries out a price, he is testing to see if buyers will accept his offer. If hands go up, the test passes.

Just as in a one-on-one negotiation, if a bid or ask is not accepted, the buyer or seller will change his price and test again. This process of testing for the right prices moves markets.

Consider how testing and passing might be reflected by technical market statistics. At a regular auction, high levels of interest are reflected by a large number of bids or hands in the air. When many hands go up quickly, you know prices will climb higher. When the number of bids decreases, you know a final price is near.

In commodities, high volume is similar to many hands at an auction. That is why price-volume theory correlates rising volume with price direction to forecast trend formation. In addition, open interest reflects different degrees of market participation. You can formulate general rules or assumptions about market behavior by considering these three elements.

You can expect an uptrend to continue based upon new buying if price, volume and open interest are all up. Buyers continue to be willing to buy with increasing enthusiasm despite higher prices, and sellers are willing to sell only if bids are more attractive.

If price is down while volume and open interest are up, the same is true on the downside as sellers and their enthusiasm become the driving force.

At an auction you can tell a final price is coming when the number of hands (bids) decreases as prices rise. Fewer hands can be associated with less volume and declining open interest.

Therefore, if price is up and volume and open interest are down, you can expect a possible top, dip or reversal based on decreasing buyer participation. Fewer and fewer buyers are willing to bid as prices rise. Previous buyers are taking profits as shown by falling open interest. While prices may still go up, you know enthusiasm is waning.

You can expect a possible bottom, rally or reversal of a downtrend if price, volume and open interest are all down. In this case, seller enthusiasm is decreasing as fewer and fewer are willing to take chances.

These general rules seem logical enough and are the basis for accumulation and distribution theory that has gained considerable popularity. When open interest and volume rise, an "accumulation" is taking place. When open interest and volume fall, "distribution" dominates.

Accumulation and distribution patterns were the focal point of preliminary studies that Edward B. Gotthelf used to develop his proprietary COMMODEX system. In developing the system, Gotthelf knew his overall market perceptions were based upon basic price/volume/open interest assumptions. The task was determining which time frames and what changes in price/volume/open interest were significant enough to move markets.

Gotthelf noticed his "feel" for a trend usually developed over several days. Therefore, he concluded that an effective system would have to measure "on-balance" accumulation and distribution over time: Rarely react to a single day . . . rarely react to a single move on a chessboard.

In fact, most historical simulations show major trends do not happen overnight. Usually, accumulation patterns develop well in advance of major price movements.

Day-to-day changes in volume and open interest appear to be random. A serial correlation of consecutive volume or open interest changes supports the theory that daily differences are random.

Gotthelf realized the difficulty in sorting out true accumulations. The statistics do not provide a clear picture. For example, on the floor he could see buyers or sellers coming into the market during the day. At the end of each session, he had a feel for who was doing what. Perhaps a series of upticks were the result of active buying where open interest expanded only to be followed by a lull and inactive downticks.

On the floor, you might see most of the accumulation was on the long side. Yet, newspaper statistics might show little price change and no way of exactly correlating open interest changes with price direction.

In his first empirical approach, Gotthelf developed a relatively simple method of measuring accumulation. He called it "On-Balance Volume and Open Interest Method." Interestingly, his on-balance term, with a variety of different definitions, has been used by many other analysts since its inception. However, his notes reveal the development of this term as far back as 1948.

When prices closed above the previous day's level, he would assign a "+" to the price for that day. If volume increased on the same day, his volume component would receive a "+". A rise in open interest would also receive a "+".

In accordance with general assumptions, when prices moved up and volume moved down, the value would be " - ". Remember, if volume moves opposite to price, a reaction is anticipated. Thus, each day's action could be measured in a series of pluses and minuses (see Figure 13.1). This method was a crude way of converting his assumptions into a quantifying method.

FIGURE 13.1

Date	1	2	3	4	5	6	7	8
Price	+↑	+↑	+↑	–↓	–↓	–↓	+↑	+↑
Volume	+↑	–↓	–↓	–↑	+↓	+↓	+↑	+↑
Open interest	+↑	+↑	–↓	–↑	+↓	–↑	–↓	+↑
Value	↑	0	↓	↑	↓	0	0	↑

Effect on value ↑ Up ↓ Down

Obviously, some days would be net pluses while others would be net minuses. Over time, he would count the number of net plus days against net minus days. If, on balance, pluses outnumbered minuses, he would be a buyer. If minuses exceeded pluses, he would sell. If pluses and minuses were about even, he would stay neutral. Hence, his term "on-balance."

Using his on-balance method, Gotthelf expanded his theory, using further market observations. He found that long periods of accumulation usually led to dramatic corrections. He called these situations "overbought" or "oversold" markets.

He concluded that when buyers continued to buy over extended periods, they would all have to take profits before contract expiration. The longer the period, the less time until expiration. At some point, liquidation pressure would build. If all buyers began closing longs at the same time, a strong correction would result. In fact, this type of action frequently takes place during the last trading days of many contracts. Sometimes too many traders hold too long.

If futures is truly a zero-sum game—for every buyer, there must be a seller; for every loss, there is an equal and offsetting gain—some might argue that you cannot distinguish between "long accumulation" and "short accumulation" and cannot separate "long distribution" from "short distribution." After all, as open interest rises, an equal number of buyers and sellers must be adding to the number of contracts. As open interest falls, both must be liquidating.

Obviously, this view shows a lack of understanding. Some longs and shorts will be hedgers, who always have corresponding cash positions not represented in open interest and volume statistics. Hence, the market is far from a zero sum.

Further, Gotthelf noted a measurable bias when accumulation is taking place on either the short or long side. Price direction determines where actual cash balances are building. For example, assume a gold transaction takes place at $400 per oz. If gold moves to $410, actual cash (variation margin) is transferred from seller to buyer—the buyer "accumulates" cash. Unlike other financial vehicles, accumulation in futures can be used to add more positions—pyramiding.

Why is this so important? Gotthelf discovered subtle psychological pressures associated with accumulation and the pyramiding process. He found the action of traders under these pressures so fascinating that he developed an entire set of theories on the "psychology of the market," another phrase used frequently today. However, Gotthelf's old definition added fresh new perspectives to the term and its application.

Gold is a 100 oz. contract. Therefore, each $1 change in price is worth $100 in value. If initial margin—the amount required to open a position—is $2,000, a $20 per oz. move in gold prices would add enough accumulated cash to add another contract ($20 × 100 oz. = $2,000 initial margin).

Assume you are long gold at $400 per oz. and the price does advance to $420. Because initial margin is only $2,000, you have several choices:

1. **Buy another contract.** Here, you show you have confidence the market will continue to rise. All things remaining equal, your bid for another position will be reflected by an increase in volume of one and in open interest of one. In addition, your bid is likely to pressure prices even higher. Thus, price, volume and open interest all increase from this decision.

2. **Hold just your existing contract.** This behavior indicates you have faith in your existing position but insufficient confidence to expand your exposure based upon the $20 price rise. All things remaining equal, this decision would have no effect upon price, volume or open interest.

3. **Take the profit.** This decision reflects a loss of confidence in the long side. You must be satisfied with your profit and believe prices will not advance sufficiently to justify risking an already handsome gain. All things remaining equal, this action would cause volume to increase by one and open interest to drop by one, and the offer might cause a dip in prices.

Now, assume again that you are long gold at $400 per oz. but that the price declines to $390 for a variation margin loss of $1,000. You are called for margin money. Your choices:

1. **You margin up and buy more.** You are showing continuing confidence in the long side by "averaging in" with additional resources. Prices are likely to find support or rebound. Open interest and volume will increase by the amount you buy.

2. **You margin up.** While you are willing to support your existing position, you lack sufficient faith or resources to add more positions. Your inaction does not affect open interest or volume. Whether your inaction impacts price probably is debatable.

3. **You liquidate.** Faced with a margin call, you think it is better to cut your losses short rather than throw good money after bad. Volume increases, open interest decreases, and price probably dips under your offer.

Δ OI $\times$ Δ P = money

Any change in price coupled with a change in open interest results in money entering or leaving a market. The greater the open interest and price, the more money in the market. The amount available (accumulated) is important for forecasting potential squeezes, tops, bottoms and momentum shifts.

Accumulation

1. Δ OI × initial margin = new margin

2. Δ OI × Δ P = new variation margin

3. OI × Δ P = variation margin from existing positions

Example:

OI = 1,000 gold contracts bought @ $400 per oz. average
1,000 × ($400 × 100 oz.) × 10% = $4,000,000 margin existing

1. Δ OI = + 100 contracts
   100 × ($400 × 100 oz.) × 10% = $400,000 new margin

2. Δ P = $10 per oz.
   100 × ($10 × 100 oz.) = $100,000 new variation margin

3. 1,000 × ($10 × 100 oz.) = $1,000,000 variation on existing margin

(Money enters market in cash and position accumulation.)

Distribution

If Δ is negative:

1. Δ OI × initial margin = margins leaving

2. Δ OI × Δ P = variation margin taken out

3. OI × Δ P = smaller variation transfer

Example:

Δ OI = - 100 gold contracts

100 × ($400 × 100 oz.) × 10% = $400,000 margin leaving

Δ P = $10

100 × ($10 × 100 oz.) = $100,000 in variation margin that is transferred or leaves

Three margin components make up the accumulation process: initial, variation (amount transferring from losers to winners) and new initial and variation margins resulting from increases in open interest. Distribution is the net process of liquidation of this money, signaling the end of a trend.

By observing position accumulation during a consolidation pattern (see Figure 13.2), you can measure intermediate trending potential and levels of "significant penetration" based upon margin call areas. The greater the accumulation during consolidation, the more likely a strong reaction when maintenance margins are violated. Each individual reacts differently to risk and exposure. However, within a group, there is likely to be a statistically consistent and measurable number of individuals who will act in the same manner when faced with the same circumstances.

FIGURE 13.2

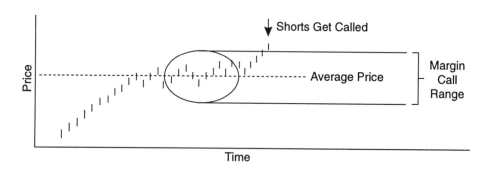

Find a consolidation pattern on a chart (trading range area, flag, triangle, etc.). Place a compass point at the approximate middle of the consolidation (average price), measure the distance in points equal to maintenance margin using the chart scale and draw a circle. Extend parallel lines from the top and bottom of the circle. As long as prices remain within the lines, a trading range exists. If either line is penetrated, margin calls must be answered. A liquidation by large numbers of traders (noted in volume/open interest statistics) will accelerate the breakout and lead to a technical follow-through.

"The behavior of investors is consistently reflected by changes in price, volume and open interest," Gotthelf said in describing his version of technical analysis that correlated price, volume and open interest with accumulation and distribution patterns and became the foundation of the proprietary COMMODEX system.

Essentially, he believed an astute market observer could read the disposition of traders, in mass, through precise measurements of changes in market statistics.

Applying the gold example to real markets, thousands of investors with hundreds of opinions and thousands of decisions make similar choices every day. Sorting out the "psychology" becomes somewhat complex. In a vacuum, your decision is easy to spot. But what if someone else takes over your position? Suppose another trader gains confidence when you think all is lost.

The approach to the more complex real world actually remains the same. Suppose another investor does take over your position. What will happen to volume, open interest and price?

In his coppyrighted book on COMMODEX, Gotthelf writes about the "woofle dog"—a very hairy dog that walks backward to see where it has been. He likened chartists to this rather unfortunate creature.

Again, with a unique humor, Gotthelf described the application of charts: They tell you where markets have been.

While random walk advocates will insist such history cannot tell you where markets are going, my father took a different view. When combined with his logical explanations and analysis of behavior, charts can provide insights into where, when and how traders are likely to react.

Assume silver is trading at $5 per oz. For no apparent reason, prices move to $5.30. Once at $5.30, prices retreat back to $5. Obviously, you would see a "top formation" on a chart as the market tested consecutively higher levels until the $5.30 and higher test "failed." Can you draw a conclusion from that?

You know buyers continued to be willing to buy from $5 to $5.30. They were confident prices would move higher. If you also knew how many buyers participated at each "test," you might determine a behavior pattern that could repeat if the distribution of buyer participation remained the same in the future.

This is a key concept. For example, you may know through statistical sampling that the average height of a mature male in the United States is 5 ft., 7 in. and that remaining heights fall in a normal distribution around that mark. This is the popular bell-shaped curve of a normal probability distribution.

What if the behavior of the average commodity trader could be distributed around an average? You could measure how many buyers entered silver at $5, $5.01, $5.02 . . . all the way up to $5.30.

If market behavior remained consistent, you could predict future reactions based upon the constructed behavior distribution with associated probabilities of confidence. Just as you know the probability that a U.S. male will be 5 ft. 7 in., you could know the probability that a specific number of traders will test particular prices at particular times.

Let's assume you want to measure the number of investors entering or leaving a market at different price levels by examining changes in volume and open interest in relation to popular moving averages. Your objective would be to determine how many investors were using such averages as decision rules. For example, how many traders buy when the price crosses a 5-day average on the upside? Or a 10-day average, a 20-day, etc.?

By measuring the number of trades executed in and around the various moving averages, you could determine if there was a distinct and consistent pattern. You would discover which moving averages seemed to have the greatest following and, thus, the greatest market impact.

Gotthelf concluded that the cumulative effect of moving average crossings was more significant than any one penetration. Therefore, he decided to observe levels of accumulation and distribution taking place when different moving averages were violated.

Based on his studies, he further concluded that, when prices were above or below particular averages, certain "conditions" existed. He believed each of these conditions should be given a quantitative value so it could be followed and evaluated objectively when it occurred.

Suppose a market moved favorably 30 percent of the time a 20-day moving average was violated and 20 percent of the time when a 10-day average was penetrated. Or suppose you measured a "30 percent participation" based upon volume and open interest changes when a 20-day average was crossed and a "20 percent participation" using a 10-day average. Under such circumstances, you might assign a value of 0.3 to a 20-day condition and 0.2 to a 10-day condition. Therefore, these two market components would have a total value of 0.5.

Consider the potential value of increasing open interest correlated with rising prices and the potential value of increasing volume with rising prices. Your real-time observations might suggest a value for the volume component of 0.2 and open interest of 0.2.

Then you might compare the 10-day average to the 20-day average. Let's assume this relationship had a value of 0.1. You can see the maximum value of all components is 1.0. Using this approach, you could measure the "index value" of any trading session on a scale of 0 to 1.0.

By the same token, you could measure accumulation and distribution associated with a downtrend by assigning negative values to the same weights. The scale would expand to include -1.0 as well as +1.0.

Gotthelf called this his "indexing method," a method that eventually was transformed into the proprietary COMMODEX system by adding trading rules and automatic stops.

During the late 1940s and through the 1950s, moving averages gained considerable popularity among traders. The basic moving average system linked trading decisions to specific price penetrations.

For example, early systems required followers to "buy when the price crosses a moving average on the upside and sell when the price crosses on the downside." Obviously, a trader would always be either long or short. Of course, this simple system was vulnerable to whipsawing during trading range markets. In effect, any follower would need considerable cash reserves for staying power while markets remained trendless.

The crossing was an "event." While prices remained above a particular average, a "condition" existed whereby followers were all long. Over time, Gotthelf determined the "condition" was more important than the "event."

How long a market remained above or below a particular average became more significant than when crossings took place. If accumulation (rising open interest) extended for several weeks while prices remained above specific moving averages, he found markets became "overbought." Or if prices remained below these moving averages for an extended period, "oversold" conditions prevailed.

These conditions had to be qualified through extensive research and quantified into an exact system. This was accomplished by measuring every day's "index" and examining the pattern over several days, weeks and months.

Using his indexing method, Gotthelf constructed patterns that he called "index series." High index values over several days indicated steady accumulation and was labeled "series high." Consistently low values were called "series low." Values between -0.2 and +0.2 were "series neutral." Bear in mind that the series had to be consistent. If daily index values jumped from high to low and back, it was called "index erratic."

From the late 1940s through 1954, Gotthelf's indexing method gained him a considerable fortune. By 1950 he was one of the largest traders in eggs and grains and, in fact, was thought to have cornered the egg market with Great Western Foods in 1950.

But, even with his remarkable record and highly accurate indexing method, something was missing. Index interpretation still required Gotthelf's personal attention. Too often, his trading still relied upon subjective analysis. The only way to vacation or spend time with the family and friends would be to either stop trading or delegate authority.

After an extremely tense bout with the markets in 1955, Gotthelf decided it was time to refine the indexing method into a less emotional technique that could be used by others as well as himself. With a room full of mechanical calculators and green visors, the final development of the proprietary COMMODEX system began.

Gotthelf had two objectives: (1) The series relationship had to be objectively qualified and (2) precise decision rules needed to be formulated to have a system. With the help of Hertzel Gottfried, Gotthelf discovered that a moving total of daily index values acted as a very accurate oscillator. A mathematician would have found this obvious because high index values would make a moving total rise while lower values would turn a moving total down. In addition, overbought conditions would be reflected by extremely high moving totals while oversold conditions would cause a very low moving total.

Watching the moving total of daily index numbers gave a very accurate indication of on-balance accumulations and distributions. Gotthelf named the moving total his trend index because it measured trending potential as well as possible tops, bottoms, rallies and reversals.

As an oscillator, the trend index becomes sensitive to change after a consistent series because uniform values are dropped from the beginning of the moving total while extreme values are added to the end. Unlike a moving average, a moving total is not divided by the summation factor. Numbers are simply added in a moving series. Therefore, a 10-day moving total would add the most recent day and subtract the 11th preceding day.

Example: +8 +6 +10 +8 +8 +6 +2 + 0 +6 -6 = +48
        +8̶ +6 +10 +8 +8 +6 +2 + 0 +6 -6 -8 = +32
        +8̶ +6̶ +10 +8 +8 +6 +2 + 0 +6 -6 -8 -2 = +24

Thus, a -10 in a series of +10s would result in a 20-point decline.

After more than three years of research, the trend index oscillator revealed a strong correlation to overbought and oversold markets when extreme values were registered. Gotthelf's "discretionary rules" (reprinted with permission) state:

1. In an advancing market, if the trend index reaches +50 or higher and a substantial profit has accrued, protect it by close stops. Similarly, in a declining market, if the trend index reaches -50 or below, protect profits with a close stop.

2. If the trend index reaches + or -60, the market is frequently overbought or oversold and at least some reaction is anticipated. Thus, it is advisable to take some profit in that area, particularly if the trend

index reverses 16 points or more. Thus, a decline from +60 to +44 might suggest caution as would an advance from -60 to -44.

When the trend index was correlated with the daily index, Gotthelf found that certain conditions led to a high probability that a trend was in progress. These correlations were translated into his famous "mandatory trading rules" and the proprietary COMMODEX system (the name came from "COMMOdity inDEX"), which has been published every day since it was introduced in June 1959.

(The system was so successful that it attracted the attention of federal regulators. They determined that it constituted "inside information" and barred Gotthelf from personal trading and from all forms of advertising. But this is a technical analysis volume, and that's a story for another time.)

FORGET VOLUME: LOOK ONLY AT OPEN INTEREST

By Earl Hadady

The following excerpt and tables are from an article that appeared in the July 1987 issue of Futures *magazine. It is reproduced here with permission. See the next chapter for the background on Earl Hadady, perhaps best known for his work with Bullish Consensus and contrary opinion thinking. Some of the material here is an extension and expansion of work done earlier by James H. Sibbet.*

Because trading volume does not have a fixed relationship to changes in open interest, volume is unimportant in forecasting the market. For example, high volume can occur as a result of a large number of eager new bulls entering the market. Likewise, high volume could occur as a result of a large number of shorts covering their positions. For analysis, you need be concerned only with whether open interest is expanding or contracting on rising or declining prices.

Every futures trade must be balanced—a seller for every buyer and a buyer for every seller. Therefore, all combinations of buying and selling and their effect on open interest are shown in Figure 13.3.

Prices rise or decline as a result of the eagerness of either buyers or sellers to acquire positions. If buyers are more eager than sellers, their trading aggressiveness will cause prices to rise and vice versa. All possible combinations of changes in open interest from buying or selling pressure are shown in Figure 13.4.

You can combine the information from those two tables to illustrate all nine possible conditions involving the interaction of price and open interest (see Figure 13.5). The most complicated situations are the transitional conditions when open interest is contracting (Conditions 3 and 9).

FIGURE 13.3

Market participants		Effect on open interest
Buyer	Seller	
New bull buying	New bear selling or	Expands
	Old bull liquidating (selling)	No change
Old bear covering (buying)	New bear selling or	No change
	Old bull liquidating (selling)	Contracts
Market participants		Effect on open interest
Seller	Buyer	
New bear selling	New bull buying or	Expands
	Old bear covering (buying)	No change
Old bull liquidating (selling)	New bull buying or	No change
	Old bear covering (buying)	Contracts

FIGURE 13.4

Prices moving	Market participants responsible for direction of price move	Other market participants	Effect on open interest
Up	Aggressive new bulls buying	New bears (sellers) or	Expands
		Old bulls (sellers)	No change
	Aggressive old bears covering voluntarily or involuntarily (their stops being hit)	New bears (sellers) or	No change
		Old bulls (sellers)	Contracts
Down	Aggressive new bears selling	New bulls (buyers) or	Expands
		Old bears (buyers)	No change
	Aggressive old bulls liquidating voluntarily or involuntarily (their stops being hit)	New bulls (buyers) or	No change
		Old bears (buyers)	Contracts

FIGURE 13.5

Prices	Open interest	Market condition	Market action on balance	Effect
Rising	Expanding	1	1. New bulls aggressively buying from new bears cautiously selling	Bullish
	Steady	2	1. New bulls aggressively buying from old bulls reluctantly liquidating (selling), and/or 2. Old bears aggressively covering* (buying) from new bears cautiously selling, and/or 3. New bulls aggressively buying from new bears cautiously selling (increases OI) balanced by old bears aggressively covering* (buying) from old bulls reluctantly liquidating (selling) (decreases OI)	Bullish (gradual rise in prices)
	Contracting	3	1. Old bears aggressively covering (buying)* from old bulls reluctantly liquidating (selling)	Bullish to bearish
Steady	Expanding	4	1. New bulls buying from new bears selling, both equally aggressive	Neutral
	Steady	5	1. New bulls buying from old bulls liquidating (selling), both equally aggressive, and/or 2. New bears selling from old bears covering (buying), both equally aggressive, and/or 3. New bulls buying from new bears selling (increases OI) balanced by old bulls liquidating (selling) to old bears covering (buying) (decreases OI)	Neutral (narrow trading range, sideways market)
	Contracting	6	1. Old bulls liquidating (selling) to old bears covering (buying), both equally aggressive	Neutral
Declining	Expanding	7	1. New bears aggressively selling to new bulls cautiously buying	Bearish
	Steady	8	1. New bears aggressively selling to old bears reluctantly buying, and/or 2. Old bulls aggressively liquidating* (selling) to new bulls cautiously buying, and/or 3. New bears aggressively selling to new bulls cautiously buying (increases OI) balanced by old bulls aggressively liquidating* (selling) to old bears reluctantly covering (buying) (decreases OI)	Bearish (gradual decline in prices)
	Contracting	9	1. Old bulls aggressively liquidating* (selling) to old bears reluctantly covering (buying)	Bearish to bullish

* Voluntary and involuntary exiting (protective stops being hit)

Condition 3 (rising prices and contracting open interest), for example, is bullish to bearish, depending upon whether prices are rising more rapidly than open interest is contracting. It is bullish if prices are rising more rapidly than open interest is contracting. On the other hand, if open interest is contracting more rapidly than prices are advancing, it is bearish and generally is referred to as a short-covering rally.

A short-covering rally is defined as bears exiting the market, either voluntarily or involuntarily as their stops are being hit, because they are precariously positioned and believe that prices are going higher. Otherwise, open interest would be expanding as new bulls would be expecting prices to rise and entering the market. Because the exiting bears must buy to cover their short positions, this puts upward pressure on prices and, therefore, causes prices to rise. When open interest stabilizes, it is an indication that the bears whose positions were precarious have exited. As this short-covering buying pressure diminishes, a decline in prices can be expected.

CHAPTER 14

COMMITMENTS OF TRADERS: TRACKING THE BIG ONES

By Steve Briese

One of the best clues to participation in U.S. markets by various types of traders is provided by the Commitments of Traders *report from the Commodity Futures Trading Commission. However, you can't just read raw numbers from this report and come up with absolute answers. As with most areas of technical analysis, analyzing COT figures involves some subjective conclusions based on years of experience. Steve Briese, editor of* Bullish Review *in Rosemount, Minn., has specialized in analyzing and interpreting COT reports and has gained a widespread reputation for his trading recommendations based on this analysis. This information is from his article in the March 1994 issue of* Futures *magazine.*

The U.S. government has been quietly providing genuine insider information on a regular basis in the *Commitments of Traders* (COT) report for more than two decades, but it is just now becoming common subject matter among market watchers.

The COT report, published by the Commodity Futures Trading Commission, breaks down the open interest in futures markets by trader type, providing an insider's survey unavailable anywhere else.

The CFTC has established reporting levels—not to be confused with position limits—for each of the futures markets. Traders holding positions in excess of reporting levels must report their actual positions to the CFTC on a daily basis, forming the basis of the COT report. Large trader reporting levels are adjusted periodically, but traders holding more than, say, 500,000 bushels of wheat or soybeans or more than 500 T-bond contracts might be required to report their positions daily.

The CFTC separates large traders in "commercial" and "noncommercial" categories. Commercial hedgers are required to qualify with the CFTC by showing a related cash business for which futures are used as a hedge; they are persuaded to register through lower margin requirements and exemption from position limits.

The non-commercial category is comprised of large speculators, most notably commodity funds. The balance of the open interest is carried under the "nonreportable" classification, which includes both small commercial hedgers and speculators.

The report has been published since the 1970s. After being abandoned for the year 1982, the report was reinstated and COT data was released on a monthly basis from 1983 to November 1990 and then twice monthly until October 1992, when a biweekly reporting schedule was adopted. Even with this long history, traders ignored the COT report for years, thinking of it as "old news." But that attitude changed as the CFTC took steps to increase the frequency and speed of reporting the numbers.

The COT report is calculated after the market close each Tuesday. Due to auditing restraints, two weekly reports are issued on alternate Fridays. Because the report is issued electronically, reported trader positions for the most recent week are three days old.

The report is no longer available by mail subscription, and modem collection from the CFTC is expensive. However, most of the commodity news wires retransmit the data soon after it is released, and a number of vendors offer updates by fax, modem or mail as well as historical data for those who want to study this approach.

There is good reason for the increasing interest in the COT report. Reliability studies conducted by the *Bullish Review* across 36 futures markets from 1983 to 1989 show that extremely long or short positions by commercial hedgers correctly forecasted significant market moves 67 percent of the time.

That commercials have shown an uncanny ability to position heavily just before important market turns is only logical. As large cash merchants in the business, commercials maintain their own intelligence-gathering networks and analysts.

In fact, in some markets—such as coffee, cocoa and sugar—commercial trade houses are the primary source of fundamental supply and demand statistics available to the trading public. Assuming the statistics are reported accurately, you can be sure they already have been acted on in the market before the data is disseminated to the public. The COT report detects these actual market manipulations.

In addition to a decided informational advantage, large commercials by definition trade in sizes large enough to move markets. Given these advantages, their futures trading prowess is not surprising. Positioning with commercial hedgers—when they become one-sided in their market view—has proved far more profitable than either riding the coattails of large speculators or fading small traders. Large speculators were reliable only 46 percent of the time, small traders only 45 percent, in predicting significant market moves in the *Bullish Review* study.

Even so, some market books recommend following the large speculators under the theory that they must be pretty good traders to get that large. While that may have been true 10 years ago, the individual large trader of yesterday has been displaced by commodity funds in the modern data. The growth of these funds can be attributed more to a knack for fund-raising than trading.

Others advise fading small traders to follow the market adage that the public is always wrong. This has not been a successful approach—probably because the COT's "small trader" category includes small commercial hedgers.

Other COT analysts have centered their studies on divergences from seasonal average positions. However, my work has shown there is no statistically reliable seasonality present in the data, even for agricultural markets where one would suspect hedging is a seasonal consideration.

So what approach works best when analyzing COT data? Although each report contains many statistics, the two lines that are a primary concern to futures traders are the actual positions of traders and the changes from the prior report shown directly below. Some analysts work directly from the raw numbers, but the data is analyzed most easily when graphed as net positions opposite a price chart.

To derive the net position for each trader category, simply subtract the number of short contracts from the long. A positive result indicates a net long position (more long than short contracts) and a negative difference denotes a net short position (more shorts than longs).

Whether a particular trader group is net long or short is not important to the analysis; net positions relative to historic levels are. For example, commercial traders provided key buy signals with unusually large purchases of both gold and silver contracts at the major bottom in March 1993. Commercials held a net long position in gold (+30,584 contracts) but were net short in silver (-27,657 contracts). Yet, both were bullish indications. How can this be?

Each futures market is made up of a unique mixture of traders. In silver, large hedgers are primarily producers who hedge against price declines by selling forward in the futures market. As a result, commercials have never been net long in silver.

In gold, however, the commercial mix is more heavily weighted with fabricators who buy long contracts as a hedge against future inventory needs and rising prices. In aggregate, commercials are as often net long as net short in gold. Therefore, a simple net position is meaningless; it is imperative to compare the current net position with recent historical levels in the respective market.

A glimpse at a financial and an agricultural market illustrates a better analysis technique. On the hog chart (Figure 14.1), important market bottoms at points A, B and C were accompanied by commercial buying that moved the commercial net position to above +2,500 contracts. In other words, commercials held 2,500 more long than short contracts at important lows. At points D and E, commercial selling moved net positions below -2,500 contracts, causing a market drop. (The net po-

FIGURE 14.1   LIVE HOGS

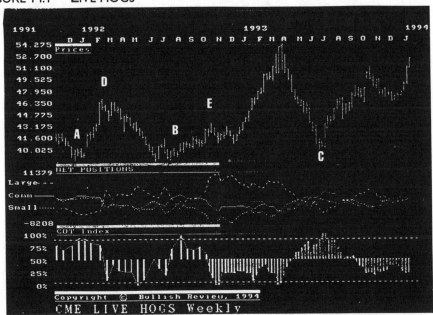

Source: The Bullish Review

sitions—long minus short contracts—are graphed below the price chart. They revolve around the zero line at which point long contract holdings are equal to short contracts.)

The increased timeliness of the COT report has been especially helpful in the pork complex, which is noted for "V" bottoms and tops; the June low at point C is an example.

The COT report issued June 25, 1993, showed commercials had increased their net long position to +3,335 contracts on June 22, an increase of 1,838 contracts in just two weeks. The data was published just three days ahead of an important U.S. Department of Agriculture Hogs and Pigs Report, and live hog prices had been ranging sideways for two weeks as traders awaited the report.

The COT figures were a clear tipoff that commercials were betting heavily on a bullish response to the Hogs and Pigs Report. Traders who positioned long with commercials ahead of the report were rewarded with a limit-up move the day after the report's release and an exciting 3 1/2-month rally. A confirming bullish picture in the pork belly market made the June low a special situation, but only large commercial hedgers were aware of it—unless you were watching their maneuverings through the COT data.

The relative bullishness of the commercial net position is easier to see when shown as an oscillator. The COT Index, plotted underneath net positions on the charts, compares the latest commercial net position to a historical range of net positions using the following formula:

$$100 \times \frac{\text{Current Net} - \text{Minimum Net}}{\text{Maximum Net} - \text{Minimum Net}}$$

Where:
Current Net = commercial long position - short position
Minimum Net = lowest net position over the period
Maximum Net = highest net position over the period

(The period can vary between 1.5 to 4 years, depending on the market. Too short a period generates constant signals, too long produces none.)

The scale is 0-100 percent, zero representing the most bearish net position over the period and 100 the most bullish. We are primarily interested in markets that reach the extremes of the range: Above 90 percent indicates a one-sided bullish commercial bias, below 5 percent conveys consensus bearishness.

Moving to financial markets, commercials—generally referred to as institutional traders including banks, mutual funds and dealers—have proven as astute as their agricultural counterparts in positioning for important market turns. When commercials have held 25,000 more long than short S&P 500 Index futures contracts, it signals a buying opportunity (points A, B and C in Figure 14.2). Sell signals were gen-

FIGURE 14.2   S&P 500

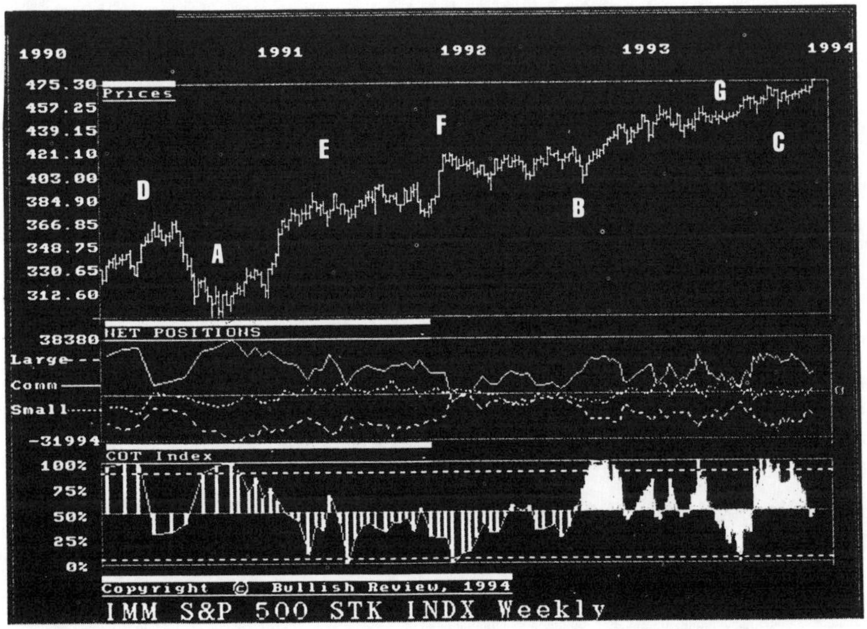

Source: The Bullish Review

erated when the net position dropped below +7,500 contracts (points D, E, F and G).

Point G is of particular interest. The market consolidated in a sideways pattern for most of 1993. In August, as the trading range narrowed, commercials bet heavily on a downside price breakout by selling futures. The breakout was to the upside and commercials quickly reversed positions, buying into the rally—the only COT signal failure on record for the S&P 500.

Of course, you can't discuss stock market indicators without highlighting the October 1987 crash. How did commercials fare? They provided a clearcut sell signal by moving to a rare net short position on the Aug. 30, 1987, COT report and held that position through the crash.

Legendary trader Daniel Drew is credited with the adage, "Anybody who plays the market without inside information is like a man buying cows in the moonlight." Large commercial hedging firms enjoy an enormous inside informational advantage over other market participants. The COT report levels the playing field by exposing the players behind the trades. Indeed, trading without reference to it might well be likened to "buying cows in the moonlight."

CHAPTER 15

MARKET SENTIMENT—
BEFORE IT IS FACT

The evidence of what people think about the price level of a particular contract is clearly visible on a bar chart: If the consensus is that the price is too high, traders make decisions that send prices lower; if they think the price is too low, they drive prices higher. The collective psychology of the marketplace shows up in the tracks on a chart.

If traders' interest in a market grows as they become more excited about a price level, volume and open interest may increase. Exchanges will provide you with lots of numbers for these measures of market activity, typically a day after they occur, and you can determine the attitude of the market by comparing changes in price with changes in volume/open interest.

If commercial traders or large speculators decide to establish a position or decide to change their minds about their positions, the result of this group thinking in U.S. markets shows up in the biweekly *Commitment of Traders* report, released to the public only a few days after these large traders themselves must reveal to the government where they stand.

While all of this information is valuable and useful, especially in the hands of analysts who can interpret its meaning for you, everything we have discussed in this section so far has been based on trades that have already taken place—old thoughts and old opinions that have already been expressed in decisions in the marketplace. What you would like to know, ideally, is what people are thinking about doing next—before they actually make the trade.

Several approaches attempt to get a reading on trader thinking before it shows up in the *Commitment of Traders* report, in volume and open interest statistics or as a price chart pattern. Whatever the approach, the intent is to discover trader sentiment early, anticipate what that means for current prices and use this information as another clue to support a trading decision.

Of course, like other areas of technical analysis, there is some art to this analysis, too. Sentiment may turn on a dime with the next report or the next rumor, or your information may be too early or too late. But however you get it, it clearly is to your advantage to have some insight into what other traders are thinking, no matter what your own trading style is.

Typically, the way this information is used is in a "contrary opinion" approach—you don't want to go against the flow and fight the market too soon, but, based on the assumption that the crowd is always wrong at major turns, you do want to go against the crowd at some point. If that concept is correct, what you obviously need to know first is what the crowd is thinking and then, second, when the crowd is likely to start being wrong.

BULLISH CONSENSUS

Perhaps the best-known gauge of market sentiment in modern futures trading is *Bullish Consensus*, introduced by James Sibbet in 1964. After studying Humphrey Neill's book, *The Art of Contrary Thinking*, published in 1954, and building on a stock market advisor index created by Abraham Cohen in 1963, Sibbet developed his own "bullish consensus" reading to measure the degree of bullish sentiment for a given futures market and devised ways to use this knowledge in trading.

In 1971 he joined with R. Earl Hadady, an engineer and successful futures trader, to form Sibbet-Hadady Publications. When Sibbet decided to concentrate on the metals markets in 1974, Hadady purchased his shares in the company and continued to refine the Bullish Consensus/contrary opinion concept further over the years. His *Market Vane* newsletter became the "bible" on the subject among traders. Consensus figures are now reported daily for 33 markets by Market Vane Corp. in Pasadena, Calif.

The original premise was that most traders, after losing money trading on their own, would turn to professional market newsletters or advisory services to help them with their trading decisions. Therefore, if you could find out what these professional advisors were recommending and knew how many followers each had, you could quantify the sentiment of a large group of traders coming to the marketplace.

Looking at dozens of newsletters every week, analysts would determine the trading recommendations for the various markets. Then, assuming larger brokerage firms or advisory newsletters with a large subscriber following influence more traders than smaller firms or lesser-known advisors, the impact of each recommendation can be weighted to quantify the consensus more precisely.

That completes the first step: Finding the market sentiment at a given moment. Carried out week after week, this research gives you a good feel for what traders are thinking and how changes in their opinions are reflected in price action. You have an idea of the consensus view.

The second step is analyzing this consensus number and determining when to trade contrarily. The principle of contrary opinion is that if a majority of traders have taken a long (short) position in the market because they believe it is going to go up (down) and if these traders have no more money to take further positions, the market is overbought (oversold). When there are no more buyers (sellers) to push a move onward, prices can only go one way—the opposite direction of the opinion of the majority.

Knowing exactly when this will occur is not a science. As with the indicators in the previous section, a bullish consensus reading above 70 percent often is considered overbought and a reading below 30 percent oversold. However, this is not true for all markets and all times, and sometimes it is the change in the reading that is most important. It often depends on the makeup of the traders in a particular market, the size of the market, previous price history, etc. In fact, some doubt the Bullish Consensus/contrary opinion techniques are useful at all any more in the 1990s because large traders and commodity funds have changed trading from what it was when the concepts became popular in the 1970s.

Like other areas of technical analysis, Bullish Consensus should not be considered in a vacuum, as Hadady emphasized in articles in *Commodities* and *Futures* over the years.

By itself, Bullish Consensus does provide useful information. As Hadady noted in one article, if 80 percent are bullish, then 20 percent are bearish. Because of the nature of futures trading—a short for every long and a long for every short—that means the 20 percent side represents the big money because each short holds an average of four times as many contracts as each long in the 80 percent bullish group. (If the Bullish Consensus hits 90 percent, shorts have nine times as many contracts as longs!) You normally want to know where the big money is: The money side of the market always wins.

Generally, however, consensus figures should be analyzed in conjunction with other tools. As the consensus figure moves to extremely high or low levels, open interest, for example, might be expected to level off or decrease because fewer and fewer are left to establish new positions. But if open interest continues to rise at extreme consensus readings, it indicates new money is still coming into the marketplace (see Chapter 13).

Bullish consensus also can be used with fundamental information as a clue to market direction. If a consensus reading is very high, for example, and a report or news event that would normally be considered bullish fails to move prices higher, that would be a strong indication of an overbought market and a time to sell.

ATTITUDE INDEX

Glen Ring, editor of *Trends in Futures* in Cedar Falls, Iowa, uses Market Vane's Bullish Consensus figures in a little different way to produce what he calls an "attitude index." This index looks at how many of the 23 physical commodities tracked by Market Vane have a bullish consensus of 50 percent or higher. It's rare, but occasionally as many as 20 or 21 of the 23 commodities will have a consensus reading above 50 percent.

When that happens, as it did several times in 1993 and 1994, Ring has found such extreme moves to be reliable indicators of upcoming trend changes for the market as a whole or at least a signal for significant corrections within trending moves.

DAILY SENTIMENT INDEX

While the Bullish Consensus figures are based on brokerage and advisory service opinions and recommendations, which presumably do influence a large number of traders as they make their trading decisions, another index attempts to capture the sentiment of the traders themselves. Developed in 1987 by Mark and Deb Lively and Jake Bernstein of MBH Commodity Advisors Inc. in Winnetka, Ill., the Daily Sentiment Index is based on a daily random sampling of the trading public.

The premise is that the thinking of a sample of traders, extrapolated to the broad cross-section of traders, will indicate how much buying and selling pressure will actually come into the trading pits. When the Daily Sentiment Index reaches bullish or bearish extremes—above 90 percent or below 20 percent, for example—it may be the first sign that a market is overbought or oversold and that a market turn is coming. The extremes for gold are quite different than they are for stock indexes so, as mentioned for Bullish Consensus above, one scale won't fit all markets.

Obviously, people's opinions can change dramatically from one day to the next, depending on a news event, a political development or some other factor. Traders caught at an emotional moment could cause wild swings in the Daily Sentiment Index, but that can be smoothed by using a moving average of the daily readings.

Of course, the input you get for this index will only be as good as the sampling technique you use. Like other areas of technical analysis, you probably will have to develop a feel for this approach before you can become comfortable with it.

SECTION IV

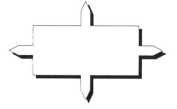

PRICE AND
PROJECTION:
MARKET STRUCTURE

INTRODUCTION

To keep our alliteration intact, I've stretched our Ps to a point here that may be reaching a bit. Perhaps the title could have been "Price and Predilection" or "Price and Predestination" or "Price and Predisposition." Whatever your preference, the thrust of this section is to look at price in light of market structure.

Normally, when you look at price action on a chart, you try to identify the trend and pick out the formations that can help you determine what prices might do next—the prices make the pattern. Another approach to technical analysis is that the pattern makes the price. For whatever reason, price follows a course set out for it by the structure of the market; if you can identify that structure, then you may be able to project price and time, according to this theory.

The various "structures" we'll discuss happen for a reason, of course. As Bill Williams of Profitunity Trading Group says in his seminar presentations, if you want to go from your office to the bathroom, chances are good you'll go through a doorway and down the hall instead of walking through a wall—you'll take the path of least resistance and go with the structure of the building, not the shortest distance.

Markets operate much the same way. While you may not be able to predict one trader's action accurately, you can, with some statistical assurance, predict the behavior of the group of traders collectively. The mass psychology of the trading crowd shows up in waves on price charts often enough that some analysts can put a structure on the marketplace that projects the next wave and how far it will go. Or, based on previous repetitions, they can project the timing and degree of the next low or high of a cycle or seasonal pattern.

Jake Bernstein of MBH Commodity Advisors, talking to a farm audience in the late 1970s, projected hog prices would drop dramatically, maybe below $30 per hundredweight. At the time, hog prices were well above $50. Inflation was heating up, and "everybody knew" cattle were headed for $100 per hundredweight, soybeans to $20 per bushel, gold to $5,000 an ounce, etc.

"We'll never see hog prices that low again. What could possibly cause hog prices to fall as much as you predict?" the skeptical audience wondered.

"I don't know. I just know what the cycles tell me, and they say prices will go lower," Bernstein responded. "Something will happen that will cause the cycle to work."

That answer wasn't very convincing to farmers that day, but prices did slide below $30 again not too many months later, making Bernstein's outlook seem almost like an eerie premonition of disaster for these producers—or the best hedging tip they might ever have gotten.

Anyone associated with agriculture—or almost any free market, for that matter—knows prices go up and down and that they seem to do so with some regularity. Generally, this happens for sound economic reasons—the "low prices are the cure for low prices" or "high prices are the cure for high prices" reaction, accompanied by psychological mood swings that may show up clearly in price action.

If there is a pattern to this process, how can you see what it is in time to make profitable trades? This section focuses on how some analysts see the market's structural framework that may direct, but not dictate, price action.

CHAPTER 16

SPREADS: MAINTAINING ORDER

Credit for background for this section should be given to various people including Keith Schap, a former Futures *associate editor who is now devising strategies for the Chicago Board of Trade; Phil Tiger, editor of* Tiger on Spreads, *and Tom Cronin, president of Trade Search Inc. and editor of* Just Spreads.

Perhaps the most logical place to begin a discussion about market structure is with spreads, the difference in price between two contracts. You may not be able to accept—indeed, you may not even be able to see—the cycles or waves or angles or other structural patterns that have been applied to a market. However, intuitively, you can sense that markets should have some natural price relationships with each other based on economic reality alone.

To trade spreads, all you need to know is what should be "normal" in these relationships in the current circumstances. When something gets out of line and is not normal, buy what is undervalued and sell what is overvalued. That, in a nutshell, is all there is to spread trading.

A spread trade is a position in which you are long one contract and short another. Industry practice lists the long contract first. Your goal is not to make money on absolute price changes but to capitalize on a change in relationship between the two contracts.

Assume you buy contract A and sell contract B. You can make money if the price of A advances and B stays flat, if A stays flat and B falls, if A rises more than B as both advance, if A decreases less than B as both decline. You do not have to be right about price direction.

For someone who has already found it difficult to assess the price prospects for just one contract, this adds a new dimension to technical analysis. One of the main advantages of spread trading, in fact, is that you may not need to be concerned as much about the more exacting technical analysis techniques covered in this volume.

Based on what you know about the fundamental situation, you may conclude that wheat should be worth more in March than in July when the new crop is available. You don't have to worry whether the overall price direction is up or down or where your entry point should be. You will want to analyze the spread situation, of course, to see how it has worked in the past (the more years, the better), its "cost-of-carry" status (see below), seasonal tendencies and the overall technical and fundamental picture. But precise timing for a spread often is less important than it is for a directional trade, and you are not as subject to whipsaws that may result from in-and-out trading.

Of course, you can trade spreads technically, too, by applying some of the same trendline and other bar charting techniques to a spread chart (see Figure 16.1).

Other advantages generally cited for spread trading include limited risk, lower margins and, consequently, more favorable risk/reward ratios. You may find a market too volatile or requiring too large a margin for an outright position but manageable with a spread. However, a spread is certainly no guarantee you are taking on less risk. It is quite possible to lose on both legs of the spread and magnify your risk.

Note on some of the spread charts that the moves can be rather substantial: What looks good going with you can also go against you. You

FIGURE 16.1   TRENDLINE BREAKOUT ON A SPREAD

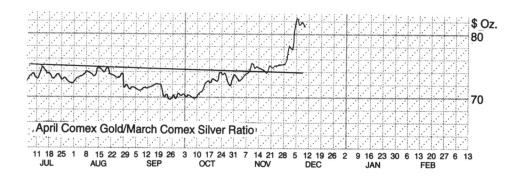

Source: Commodity Price Charts

must have the same discipline to get out of a losing spread trade as you do with outright position trading.

Some may find a spread trading style too "boring"—like watching paint dry, some say—but commercials and professional traders have proven it may be better for longevity and financial health. As you become a more accomplished trader and make your trading more business-like, it's quite likely an approach you'll want to consider. If so, you have many varieties of spreads from which to choose, using strategies ranging from arbitraging for nickels and dimes to long-term position trading for big changes in price relationships.

INTRAMARKET SPREADS

Same commodity, same exchange, different delivery months. Example: long February cattle, short June cattle (see Figure 16.2).

For the agricultural crop commodity contracts, there should be two distinctions:

FIGURE 16.2

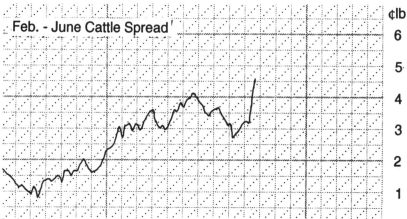

Source: Commodity Price Charts

a. Intraseasonal—Two contracts within the same crop year. Example: long March soybeans, short July soybeans. The concept of "cost of carry" or "carrying charges" is important in these spread trades.

Look at your array of prices for various futures contract months. If March soybeans are at $6 per bu., for example, July soybeans might be at $6.25. The difference is due to the cost of storage, insurance, interest expense, etc. Somebody has to account for the costs of holding soybeans four extra months until July.

Depending on the price level and a variety of other factors, it might be "normal" for these carrying charges to be 10¢ per bushel per month or 40¢ from March to July. Seldom will the actual price difference reflect the full cost of carry so it might be "reasonable" to expect a 25¢ difference in the price for soybeans between the March and July futures contracts. If the actual difference is somewhat more or less than that or you suspect there is good reason it could be, you might have a spread trade.

In a "normal" situation, the cash price would be the base level and each futures month would be at a progressively higher price to account for carrying charges. The term for this alignment is a "contango" market (used mostly in international markets). When the cash price is higher than the futures price or a nearby futures month is higher than the next month, it is called "backwardation." These are important to the spread trader trying to capitalize on what is "normal" or "abnormal."

Of course, just because a market is in backwardation does not mean it will jump into a "normal" contango setup or that it won't go further into backwardation—energy markets, for example, or copper in 1994 have provided plenty of evidence for that.

b. Interseasonal—Two contracts in two different crop years. Example: long July 1995 soybeans, short November 1995 soybeans. Although they are the same commodity, same exchange, etc., there may be a tremendous difference in price relationship dynamics between the intraseasonal spread and the interseasonal spread due to differences in crop sizes, demand and other fundamental factors in the two seasons. Each crop season naturally affects the next, but this often is not a normal carrying charge situation.

Note: Another July-November spread—July *1996* and November 1995—would be in the same season and would have carrying charge and other intraseasonal spread characteristics. It's important to distinguish exactly which months you are trading.

You can categorize the tactics for intramarket spread trades several ways:

"Bull spread"—Long the nearby month, short the more distant month. Basically, the situation is bullish. The assumption is that demand (or lack of supply) will make the market willing to pay more in the near future than it would be willing to pay at a later time. You perceive the market's message to be, "We want it sooner rather than later."

But being bullish doesn't automatically suggest a bull spread trade. For one thing, the nearby month may already be priced at a historically high level relative to the more distant month, and the spread may not be likely to widen any further. And, in some cases, an increase in prices for a commodity—precious metals, for example—will mean higher carrying charges so the more distant months may need to rise more than the nearby months to cover these added costs.

"Bear spread"—Long the back month, short the nearby month. The reverse of the bull spread, in this situation the mood is bearish. The assumption is supplies (or lack of demand) will be greater than the market wants in the near future so it will pay someone carrying charges to hold the supply for use at a later time. The market's message is, "We don't want it now."

As with the bull spread, the caveats apply: The more distant months may already have built in sufficient carrying charges, and the spread may have no further to go.

One important reminder about bull and bear spreads: The market does not have to go up or be bullish for a bull spread to be profitable; the market does not have to go down or be bearish for a bear spread to be profitable. In a bull spread in a market decline, the nearby month just has to go down less than the more distant month.

INTERMARKET SPREADS

Same commodity, same delivery month, different exchanges. Example: long December wheat at the Chicago Board of Trade, short December wheat at the Kansas City Board of Trade or the Minneapolis Grain Exchange. The commodity is wheat at all three exchanges, but the type of wheat, its uses, delivery points, etc. are different at each exchange so the fundamentals that affect one may not affect the other in the same way.

Other examples that could be placed in this classification include the energy contracts, cocoa, sugar, coffee, copper, Eurodollars, Japanese government bonds and currencies, among others. Some stock indexes also might fit here—the S&P 500 Index versus the Value Line or NYSE Composite Index because the "commodity" is U.S. stocks (although the number and type are different in each futures contract). Other stock indexes in London, Paris, Tokyo, Singapore, etc. are on different stock markets and probably fit more correctly in the next category.

INTERCOMMODITY SPREADS

Same delivery month, different but related commodities, may or may not be on same exchange. Example: long December silver, short December gold.

You probably won't be able to convince your broker to give you a spread margin for, say, long cocoa/short pork bellies, but many other relationships are traded as spreads in markets every day. Currency cross-rates and many arbitrage techniques fit here.

In the financial markets, the most popular U.S. interest rate spreads are probably the "NOB" spread (involving the 10-year Treasury note and the 30-year Treasury bond contracts traded at the Chicago Board of Trade) and the "TED" spread (T-bills versus the Eurodollar contract at the Chicago Mercantile Exchange). The "MOB" spread (CBOT municipal bond index and T-bond futures contracts) is another less active example.

The spreads covering different maturities have little to do with the overall direction of interest rates but essentially are a view of the yield curve, which tends to get out of "normal" alignment depending on the market's perception for interest rates at various maturities. If you expect the yield curve to steepen, with the rate for shorter maturities increasing over the more distant T-bonds, you buy the NOB—buy T-note futures, sell T-bond futures. If you expect the yield curve to flatten, you sell the NOB—buy T-bond futures, sell T-note futures.

This can be a straightforward 1-to-1 trade for arbitraging or short-term situations, but portfolio managers or other institutional traders looking for a more precise balance will want to take into account duration risk or the price value of a basis point for both instruments.

The TED spread involves two short-term interest rates and is viewed as a gauge of early market reaction to world fiscal, monetary or political changes. It is a quality spread: the safer T-bill versus the more risky Eurodollar.

Many other intercommodity spreads work for logical seasonal or economic reasons. For example, corn and soybeans are kept somewhat in alignment because they compete for the same acreage in much of the United States. Because of yield differences, the price of a bushel of soybeans "normally" is about 2 1/2-3 times the price of a bushel of corn so the return per acre is about the same for either. If corn prices get "too high" relative to soybeans, farmers will shift more acreage to corn, adding to the corn supply and subtracting from the soybean supply enough to cause price shifts that get the economics back in line.

Cattle versus hogs is another economic spread (see Figure 16.3) influenced in part by the demand side as shoppers buy one or the other (or poultry or fish) based on price at the supermarket. Demand (not consumption) based on consumer tastes is harder to gauge than supply so it may be more difficult to quantify "normal" for this aspect of the spread.

Combining seasonals (see next chapter) and spreads, a corn-wheat spread works because different harvest seasons produce supply pressures at different times—buy wheat at its harvest lows in June-July and sell corn; buy corn at its harvest lows in the fall and sell wheat (see Figure 16.4).

FIGURE 16.3

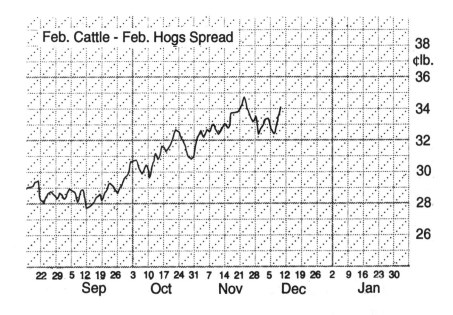

Source: Commodity Price Charts

FIGURE 16.4

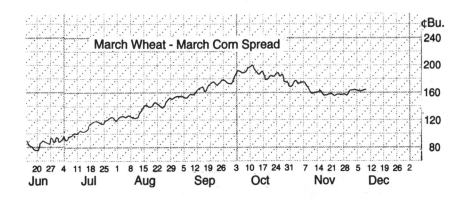

Source: Commodity Price Charts

SOURCE-PRODUCT SPREADS

Between a commodity and one or more of its products. Example: long February crude oil, short February unleaded gasoline, short February heating oil. These are expanded versions of intercommodity spreads where the trader can be in the "business"—on paper. While the math may seem to be a little cumbersome, these spreads are excellent candidates for spreadsheet programs and simple graphics—you just plug in the new values each day. Some of the more common spreads in this category include:

Soybean crush/reverse soybean crush—This is the oldest and probably best-known spread of this type because futures have been available on both sides of the trade for many years and because it reflects, in essence, the soybean processing business. When prices for soybean meal and oil relative to soybeans are attractive, processors are likely to hedge; when soybean product prices are too low or soybean prices too high to make a profit, processors will not crush soybeans at a loss for very long. These forces help to keep the economic relationship in line and make these spreads work.

You need to have a little background in fundamentals to understand the technical analysis of this spread. A 60-pound bushel of soybeans yields roughly 47-48 pounds of soybean meal and 10.5-11 pounds of soy oil. (Those figures can vary from year to year, depending on crop quality and other factors, so any calculations you make will have to allow for these fluctuations.) Using the current price, you can calculate how much value each of those components bring to a bushel of soybeans. Here's an example:

	Soy oil	Soybean meal
Prices:	27¢ per lb.	$160 per ton
Yield:	10.8 lb./bushel	48 lb./bushel
Value:	$2.92 per bushel	$3.84 per bushel
		($160/2,000 lb. = 8¢ per lb. * 48)
Total value:	$6.76 per bushel	

Assume the price of a bushel of soybeans at the same time was $5.75. The difference of $1.01 per bushel is the processor margin or the crush margin. The key question, as it is with most spread trades, is, "What is 'normal'?" As the January crush chart (comparing January 1995 futures contracts for soybeans, meal and soy oil) indicates, that margin is on the high side (Figure 16.5). That suggests processors might be interested in locking in the high margin by hedging—selling product futures and buying soybean futures.

FIGURE 16.5   JANUARY "CRUSH" SPREAD

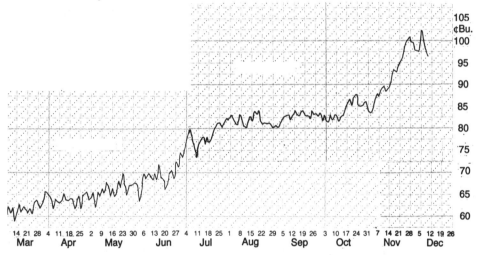

Source: Commodity Price Charts

But this chart also illustrates how demand for one or both products can widen the spread much more than you might expect, making a typical crush spread an expensive proposition. In this situation, soybeans and soybean meal peaked in May-June and then drifted down to harvest lows. Soy oil prices, however, peaked in May-June, too, slumped but then rallied back in the fall to the earlier peak. With soy oil demand adding value to the product side and with plenty of soybeans available, processors saw little urgency to hedge to narrow this spread to what might seem to be more "normal."

That makes the crush spread a little risky for the average trader. The reverse soybean crush spread is more reliable. Good business sense suggests the combined value of meal and soy oil in a bushel of soybeans should always be more than the price of a bushel of soybeans plus some margin the processor must have to cover costs. Processors wouldn't be in business very long if that weren't true. If their profit margin gets too low, you can bet they will take steps to correct it.

But what is "too low"? That's where historical analysis will help you. Where 20¢ a bushel might have been adequate in the 1970s, the minimum might be 50¢ per bushel in the 1990s to cover higher energy, labor and other operating costs. That will vary as conditions change, but if the spread starts to squeeze processors too much, it may be time for the reverse soybean crush—buy the products and sell soybeans.

A reverse soybean crush trade doesn't come along every day or maybe even every season, but when it does, you probably will find it comforting to know that the processors are working in the same direction you are trading to make the spread work in your favor.

One of the problems you have with the crush or reverse crush spread is getting a precise balance in the futures market. A Chicago Board of Trade soybean contract is 5,000 bushels on one side of the trade. On the other side, the soybean meal contract is 100 tons or the equivalent of roughly 4,200 bushels of soybeans, and the soy oil contract is 60,000 lb. or the equivalent of about 5,560 bushels of soybeans (again, that will vary depending on the yield of meal and oil in each bushel of soybeans). Using only one contract of each would leave you exposed in some area.

Unless you use mini-contracts at the MidAmerica Commodity Exchange to refine your position, you would have to have a combination of 10 contracts of soybeans, 12 contracts of soybean meal and 9 contracts of soy oil to achieve a nearly exact balance at the CBOT.

Looking at the dollar values for each side of this package may be a better way to see trading opportunities than looking at the typical cents per bushel values. Using the prices above, on the one side, you would have 50,000 bushels at $5.75 per bushel or a total value of $287,500. On the other side, the value of the meal contracts at $192,000 (100 tons * $160 * 12) plus the value of the soy oil contracts at $145,800 (60,000 lb. * 27¢ * 9) totals $337,800. The difference is $50,300.

Historically, whether you look at $1.01 per bushel or $50,300 for the typical crush spread package, the figures appear high and potentially attractive for a soybean crush spread. But are they out of line enough to trade profitably? That's what your spread analysis has to tell you.

"Paper refinery"—"You, too, can be an oilman!" a promotion piece might exclaim about what is known as "the crack spread." The basics of this spread are like the soybean crush spread above—a raw material (crude oil) is processed into products (heating oil and gasoline), and futures contracts are available on all three. However, the crack spread, considered the classic indicator of relationships in the energy market, is a little more complicated. Again, you have to have a little background in fundamentals to start your technical analysis of this spread.

First, there are different kinds and grades of crude oil. The major futures contracts are on West Texas Intermediate (New York Mercantile Exchange) and Brent (International Petroleum Exchange) crude oils, but that's not the whole oil market.

Second, based on the type of crude oil, market demand or other factors, the breakdown of the raw material into products can vary.

On paper, of course, you don't have to worry as much about such details. However, you do share a concern with real refiners that may affect you more immediately than it does them: Oil (and anything connected to it) tends to be an extremely sensitive and volatile commodity when it comes to certain political events, weather, shipping or production interruptions, etc. Sudden aberrations seem to be almost the norm, making energy an anxiety arena where even the best thought out crack spread program can fall apart.

As with the soybean crush, the crack spread defines a value added by a processing operation. Keeping in mind that there can be many variations, a barrel of crude oil generally breaks down into roughly 50 percent unleaded gasoline and a little less than 25 percent heating oil with the remainder in other products such as residual fuel oil, jet fuel, naphtha, butane and asphalt.

A number of crack spread combinations are possible, depending on the production emphasis, but the traditional one is the 3-2-1 spread: Three barrels of crude oil versus two barrels of gasoline and one barrel of heating oil. A 2-1-1 spread is also common and may be easier to compute at a glance.

Crude oil is priced in dollars per barrel and the products in cents per gallon. For comparison, translate the oil price from barrel to gallon by dividing by 42 (gallons in a barrel). Using the 3-2-1 spread, here is the formula:

Crack spread = (((2 * gasoline price) + heating oil price) - (3 * (crude price/42))) / 3

 If the price of unleaded gasoline is 54¢ per gallon, heating oil 52¢ per gallon and crude oil $18 per barrel, the crack spread is:

(($1.08 + 52¢) - (3 * 43¢)) / 3

$1.60 - $1.29 = 31¢ / 3 = 10.3¢ per gallon

Or, if you prefer barrels, you can multiply product prices by 42 to translate to dollars per barrel or multiply the 10.3¢ figure above by 42 to get $4.326 per barrel (which is how the crack spread is shown in Figure 16.6).

FIGURE 16.6

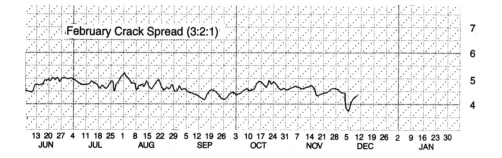

Source: Commodity Price Charts

Now you're ready for the same question for all spreads: Is that price "normal" for the current circumstances? If the price of crude oil were to go up $2 per barrel and product prices remain flat, the crack spread would drop to 5.6¢. Is that "too low" to encourage refiners to maintain the pace of production?

In the early 1990s, an average break-even figure was considered to be 4¢ a gallon (or, multiplied by 42, $1.68 per barrel). Refiners, of course, will want something above that for their profit, for taking on risk, etc.

As an "oilman," what looks "right" to you? As you analyze the relationships in the crack spread, you will see trading opportunities but you'll want to stay in tune with what the "real" refiners are telling you.

"Paper feedlot"—Instead of being an oilman, maybe you've always wanted to be a cattleman. However, you may not be excited about the prospects of shoveling manure, early morning feeding chores and thaw-ing frozen water lines. Well, you can still realize your dream to be a "cattleman" in futures markets. But it isn't easy. One problem is you can't slow or stop production or store the raw or end products as easily as you can with the previous two spreads.

Futures contracts are available for the basic ingredients: feeder cattle, corn, soybean meal and live cattle. They're not in the same month in the same sizes so it does take some maneuvering and astute timing to accumulate your "supplies" and liquidate your "herd." And, of course, this arrangement doesn't take into account all the factors actual feedlot operators face such as veterinary bills, death losses, interest rates, etc.

If you're serious about this spread, you'll have to do more calculations to determine your feed needs, break-even points, timing of purchases and sales, etc. But here are the basics. Assume you "feed" 650-pound feeder cattle to about 1,050-pound animals. If you buy one November feeder contract (50,000 pounds), you have roughly 77 head. When they are fed out in five months, you will have the equivalent of two live cattle futures contracts (a 40,000-pound contract). You will prob-ably use April cattle futures to sell.

Each calf will eat about 45 bushels of corn (3,465 bushels total for 77 head) and 215 pounds of soybean meal (a little over 8 tons total) in the five-month feeding period. One contract of feeder cattle is not enough for a full futures contract for corn and far short of a soybean meal contract. If you want to achieve a balance here, you'll have to make an adjustment into multiple contracts. You would need to feed about 920 head of cattle (about 12 feeder contracts) for a full meal contract, for example. Your feed inputs will probably be in December futures.

To assess the potential of the spread, total the values of the contracts on the input cost side. Then look at the total value of your live cattle futures contracts. "Real" cattleman can attest that sometimes what you get from selling your cattle can be less than your costs. That's true on paper, too. This is a tricky spread to execute, but it's a good way for speculators to look at this market just as an actual cattle feeder does in his business.

If you'd rather "raise" hogs, you can set up a similar program using futures contracts for live hog futures on one side and corn and soybean meal on the other. However, there is no futures contract (yet) for feeder pigs, one of the key input costs. Some watch the hog/corn ratio, but that can stay "out of line" for extended periods before it adjusts.

CHAPTER 17

'TIS THE SEASONAL

Many markets exhibit seasonal tendencies—that is, prices tend to rise or fall about the same time each year due to production cycles, demand influences, etc. While seasonal patterns are particularly notable in agricultural markets, they show up in some other rather surprising places, too. But how can you identify this seasonal structure that influences so many markets?

As with technical indicators, you may turn to a research service to give you all the answers you need for your trading. But to give you some insight on seasonal patterns and how to read them, this chapter looks at several approaches to seasonal analysis.

INDEX METHOD

By Jake Bernstein

Jake Bernstein, president of MBH Commodity Advisors in Winnetka, Ill., first made a name for himself in the futures industry in the 1970s with his work on seasonals/cycles and the psychology of trading. He didn't discover seasonality, of course, but did much to publicize its use in trading in several books and articles in Commodities *magazine. The following comes from an article in the November 1981 issue. It is reproduced here with permission. His research since then has gotten much more extensive and sophisticated, resulting in 27 books on trading, and he has become one of the most widely known analysts among individual futures traders.*

One method to detect seasonal patterns, and perhaps the most basic of all approaches, is the "eyeball" technique. It involves nothing more than visually examining price charts covering a similar time span over a given period of years.

Based on this, you reach a conclusion about what is normal or typical for the time span examined. This not only is the fastest way to inspect for seasonality but it also is the least accurate and least specific.

A more effective way involves constructing a normalized seasonal change index and a percentage comparison table. This can be used to isolate seasonals in many different areas, including cash markets, futures contracts, government data and even spreads.

To construct a weekly seasonal price change index, your first step would be to obtain the weekly closing price of each year's contract for as many years back as you wished to study—as far back as possible.

Compute the normalized price for each week by converting the raw weekly data to a standardized price. In other words, convert the lowest weekly close of the year to a reading of 0 and the highest weekly closing price of the year to a reading of 100. This is a fairly simple, but time-consuming, procedure. The purpose is to minimize the effect of very high or low prices in given years because you are interested primarily in trend and not magnitude.

Upon completing the conversion, determine the price change from one week to the next. Remember to line up prices using the last week of trading as the starting point. Futures contracts begin trading at a slightly different time each year so your best guide is by week of expiration because these are fairly similar historically.

The next step is to determine the number of +, - and 0 change signs for each given week. For example, assume that week number 15 prior to contract expiration showed 11 gains and four declines from week 16 during a 15-year span.

You now know the market has gained in price from week 16 to week 15. In other words, the fraction 11/15 expressed as a percentage probability is 73.3 percent. This means prices have moved up over 73 percent of the time from week 16 to week 15 over the last 15 years. This is an important piece of trading information, particularly for the short-term trader.

You then could add the normalized price change figures from week to week, thereby arriving at a cumulative price trend plot. This is done by algebraically adding the figure for each week and taking the arithmetic average. This yields one price entry for each week.

These entries then are cumulated on a week-to-week basis and plotted on a chart (Figure 17.1). You end up with a composite seasonal chart showing the usual trend(s), price moves in terms of normalized magnitude and a weekly probability reading of higher or lower prices based on the historical action of the given market. You could perform the same basic analysis on weekly cash data or government report data, as long as it is available on a weekly basis.

FIGURE 17.1

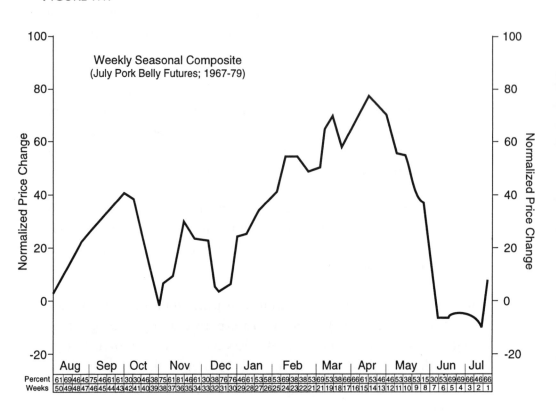

Source: MBH Commodity Advisors

Remember that the composite seasonal chart and weekly price move probability are based on historical data and do not necessarily predict what will occur. They merely tell you what likely will occur based on past performance.

Some traders attribute much credibility to inflation indexing and use still another method. Assume you wanted to do the same type of analysis to adjust for inflation. This would be a relatively simple addition to the method. All you need to do prior to converting the raw data to normalized data is subtract the effect of inflation. Do this by taking the inflation rate reading for the given week, multiplying it by the price reading and subtracting this figure from the weekly closing price. The new price (inflation-adjusted) then could be used in your data analysis in place of the previous raw data.

How high should the reading be? Generally, I prefer to use readings above 65 percent (plus or minus) for trading purposes—that is, the market that week was up (or down) from the previous week about two-thirds of the time in the past. The higher the reading, the more likely the move. To maximize timing, you could use short-term timing signals in conjunction with seasonal readings that have high percentage readings.

COMPUTER SELECTION

By Steve Moore, Jerry Toepke and Nick Colley

One analyst who has done perhaps more research on seasonal trends than anyone else in recent years is Steve Moore, president of Moore Research Center in Eugene, Ore. He has taken the computer to the max to ferret out reliable seasonal trade possibilities, going well beyond the commodities normally associated with seasonals to interest rates, currencies and other markets that, on the surface, might not seem to be candidates for seasonal trading. I'm still a little skeptical about calling some of these moves "seasonals," especially those that run only a few days and seem to have little reason to move in a consistent pattern every year. But Moore's research has shown they will work. The following is from an article by Moore and two of his associates that appeared in the April 1994 issue of Futures *magazine. It is reprinted here with permission*

Certain annual supply/demand factors repeatedly exert pressures on price, creating a natural fundamental-cause, seasonal-effect relationship. In addition, because annually repetitive price activity translates into seasonal tops, bottoms and trends, seasonal effects can be analyzed technically.

So not only do seasonal studies offer a means to research a trade or better understand a market, they also can be integrated with fundamental and/or technical techniques to provide a more comprehensive perspective and trading approach.

Better yet, the seasonal approach isn't limited to markets directly influenced by weather. Though traditionally more associated with agriculture, seasonal analytical properties and trading principles apply in every market.

For instance, annual changes in the weather pattern obviously affect heating oil prices, but is it just a statistical aberration that the beginning of the most significant period of weakness during the year for Treasury bond futures is coincident with the new U.S. tax year? What meteorological event recurs every April 15 that could create such a distinct pattern in trading the future of long-term interest rates (see Figure 17.2)?

FIGURE 17.2   THE TAX MAN COMETH—SEP. 30-YEAR T-BONDS
15-YEAR SEASONAL (1979–93)

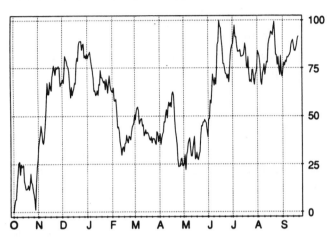

Source: Moore Research Center, Inc.

Prices move most dramatically when anticipating—and adjust equally dramatically upon realizing—changing conditions in the supply/demand equation. This recurring phenomenon is intrinsic to the seasonal approach to trading, which is designed to anticipate, enter and capture the recurrent trends as they emerge and exit before doomed by the adverse psychology of realization.

The logic underlying seasonal research begins with the premise that for each and every market, annually recurring fundamental factors specific to that market occur, forcing price to react. Supply/demand factors—whether in real estate, T-bonds or soybean futures—are determined by fundamentals, some of which (school years, quarterly Treasury refunding auctions and tax deadlines or specific characteristics of futures contracts such as delivery and expiration) tend to recur in more or less a timely manner and influence prices to a greater or lesser degree every year.

To quantify those reactions, we must find empirical evidence of their evolution into a basic price pattern. Accomplishing that, we then can define seasonality as a tendency to consistently repeat similar price movement at a given time every year.

Computers can mathematically construct a daily seasonal pattern, derived from a composite of historical daily activity for any market for any designated number of years. To more accurately depict historical price behavior, each calendar day is assigned a value representing where its price typically traded relative to the year's eventual range.

So if price on calendar day one of year one was $4, falling within the eventual range of $2 and $12 for year one, a value of 20 (percent) is assigned ($4 is 20 percent off the $2 bottom). If on calendar day one of year two the price was at $16 in an eventual range for that year of $8 and $24, a value of 50 is assigned. That goes on for each calendar day one in each of the years designated. The average of those values then is plotted for calendar day one. The process is repeated for each day of the year.

The pattern ultimately plotted against the numerical index reflects the historical tendency for that market to trade at its seasonal high (100) and seasonal low (0). Between these two points appear trends and secondary highs/lows. This seasonal pattern simply illustrates the annual cycle of increasing/decreasing demand relative to supply (uptrends/downtrends) and typical periods of greatest/least demand (seasonal tops/bottoms).

These historical price patterns not only visually display typical market movement but also suggest specific windows of opportunity. Distinct time periods within significant seasonal trends may be analyzed more closely for precise and historically reliable trading opportunities. For example, look at the highlighted portion of the 15-year seasonal pattern for April live cattle (Figure 17.3).

FIGURE 17.3   CATTLE CHANGES—APRIL LIVE CATTLE
15-YEAR SEASONAL (1979–93)

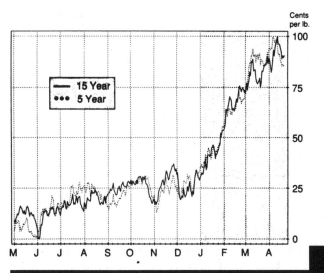

Phase one: List of live cattle seasonals									
	Futures trade	Entry date	Exit date	Win %	Win years	Loss years	Total years	Average profit	Ave profit per day	Ave % dly mgn
1	Buy live cattle (CME) — April	1/06/93	2/08/93	93	14	1	15	825	24.27	3.60
2	Buy live cattle — April	1/08/93	2/22/93	93	14	1	15	1,007	21.88	3.24
3	Buy live cattle—April	1/08/93	2/24/93	93	14	1	15	1,053	21.93	3.25
4	Buy live cattle — April	1/08/93	3/08/93	87	13	2	15	1,291	21.52	3.19
5	Buy live cattle — April	1/08/93	3/25/93	80	12	3	15	1,403	18.22	2.70
6	Buy live cattle — April	1/20/93	2/25/93	80	12	3	15	939	25.37	3.76
7	Buy live cattle—April	1/23/93	2/08/93	93	14	1	15	706	41.52	6.15
8	Buy live cattle — April	1/23/93	3/10/93	80	12	3	15	1,214	25.84	3.83
9	Buy live cattle — April	1/23/93	4/15/93	80	12	3	15	1,565	18.85	2.79
10	Buy live cattle — April	1/24/93	2/17/93	93	14	1	15	663	26.54	3.93
11	Buy live cattle — April	1/24/93	3/10/93	80	12	3	15	1,104	23.99	3.55
12	Buy live cattle — April	1/31/93	4/11/93	80	12	3	15	1,347	18.98	2.81
13	Buy live cattle — April	2/12/93	4/15/93	80	12	3	15	986	15.65	2.32
14	Buy live cattle—April	3/04/93	4/09/93	87	13	2	15	528	14.27	2.11

Final list of live cattle seasonals									
	Futures trade	Entry date	Exit date	Win %	Win years	Loss years	Total years	Average profit	Ave profit per day	Ave % dly mgn
3	Buy live cattle (CME) – April	1/08/93	2/24/93	93	14	1	15	1,053	21.93	3.25
7	Buy live cattle — April	1/23/93	2/08/93	93	14	1	15	706	41.52	6.15
14	Buy live cattle — April	3/04/93	4/09/93	87	13	2	15	528	14.27	2.11

Source: Moore Research Center, Inc.

Using a computer to calculate every possible combination of entry/exit points between specific dates, we compiled a table listing all possible strategies that meet various minimum standards, including those established for historical reliability (in this case, 80 percent), average profit and duration of time. From this initial list we can find the best—and most profitable—trades.

This can be done across all markets. A stand-alone approach to trading seasonal research requires little time or experience—just simple execution. Furthermore, methodically trading a sequence of seasonal strategies can take advantage of its diversity (across a broad spectrum of markets), balance (between long and short) and historically established patterns to reduce net risk exposure but permit ample participation in several market trends.

Seasonal research lends itself to more than just systematic execution of strategies. It can function as a check-and-balance on another trading system or perspective, confirming or contradicting conclusions drawn from technical or fundamental analysis (or vice-versa). It can also reveal an emerging contra-seasonal trend, one of the most dynamic of all market movements, by comparing unusual price activity to the "norm."

In real-time trading, seasonal analysis can compensate for limitations in pure technical or pure fundamental analysis. Too often, pure technical analysis gives false or misleading signals. Seasonal research, describing a "norm," can anchor technical analysis to a market by providing a yardstick to better judge the validity or significance of a technical signal.

Likewise, pure fundamental analysis (even assuming correct and complete input) too often lacks the element of timing, a problem associated with the phenomenon of anticipation/realization. Seasonality, a fundamental factor itself, can provide a yardstick to evaluate the timing of changes in the supply-demand equation.

One example illustrates a top-down analytical technique (from the "macro" to the "micro") and integrates seasonal analysis into a technical trading approach.

On Dec. 31, 1993, the monthly CRB Index offered the following technical picture: A seven-month period of accumulation formed a potentially major double bottom and was followed by decisive penetrations of three progressively more significant downtrend lines. A review of weekly charts in search of specific bullish candidates within the CRB family revealed a massive inverted head-and-shoulders formation in cotton—and a decisive penetration of the neckline (see Figure 17.4).

Do you jump in, knowing the risks in trading cotton with its penchant for abrupt movement? Cotton's seasonal pattern (see table) suggested that breaks during January often were buying opportunities in anticipation of the typical seasonal rally during spring.

In this instance, seasonal analysis confirmed technically bullish "macro" indications and suggested seasonal pressures favored continued strength, if not a rise, in cotton prices. Better yet, this integrated approach fortified purely technical analysis by anchoring it to typical supply/demand fluctuations.

FIGURE 17.4   MONTHLY CRB FUTURES PRICE INDEX CLOSE

	Futures Trade	Entry Date	Exit Date	Win %	Win Years	Loss Years	Total Years	Average Profit
	Cotton seasonals							
1	Buy cotton (NYCE) — May	1/28/93	4/23/93	87	13	2	15	1,330
2	Buy cotton — May	2/07/93	3/22/93	93	14	1	15	920
3	Buy cotton — July	2/22/93	5/13/93	80	12	3	15	1,287
4	Buy cotton — July	3/07/93	3/22/93	87	13	2	15	704

WEEKLY NEARBY COTTON

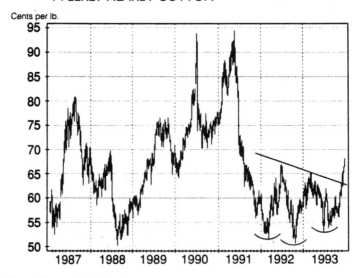

Source: Moore Research Center, Inc.

SEASONALS BY DAY

Sheldon Knight, president of K-Data Inc. in Sunnyvale, Calif., has been involved in computerized analysis of stocks and commodities for more than 30 years and has tested trading systems extensively. He used some of the same techniques as others to find the best seasonal trades, testing all possible entry and exit dates with historical data. But he didn't like the results he got in real trading.

Instead of using dates—Jan. 2, Jan. 3, Jan. 4, etc.—he decided to test the day of the week—first Monday in January, first Tuesday in January, etc.—and he found the weekday to be very important in futures price movement.

"For example," he reported, "the bond market often makes huge moves on the first Friday of each month when the employment report is released. The investment committee for a large pension fund may meet on the first Monday of each month. And traders are often reluctant to hold positions over a weekend so Friday and Monday activity is different from the middle of the week."

His research had shown that the day of the week that a trade was entered could make a big difference in a trading system's results. Applying that concept to seasonal trading, he developed the K-Data timeline. To compute it, take a specific day—the second Wednesday of July, for example—and find the average price change for the second Wednesday of July over the last five years (the second Wednesday of July will be on a different date each year, but the key is to stay with the second Wednesday). Then add the average price changes for the individual days to produce the timeline.

Example: June 1994 T-bonds, first week of May

May 2, 1994—First Monday of May
May 3, 1994—First Tuesday of May
Etc.

Price change on first Monday of May:

May 3, 1993—$1,250
May 4, 1992—($281.25)
May 6, 1991—($62.50)
May 7, 1990—($312.50)
May 1, 1989—($843.75)
Five-year average—($50.00)

Price change on first Tuesday of May:

May 4, 1993—$718.75
May 5, 1992—$250.00
May 7, 1991—($93.75)
May 1, 1990—($93.75)
May 2, 1989—$468.75
Five-year average—$250.00

Continue for first Wednesday, Thursday, Friday to get these five-year averages:

Wednesday—$131.25
Thursday—$56.25
Friday—$243.75

Timeline values:

May 2, 1994—($50.00)
May 3, 1994—$200.00
May 4, 1994—$331.25
May 5, 1994—$387.50
May 6, 1994—$631.25

(See Figures 17.5-17.9 for plotted values for all of May and for the whole contract year)

Using these timelines, Knight developed a mechanical trading system for T-bonds. Looking at the year-long chart first (Figure 17.5), note that the best projected long trade would be entered in late August 1993, exiting around the end of December (you have to ignore the higher projected prices at the end of the chart in June because they come after first notice day when you do not want to hold long contracts). The best projected short trade runs from the end of December to early May.

Now turn to the monthly timelines. The August chart (Figure 17.6) shows Aug. 27, 1993, as the exact date for the projected low when you would enter the long trade. The December chart (Figure 17.7) shows Dec. 23, 1993, as the exact date for the high when you exit the trade. You also enter the short trade on that date and exit that position on May 2, 1994 (see Figure 17.8). Knight emphasizes that you must enter these seasonal trades on the exact dates because of the day of the week effect.

Check your long-term chart (Figure 17.9) to see how these trades came out. You probably wouldn't have liked the long trade, but the short trade turned into a real winner.

There's more to the system than that, but this is sufficient to illustrate the day-of-the-week approach to seasonal trading. Each year will require new calculations for the previous five-year period and will likely produce different dates to catch the right day, but Knight's results show that further refinement of the seasonal technique can be quite profitable.

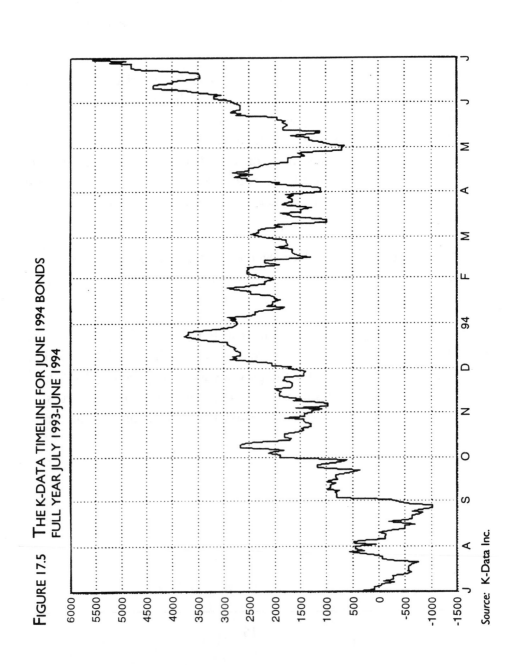

FIGURE 17.5   THE K-DATA TIMELINE FOR JUNE 1994 BONDS
FULL YEAR JULY 1993-JUNE 1994

Source: K-Data Inc.

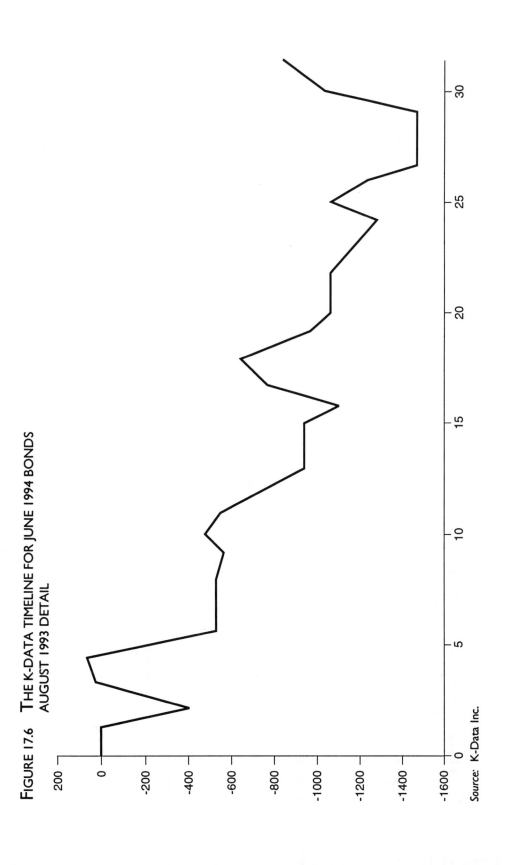

FIGURE 17.6   THE K-DATA TIMELINE FOR JUNE 1994 BONDS
AUGUST 1993 DETAIL

Source: K-Data Inc.

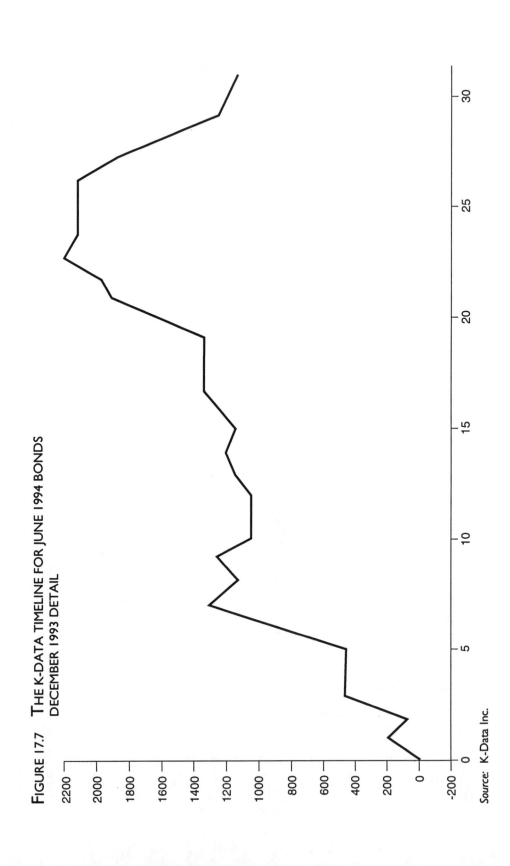

FIGURE 17.7   THE K-DATA TIMELINE FOR JUNE 1994 BONDS
DECEMBER 1993 DETAIL

Source: K-Data Inc.

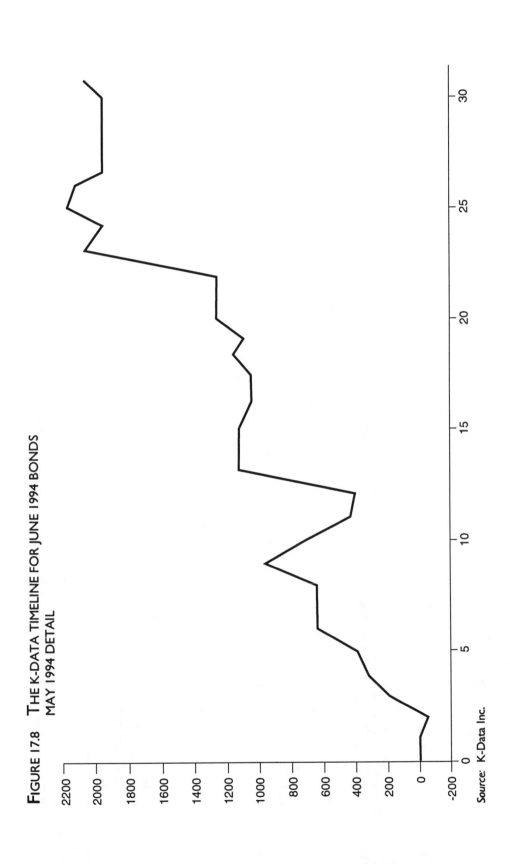

FIGURE 17.8   THE K-DATA TIMELINE FOR JUNE 1994 BONDS
MAY 1994 DETAIL

Source: K-Data Inc.

FIGURE 17.9 T-BONDS

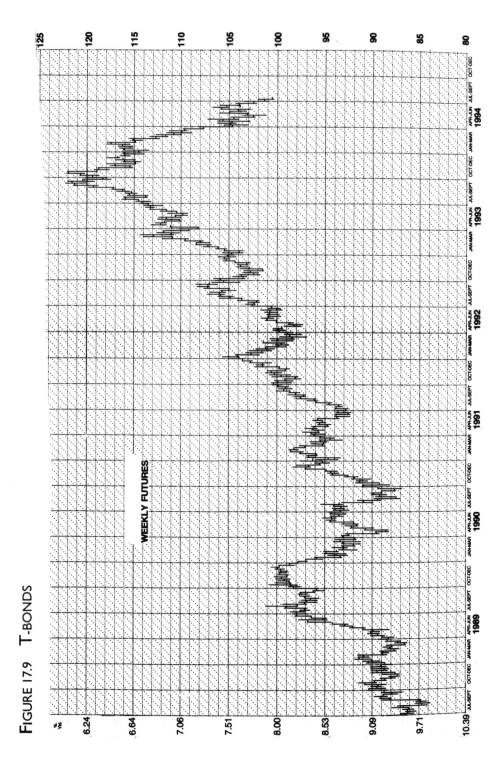

Source: Commodity Price Charts

CHAPTER 18

RIDING THE CYCLES

When you look at any traditional bar chart for any commodity for any length of time, the first thing you're likely to note is that prices go up and down. Look a little more closely and you'll see they seem to do so with some regularity, even within broader trends. As we indicated earlier, these vacillations are caused by psychological mood swings of market participants. But are these swings something you trace after the price action has occurred, or does some grand plan for market structure influence how price action unfolds?

While there is little argument that prices do go up and down, some do not see regular cycles in anything; others see cycles in everything. In fact, cycle advocates can point out cycles within cycles within cycles almost without end, from the biggest 500-year fluctuations in climate to the tiniest movements on tick charts.

Looking at the big picture, for example, you can identify major political turns of roughly 60 years in U.S. history often paralleling what was happening elsewhere in the world. In the late 1700s, the cycle was against centralized government domination as expressed by the American and French revolutions. As the mood reached extremes, the country appeared ready to fall apart into chaos. The crisis of adopting and implementing a Constitution to get the new country on its feet started a swing toward realizing the need for an increasing role for the federal government that began about 1800.

There naturally were cycles away from the trend of the bigger cycle, but a growing centralized government continued until around 1860 and the Civil War. The crisis issue then, of course, was slavery, but the battle was also about states' rights and all individual rights as some believed the government was over-reaching its boundaries of control.

After the war the trend away from centralized control and toward private enterprise boosted the development of the West and the growth of industries that formed the roots of many of today's major corporations. This more wide open era prompted economic growth but also led to abuses in the private sector and excessive speculation. It all came tumbling down with the next crisis, the Big "D" Depression.

In 1932 the country was ready to swing back toward increasing the federal government's role again with the election of Franklin D. Roosevelt. (It wasn't a particularly good period anywhere for capitalism, private enterprise or individual rights in general, as the world shifted to government domination with the Soviet Union and Germany as prime examples.) That major trend, again with counter cyclical spurts, has continued to the 1990s.

Now, some think the election of 1994 may be the signal another new era is underway to again reduce the role of the federal government. Whether a Congress controlled by the Republican party for the first time in years will be able to turn the tide remains to be seen. Has there been a crisis significant enough to cause a turn? Is the public sick enough of government intrusion into their lives (taxes, environmental and other regulations, some aspects of civil rights legislation) to follow through with actual steps that may mean personal sacrifices to down-size government control? Various countries are breaking apart or fighting strong central governments, but will that attitude extend to the United States?

That remains to be seen. If the 1990s do mark a turn, the last time this situation existed was in the 1860s, suggesting this could be the beginning of an era of less government, more private enterprise opportunities and improved prospects for "real" things such as physical commodities instead of "paper" investments. However, you should note that, with so few repetitions to date, the validity of these cycles may be questionable.

All of this background is not intended to be an economic treatise but to point out that cycles can be evident on a broad scale and that part of your market analysis should include an awareness of the economic climate at the time in which you are trading. For a futures trader, however, the problem in these Kondratieff Wave (named after the Soviet economist who developed an economic theory based on 60-year cycles) size of cycles is that they don't generate many good trading signals. They may be correct, give or take 10 years—hardly useful to the futures trader. The climate is important, but what is today's weather?

Cycle advocates would have you analyze price action for ever smaller cycles until you can define the cycle for the time period you want to trade, similar to Elliott Wave analysis (see Chapter 20). However, while cycles would seem to be a great tool for timing market entry and exit, you cannot rely on cycles alone. An 11-year cycle in cattle or a four-year business cycle may bottom a few weeks or even months before or after the projected ideal date for a bottom and still be within the definition of the cycle. In futures trading a few weeks or months can make a big difference.

As you analyze a price chart for cycles, the key is to discover where price action repeats itself again and again and determine the interval between these similar patterns. The most difficult part of cycle analysis often is just being able to see the cycle. Once you have spotted a cyclical pattern, you can use that as your basic market bias for buying or selling during your "window of opportunity"—it's your timing and direction alert but not your timing signal. Precisely when you trigger the trade should involve other technical indicators.

SPOTTING PRICE CYCLES

By Walter J. Bressert

Walt Bressert of HAL Commodity Cycles wrote a number of articles on cycles for Commodities *magazine in the late 1970s and early 1980s, introducing cyclical analysis techniques to a broad range of individual traders for the first time. Now based in Florida, he continues to publish an advisory service and develop software based on cycles. Although it may seem rather simplistic today, the following material provides a sound basis for anyone interested in cycle analysis. It includes information from articles that appeared in* Commodities *in July 1976 and October 1980. It is reproduced here with permission.*

> Everything in nature moves in cycles . . . the cycles of the seasons . . . night and day . . . the tides that occur with predictable regularity as does the full moon. Each year geese migrate . . . animals hibernate . . . salmon swim upstream to spawn . . . and every three years lemmings run into the ocean.
>
> While these cycles are very visible, many other cycles are not quite so detectable. Often, the reason these cycles are not seen is because the interaction of many large and small cycles makes individual cycles hard to see. However, through the simple process of detrending—eliminating the effects of all cycles larger than the one to be studied—it is possible to isolate each individual cycle.
>
> To detrend price data, a moving average of the same length as the suspected cycle is plotted on a chart with the price data. Instead of plotting the moving average at the current date, it is centered, or plotted in the middle of the time period used to compute the moving average. In Figure 18.1, the last 20 days of prices have been used to compute the moving average, and the moving average computed on day 20 is plotted on day 10. The moving average computed on day 15 (using the previous 15 days) would have been plotted on day 5.

FIGURE 18.1

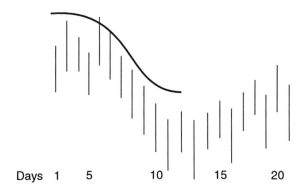

Days 1   5   10   15   20

DETRENDING METHOD

Once the moving average has been computed and centered, there are several methods of detrending. The simplest is to plot the actual distance of prices from the moving average. This has the advantage of requiring no additional mathematical calculations, once the moving average is computed, and the distance of prices from the moving average can be measured with a ruler and plotted around a zero line directly below the price for easy comparison, as shown in Figure 18.2. The distance of prices from the center of the moving average AB is measured and plotted around the straight line AB, eliminating the effects of all larger cycles.

This method is also shown on the larger chart (Figure 18.3). The moving average line looks somewhat like a wavy string; pull it taut and the lows and highs and cycles stand out much more clearly. (Also see Chapter 8 on moving averages, which shows how a moving average center line can be used to draw upper and lower channel lines or bands or an envelope in a similar fashion.)

FIGURE 18.2

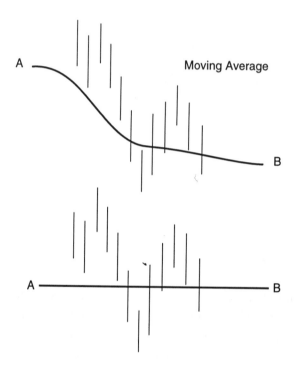

You can also detrend prices by measuring the distance from the moving average as a percentage (divide the prices by the moving average), or you can convert the prices and moving average to logarithms and plot on logarithmic paper. These methods have the advantage of eliminating the wide distortions caused by the large swings common at high prices but have the disadvantage of requiring an extra calculation.

PROJECTING THE ACTION

Knowing that cycles do affect prices is interesting information but not of much use in the markets unless a commodity can be analyzed to give a relatively accurate indication of future price activity. Cycles can be one of the most powerful analytical tools for identifying trends and

FIGURE 18.3

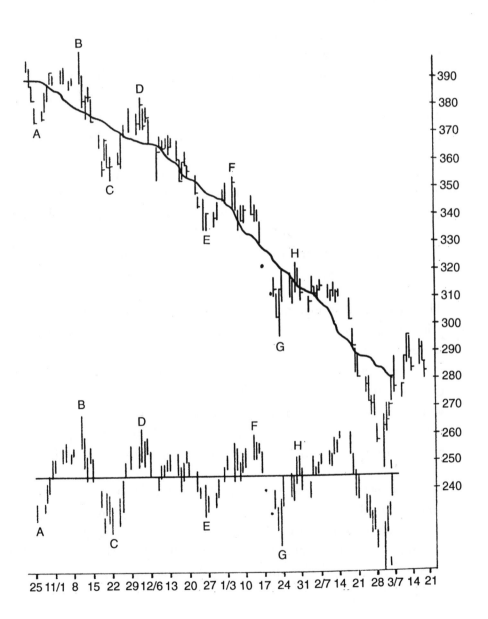

trend reversals. Once a cycle has bottomed, the trend will be up until the cycle tops; once the cycle tops, the trend will be down until the cycle bottoms.

To analyze a particular commodity, it is necessary to isolate the dominant cycles affecting price activity. Once these dominant cycles have been isolated, future price expectations can be established by combining the effects of the dominant cycles. Shorter cycles (weekly and daily) can then be used to determine exactly when long-term cycles have topped and bottomed and when to enter and exit a market.

Cyclic analysis of futures markets assumes that, at any point in time, the then current fundamental information available is relative only to the current price structure and that fundamental events will occur within a cycle to move prices in the direction of the cycle. To apply this concept to longer-term cycles, current fundamental information must be disregarded.

This may sound strange but consider that some of the largest moves in prices have occurred when no fundamental information indicated the "series of events" that forced prices to move so dramatically. This is not to suggest you ignore current fundamental information in your trading or that a knowledge of cycles affecting a commodity alone will enable you to know the price of the commodity two years from now. But it will give a time sequence with which to work and make progressive price projections within, and around, each of the dominant cycles.

These projections actually involve analyzing a series of cycles of various time frames. Every market has long-term and short-term cycles. Long-term cycles of two years or more determine a market's long-term trend. Seasonal or yearly cycles determine the intermediate trend, and a weekly cycle called the "primary cycle" determines the short-term trend.

Trading cycles average 28 days or four weeks for most commodities but can be as short as 21 days in cattle or gold or as long as 44 days in wheat. The average 20-week primary cycle would have approximately five 28-day cycles within it (Figure 18.4).

FIGURE 18.4

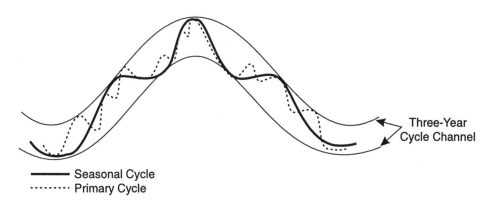

Seasonal Cycle
Primary Cycle

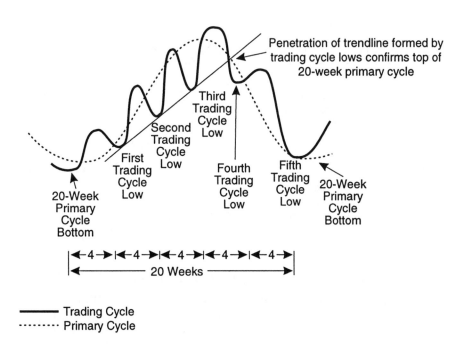

Trading Cycle
Primary Cycle

When the time is right for a cycle to top or bottom, trendlines help to confirm the end of a longer cycle. When a trendline drawn through the lows of two trading cycles is penetrated (Figure 18.4), the next longer cycle, which often is the primary cycle, has topped. Penetration of a trendline across the tops of two previous trading cycles works similarly in determining when a primary cycle has bottomed.

Of course, cycles can stretch or contract or even disappear for a time before emerging again later. In a bullish situation the peaks of the cycle tend to come later than the ideal cycle would suggest as the market continues to advance. Drawn on a chart, the peaks are to the right of the midpoint of the cycle in what is termed "right translation" (see Figure 18.5). In a bearish situation, the peaks tend to come earlier to the left of the midpoint of the cycle—"left translation"—as the decline portion of the cycle is extended.

FIGURE 18.5

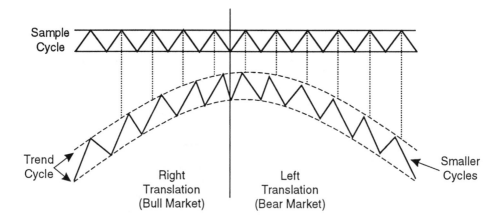

In addition to the 28-day cycle, shorter-term cycles—14-day, 7-day, 3 1/2-day . . . all the way down to a cycle based on minutes—can be used to help determine the day of trend reversal. In reality, of course, cyclical analysis is more complex than this ideal picture. Many other tools, including chart patterns and oscillators, are used to help determine cyclical tops and bottoms, often to within several days.

CHAPTER 19

TYING THE MARKETS TOGETHER

By Glen Ring

The previous chapters in this section indicate that prices often seem to fall into place rather naturally for one reason or another and suggest that this predisposition to remain within a market structure defined by a spread, seasonal pattern or cycle can be forecast well enough to help make trading decisions.

Glen Ring picks up on this theme with new observations about intermarket relationships that connect the various markets together, looking at the big picture and then bringing his focus down to the individual commodities where trades can be made. Glen is the editor of Trends in Futures, *a weekly technical newsletter published by Oster Communications Inc. in Cedar Falls, Iowa, and has closely watched and traded markets for more than 20 years.*

Individual markets may be viewed as pieces of a huge jigsaw puzzle: Each may have a peculiar shape or uncertain marking, yet, when they are all pulled together, the overall picture of the marketplace may be revealed.

While each market is an entity unto itself, each is also a piece of the bigger picture. Thus, at least to some extent, every market is related to the rest of the marketplace. Some may have a greater overall impact than others. But even the seemingly most insignificant, nondescript market pieces hold special positions in the larger puzzle.

Over the years and decades, cash has flowed from one investment arena to another and on to another and back and forth and so on. This chapter focuses on the unique position held by one particular entity in this overall marketplace: The Commodity Research Bureau (CRB) Futures Price Index. Evidence suggests it may well be the leader of the pack.

The CRB Index is a geometric average of 21 commodity futures markets. Component areas include energy, grains and oilseeds, international foods and fiber, meats and metals. Even though it tends to be weighted toward agricultural markets, it may be described as the Dow Jones Industrial Average of the physical commodity complex. However, as you will soon see, key intermarket relationships of the CRB Index are not limited just to physical commodity markets.

Before you read on about significant intermarket relationships, it could prove helpful to shed some light on where or how this information may be useful in the overall analytical or trading program. Trading can be viewed as a multi-step process. One part of the process is identifying opportunities. Discretionary traders generally use some form of analysis, at least in part, to help with this identification stage. Understanding intermarket relationships, and the major role of the CRB Index, may help build a foundation for you to spot specific trading opportunities.

Also, the role of spotting opportunities in discretionary trading can be mechanical, objective or even subjective at times. Because the role of the analyst is to spot opportunities or understand how markets function, a degree of subjectivity is tolerable. This is especially true because analysis is simply a sub-task in the process of finding a potential tradable opportunity.

Most of the relationships discussed in this chapter have been tested objectively. However, a few interesting patterns have yet to be proved or disproved but were deemed worthy to share. As such, these relationships should be viewed as "observations" or "subjective" until proven otherwise, and those items that fall into this category will be noted as such.

Many successful traders trade with the trend. So, being aware of intermarket relationships potentially signaling markets that may be ready to move—as well as the likely direction of price movement—could prove quite useful to them.

Unless otherwise noted, the various relationships between the CRB Index and other markets are made on the monthly degree. This is done to provide information that has a much longer time basis for comparison than a weekly or daily degree. Shorter time frame comparisons between the CRB Index and other markets have shown some interesting relationships, but numerous such weekly or, especially, daily relationships have not stood the test of time.

Because the grain and oilseed complex is one of the largest components of the CRB Index, it is not surprising that the closest intermarket relationship may be between the CRB Index and soybeans. There is a strong tendency for the direction of price movement in the CRB Index to parallel or lead the direction of price movement in the soybean market (see Figure 19.1). While peaks and valleys in the CRB Index may not coincide with absolute highs and lows in the soybean market, it is unusual to see these entities move in opposite directions for more than a month or so at a time.

Notice that the relationship is described as relating to the *direction* of price movement. While major trends tend to develop at virtually the same time in both the CRB Index and the soybean market, the *magnitude* of price movement in the CRB Index does not necessarily relate to magnitude of price movement in soybeans. These characteristics tend

FIGURE 19.1

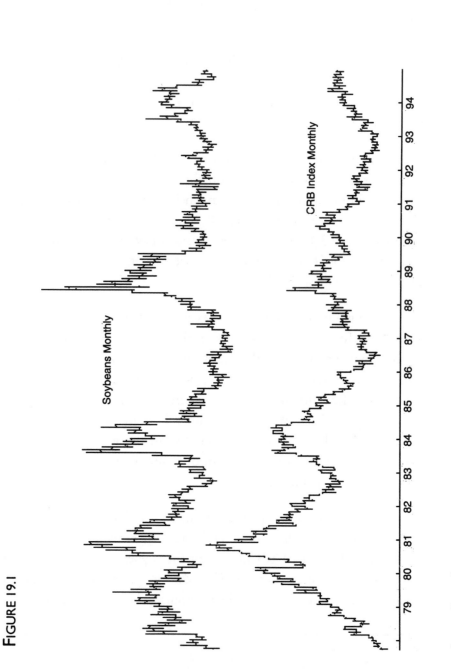

Soybeans Monthly

CRB Index Monthly

79   80   81   82   83   84   85   86   87   88   89   90   91   92   93   94

Source: FutureSource

to hold true throughout most CRB Index-based intermarket relationships—the direction of movement is a much more reliable correlation than the magnitude of movement.

Because soybean meal is a primary product of soybeans, it is logical that the relationship between soybean meal and the CRB Index would be quite strong. Cycle students may find that soybean meal, as well as soybeans, tends to track very closely with key cycles in the CRB Index (see Figure 19.2).

Growing areas and seasons in corn and soybeans overlap extensively. So it is reasonable to expect that there is also a strong correlation between price movement in these markets and the CRB Index. Over the vast majority of time, the direction of the CRB Index and the direction of the corn market tend to correlate quite well. However, there are some notable exceptions when these directions parted company for more than a month at a time (see marked areas on Figure 19.3).

In late 1979 and early 1980, the corn market sagged while the CRB Index continued to generally push higher. The CRB Index posted a major upturn in mid-1986, yet it took the corn market another seven months to find a bottom. And, when the CRB Index drifted lower through most of the 1991-92 period, the corn market waited until March 1992 to roll over and join the slide toward major lows.

The CRB Index and the wheat market also often move in tandem. However, the wheat market tends to be more of a maverick than the corn and soybean markets. The wheat market may track extremely well for years with the direction of the CRB Index. Then wheat may suddenly act as if it has a mind of its own and take off in the opposite direction. The 1991 upturn and sharp advance in wheat marked a strong divergence in the movements of these two market entities (see Figure 19.4).

337

FIGURE 19.2

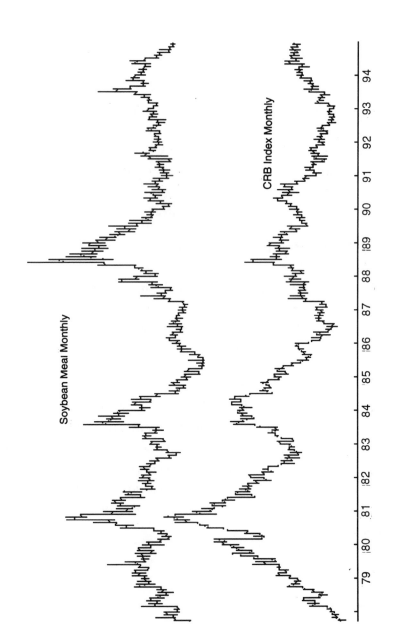

Soybean Meal Monthly

CRB Index Monthly

Source: FutureSource

FIGURE 19.3

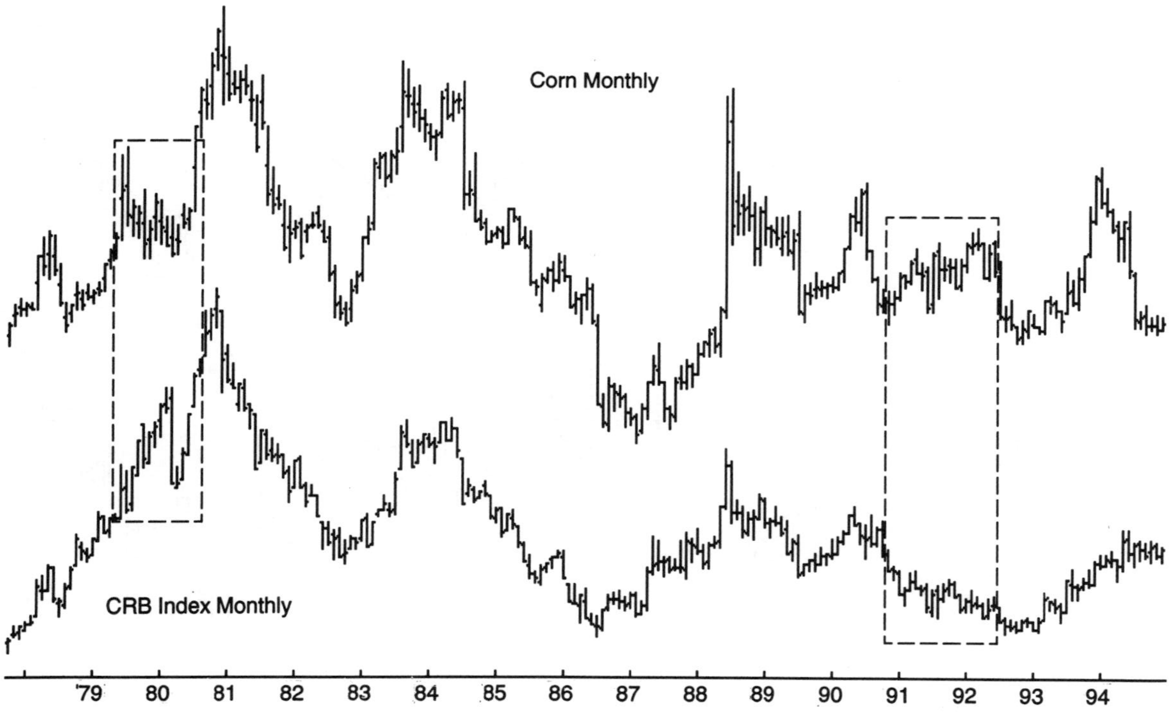

Corn Monthly

CRB Index Monthly

Source: FutureSource

FIGURE 19.4

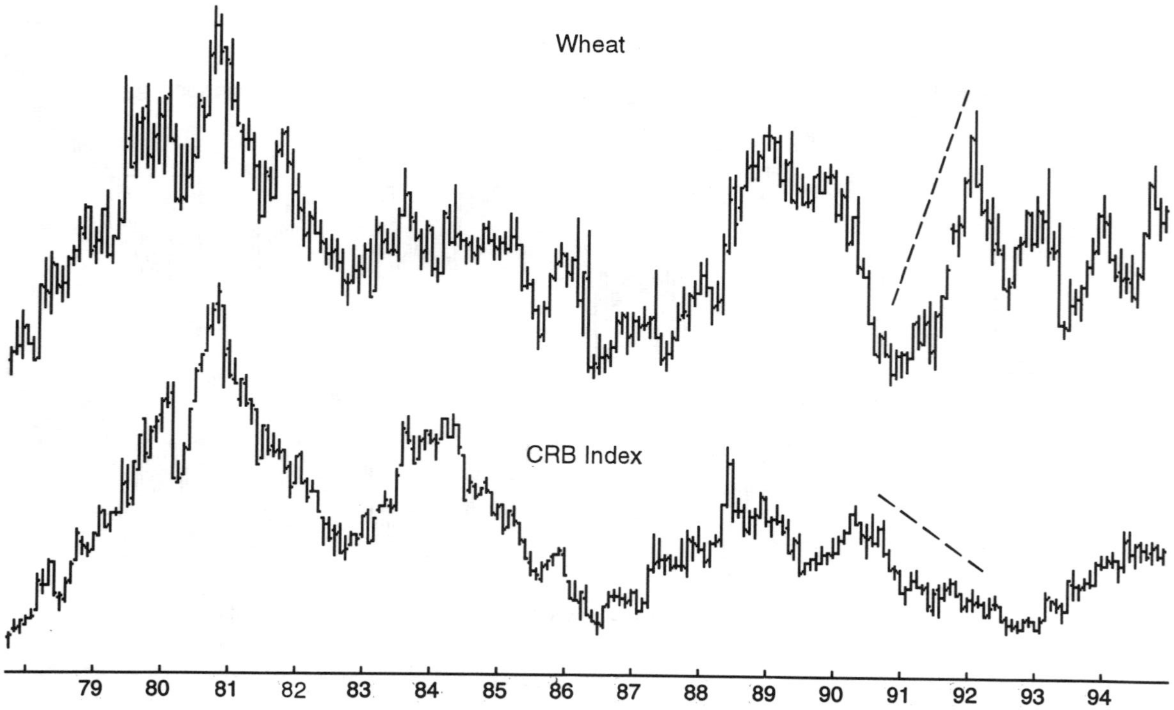

Wheat

CRB Index

Source: FutureSource

Even though the corn and wheat markets occasionally go off on their own, history shows that both eventually renew their rhythmical relationships with the CRB Index. Thus, despite the adverse adventure from time to time, odds rarely favor betting that the corn and wheat markets won't parallel or follow the lead of the CRB Index.

The oat market is no longer used in the calculation of the CRB Index. However, this market tends to track the CRB Index in a manner very similar to what the corn market does.

While the grain and oilseed markets appear to have the strongest correlation to the direction of the CRB Index, three other markets in the agricultural commodity sector have relationships that show a degree of reliability.

The cotton and sugar markets tend to track the CRB Index in much the same manner as the wheat market. As a broad generalization, sugar and cotton follow the multi-year ebb and flow of the CRB Index. However, there have been significant periods when either market breaks away from the lead of the CRB Index to post significant opposing moves. This behavior has been especially true in the cotton market, where divergent moves have occasionally turned out to be quite substantial.

The other agricultural market that often tracks the CRB Index is cocoa. However, in this relationship, cocoa hasn't tended to follow the larger degree trends of the CRB Index. Instead, cocoa often tracks the month-to-month swings of the CRB Index. A positive month in the CRB Index often is paralleled by an up month in cocoa while a down month in the CRB Index tends to result in a negative corresponding performance in the cocoa market.

With one almost baffling exception, the balance of the agricultural markets appear to show little reliable connection to the CRB Index although some members of this complex, such as the cattle market, show a slight negative relationship.

However, the one exception is the hog market. In a sense, it has been observed that the CRB Index appears to follow the lead of the hog market. Major extremes—yearly or multi-year highs and lows—in the hog market seem to precede by approximately 10 to 18 months corresponding extremes in the CRB Index. Subsequent moves tend to follow similar paths. But there appears to be little reliable correlation in the magnitude of subsequent price trends.

BEYOND AGRICULTURE

High inflation of the 1970s left the marketplace highly volatile through the mid-1980s. Not surprisingly, there appeared to be a strong correlation between the movement in the precious metals complex and the CRB Index—at least until the mid-1980s. Prior to the mid-1980s, the precious metals markets generally preceded or paralleled motion in the CRB Index. However, as inflationary pressures fell in the late 1980s and early 1990s, the leadership of the precious metals complex diminished.

Starting in the late 1980s, the precious metals prices fell into a pattern of *either* leading or following the direction of the CRB Index (note letters in Figure 19.5 showing gold and the CRB Index). As more years pass, data will become reliable. However, it appears that the "normal" pattern is for the CRB Index to slightly lead the direction of the precious metals markets.

Part of the problem in determining the monthly degree relationship between the CRB Index and precious metals markets goes back to the place of key precious metals in U.S. history. Simply, prior to the early 1970s, gold prices were fixed by the government, effectively restraining the movement of related metals prices. Thus, there is less reliable data

FIGURE 19.5

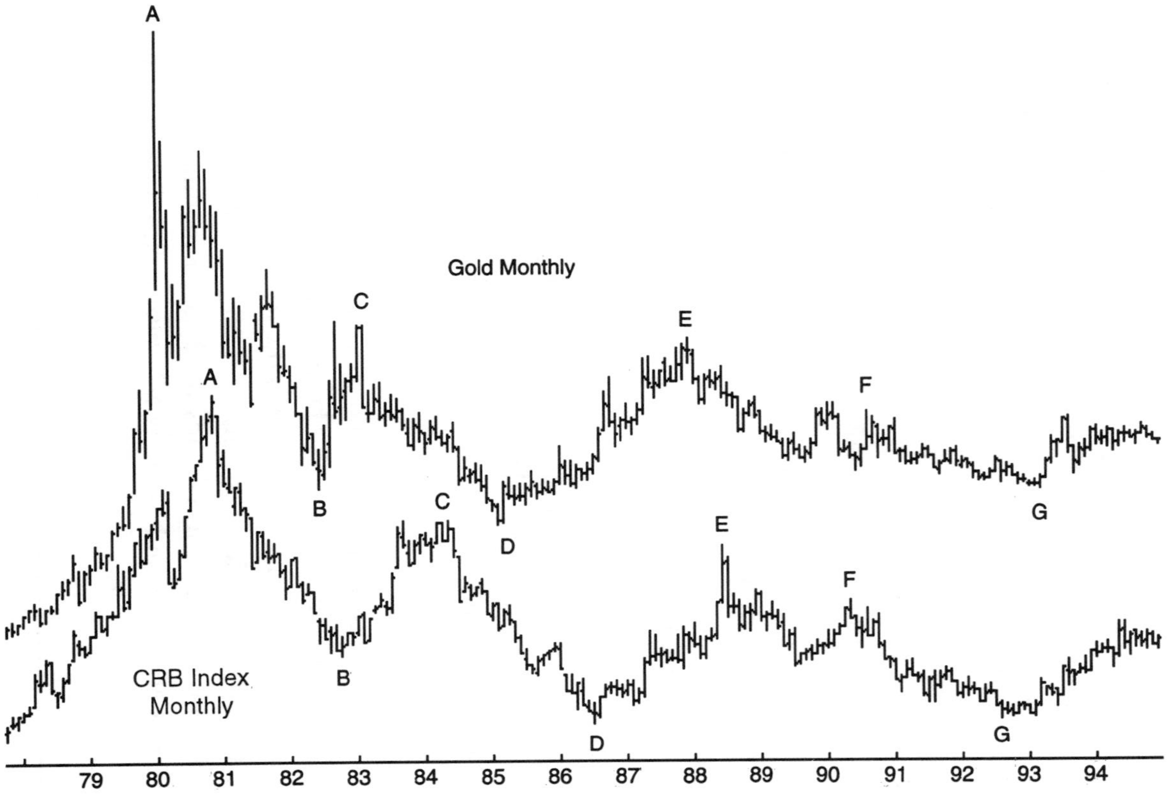

Gold Monthly

CRB Index
Monthly

Source: FutureSource

of free trading to make comparisons between precious metals and the CRB Index.

However, subjective observation strongly suggests that there is a strong relationship between the CRB Index and the precious metals markets. At this point, the likely correspondence will be for the CRB Index to parallel or slightly lead the direction of gold and silver.

This brings up a side story. During the 1970s and early 1980s you would often hear that "as silver goes, so go soybeans." The study of the relationships of the CRB Index and the soybean market and the CRB Index and silver shows that there is correlated movement. Thus, it is reasonable to assume that there is a basis for the old silver/soybean axiom.

CRB INDEX VERSUS OTHER MARKETS

The rest of the physical commodity markets show little in the way of reliable monthly degree relationships with the CRB Index. This, however, doesn't mean the end of intermarket relationships involving the CRB Index. Actually, there are some striking relationships between the CRB Index and other key markets.

One of the more striking of all monthly degree intermarket relationships involving the CRB Index is the one which is shared with the Treasury bond market. In this instance, however, the relationship is inverse in nature.

Major peaks in the CRB Index tend to precede major bottoms in the T-bond market while major bottoms in the CRB Index tend to forecast major tops in Treasury bonds (note lettered areas on Figure 19.6). Historically, the major turns in the CRB Index have preceded corresponding inverse turns in T-bonds by 2 to 10 months. On a rare occasion, the CRB Index and T-bonds will reverse directions at virtually the same

FIGURE 19.6

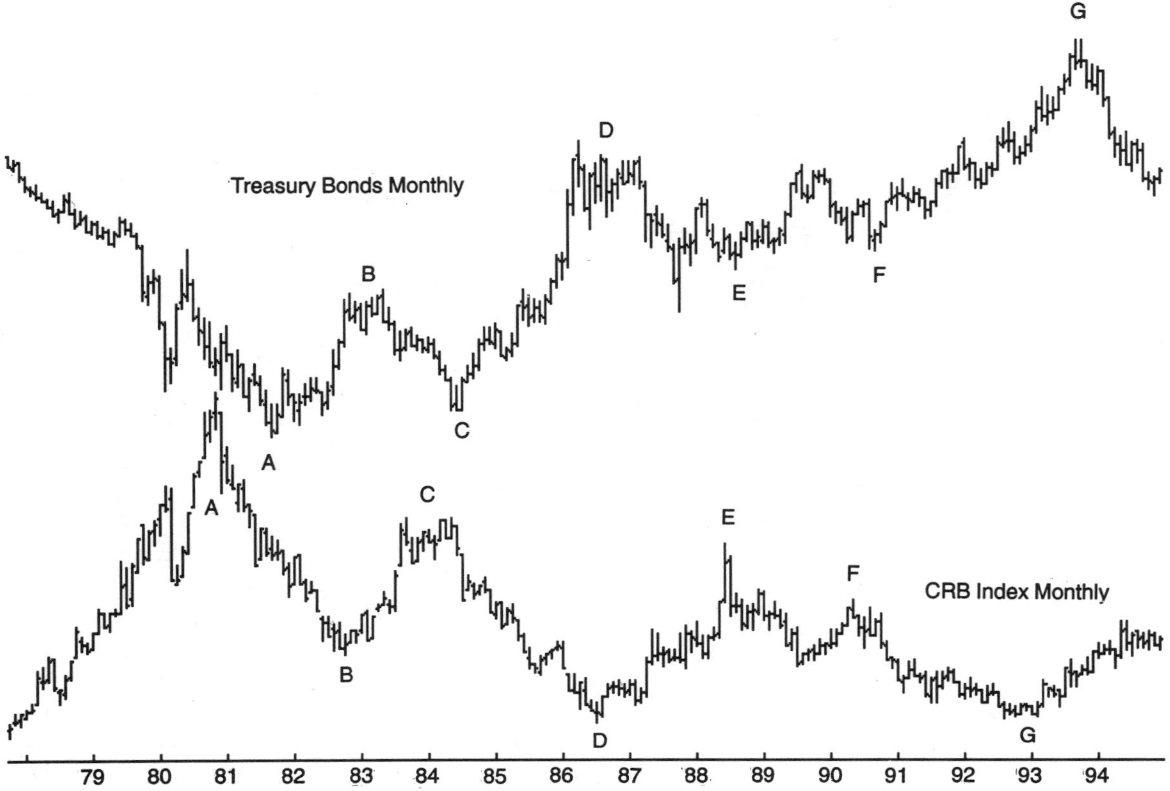

Treasury Bonds Monthly

CRB Index Monthly

Source: FutureSource

time. However, most turns in the CRB Index forecast subsequent reversals in the bond market by about 8 to 10 months.

As impressive as the correlation between the turns is, it is the moves that follow the turns that make the relationship between the CRB Index and T-bond markets striking. In this observed relationship, the magnitude of the move in the CRB Index typically impacts the magnitude of the move in T-bonds. Thus, a big upswing in the CRB Index tends to trigger a large slide in T-bonds and vice versa.

This brings up another question: What about the CRB Index and the stock market? Many believe the stock market ultimately follows the lead of the bond market. However, with the bond market having such a strong inverse relationship with the CRB Index, it is possible that the CRB Index actually is the ultimate leader.

It is clear that the major rise in the stock market that began in the early 1980s and carried into the early 1990s saw a corresponding deterioration in commodity markets. And there is some correlation between major turns in the CRB Index and the Dow Jones Industrial Average. Thus, it is safe to conclude that there is an inverse relationship between the CRB Index and the stock market (note long-term trends on Figure 19.7). However, there is indeed a stronger correlation between the stock market and monthly swings in T-bonds than the swings in the CRB Index.

A review of history, however, shows movements in the physical commodity complex (CRB Index) and stock market haven't always been on opposite sides of the arena. Prior to the industrial revolution, the U.S. economy was tied largely to raw commodities, especially agriculture and mining. Thus, when commodity markets rose, many businesses also fared well.

Following the industrial revolution, a smaller percentage of companies were involved in production and distribution of raw commodities. In-

FIGURE 19.7

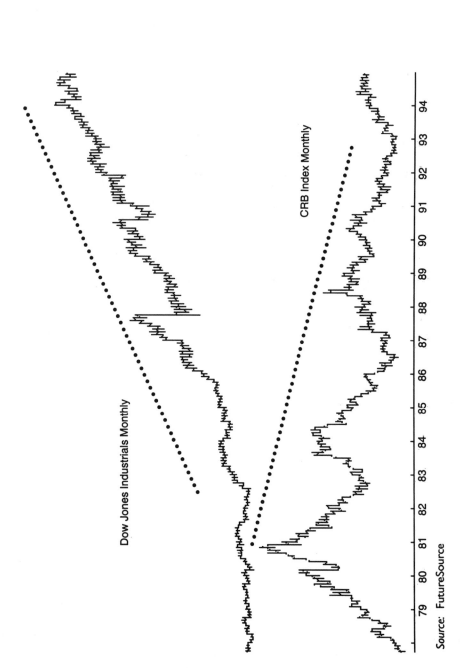

Dow Jones Industrials Monthly

CRB Index Monthly

Source: FutureSource

stead, advances in technology and refinement became more dominant. So, instead of an upswing in commodity markets adding to the bottom line of most companies, a rise in commodity prices generated a significant increase in expenses of commodity-consuming companies. In modern times, swings in commodity prices tend to have an inverse impact on the bottom line of most companies—and a corresponding negative impact on stock prices.

Other markets have had significant long-term relationships with the CRB Index. However, these are not included in this discussion primarily because they did not hold true in recent years or diverged from the dominant pattern for years at a time.

Whether you are a trader, an analyst or economist, it is unlikely that you truly come to the marketplace without a bias. Understanding the relationships between the CRB Index and many key markets should prove useful in building a foundation for that bias. Extensive monthly degree analysis of the CRB Index may provide a solid head start in researching the outlook for many other markets!

CHAPTER 20

COUNTING THE WAVES

Most analysts have little problem seeing the structure of the market-place based on the relationships some markets have with each other and the tendency some have to move in a seasonal and perhaps even cyclical pattern. But there is little agreement about the value of several other methods for looking at the big picture of market structure. You can't be involved in technical analysis of markets very long before you will run into one or all of these concepts:

❑ **Elliott Wave**—markets move in waves within waves—five "impulse" and three "corrective"—reflecting changes in the mass emotion of people.

❑ **Fibonacci numbers and ratios**—a number sequence that can be used for time and/or price targets.

❑ **Gann**—incorporates what some view as "mystical" elements and mathematical tecnhiques to arrive at specific time and price objectives.

Some of the concepts in these approaches are rather esoteric and sub-ject to wide interpretation. Traders tend to be either devoted followers, casual observers ("Hmm, that's interesting") or debunkers whose reac-tions range from "Why bother?" at best to "crackpot ideas" at worst—there isn't a lot of middle ground.

One thing that is consistent is that more analysts in these areas than in any other field of technical analysis contend they know the subject and use it properly while claiming other analysts don't understand the techniques or simply misuse or misrepresent them. We hope we have made some "correct" choices in what we present here, but someone is bound to conclude this isn't Gann or Elliott or Fibonacci as they know it.

Nevertheless, when you consider some projections that have been made by masters using these approaches (see below), they do get your attention. They should definitely be part of your technical analysis survey even it you decide they aren't your style.

We will cover Elliott Wave and Fibonacci together in this chapter because they often are so intertwined in analysis that you need to have the background for both when you are working with either of them. We'll provide the basics first, then several illustrations of how these concepts have been and are being used in the marketplace.

The danger, as with any example, of course, is that the illustrations presented may be only the ideal ones that worked and not those that didn't. Sometimes, it seems, analysts go back and "adjust" their counts or numbers to fit what actually happened and then proclaim how obvious it was to see how their approach worked so accurately on a chart. Our examples are shown as they appeared, well before the fact.

Another danger is that, like our comment on cycles, these tools for timing may not be very good timing tools. It is one thing to be "correct" about a projection but quite another to trade it if it comes three weeks, three months or three years earlier or later than projected.

However, I think you'll find the following information interesting and useful, not so much for the forecasts that were made but mostly for the application of theory to real market situations. Without examples, it would be almost impossible to comprehend these complicated concepts.

ELLIOTT WAVE

Ralph Nelson Elliott was an accountant and business consultant whose study of the stock market in the 1920s convinced him that everything in the universe, including markets, is ruled by natural law and that "all human activities follow a law that causes them to repeat themselves in similar and constantly recurring serials of waves or impulses of definite number and pattern" (quote from *The Wave Principle* written by Elliott and Charles Collins, an associate who edited a market letter, in 1938).

Developing his idea for markets, Elliott saw price action unfolding in a pattern of five "impulse" waves—three in the direction of the trend and two reactions against the main trend—and three "corrective" waves. Each wave subdivides into a similar pattern of five and three waves, each of those waves divides into five and three . . . (see Figure 20.1). Elliott described nine types of waves, ranging from the grand supercycle covering several centuries to the sub-minuette.

These waves aren't random but occur cyclically and predictably for a very good reason: People are people. Elliott concluded that, as part of natural law, human emotions and activities ebb and flow in a regular pattern. As the mood swings, collective behavior of the crowd will be much the same as it has been in the past.

Market behavior is just one facet of the universe affected by the prevailing social attitude (so are war, social upheaval, creativity, even musical tastes). In an effort to develop more reliable forecasting techniques, Elliott (and many others since) studied how the cyclical rhythm of peoples' actions affect markets, leading to the wave principle, an elaborate network of cycles into which all market action falls.

Several problems with Elliott's theory undoubtedly contribute to notions that other analysts don't know what they are talking about. First, there are no objective measurements for waves—there are rules about what waves can and can't do (Wave 4 should not drop below the top of

FIGURE 20.1   BASIC ELLIOTT WAVE PATTERN

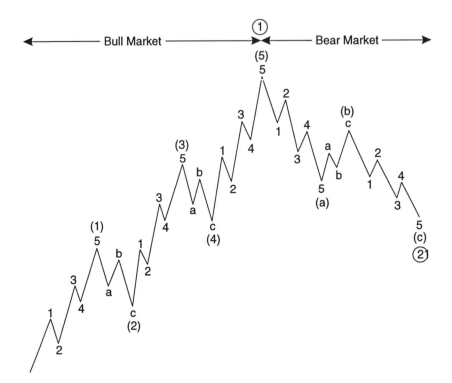

Wave 1, for example), but nothing that clearly defines what a wave is and the degree of the wave. It's almost an either-you-see-it-or-you-don't type of situation. Obviously, that leaves a lot of latitude for interpretation and room for argument.

Second, as with any chart pattern or market theory, wave "extensions," "irregular tops" or other permutations can mess up the way the pattern is supposed to look and create uncertainty. You may need a "You are here" guide if you get too baffled. Or you may think you have it all figured out, only to see prices do the "unexpected" and force you to "adjust" your wave count. It takes a lot of work to become comfortable with these concepts.

FIBONACCI

As mentioned, the waves in Elliott Wave theory seem to show up in a regular, consistent pattern. Working with Collins, Elliott began to connect his wave theory with a numerical sequence discovered by Leonardo de Pisa, also known as Fibonacci, centuries earlier.

Beginning with 1 and stretching to infinity, each number in Fibonacci's mathematical series is the sum of the two previous numbers:

1 + 1 = 2
1 + 2 = 3
2 + 3 = 5
3 + 5 = 8
5 + 8 = 13

And so on, making "Fibonacci numbers" of 1, 2, 3, 5, 8, 13, 21, 34, 55, 89, 144, 233, . . . Notice the numbers on the basic Elliott Wave pattern diagram. "Five" impulse waves and "three" corrective waves are both Fibonacci numbers as is their sum, "eight." If you go from the bottom to the top through the five main waves up, the number of waves is 21; add the waves in the corrective wave and you get 34 waves total. Within a major wave are 89 minor waves altogether. Naturally, all are Fibonacci numbers. As you'll see below, Fibonacci pops up everywhere in Elliott Wave analysis.

More important than the numbers themselves, in many cases, is the ratio between successive numbers. Once you get beyond the first few numbers, when you divide the lower number by the next higher number, the ratio works out to 0.618. Or if you divide a Fibonacci number by the preceding number, the ratio is 1.618. (Incidentally, if you started your number series with another number—3, for example, making Fibonacci-like numbers out of 6, 9, 15, 24, 39, 63, etc.—the ratios are still 0.618 and 1.618).

Those numbers are significant in calculating how far prices might go or in timing (there is some disagreement whether Fibonacci is more useful for price or for time). The ratios are often used to calculate potential price objectives or retracement levels, and their use extends well beyond Elliott Wave analysis.

If prices advance 100 points from a bottom to a top and then start to drop back, one place that serves as a target on a reaction would be 38 points below the top (a Fibonacci 0.382 of the upmove); if prices fall below that level, another target would be a decline of 62 points (0.618 of the upmove). Those aren't the only targets analysts see but may be significant ones, especially if they coincide with key chart points or targets identified by other analysis. Or the next move up might be 162 points (1.618 × 100) or some other Fibonacci ratio of the previous move.

Related to timing and cycles, you should not be surprised to see moves take 34 days or 21 weeks or some other Fibonacci number, or you'll find that a bull or bear move lasts a Fibonacci 0.618 or 1.618 times as long as the previous bull or bear move.

If you do your Elliott Wave analysis thoroughly, it can be a complicated and sometimes confusing process. But you may want to track at least the major waves. All you have to remember is that Elliott said prices follow pattern, time and ratio and that you can predict each of these functions with the help of Fibonacci.

ELLIOTT WAVE AND THE DOW

By Robert R. Prechter Jr.

The foremost master of the Elliott Wave Principle in our generation may be Robert Prechter, president of Elliott Wave International in Gainesville, Ga. As publisher of the Elliott Wave Theorist, *co-author with A.J. Frost of* Elliott Wave Principle—Key to Stock Market Profits *and editor of Elliott's collected works, Prechter has probably studied and written more about Elliott and his theory than anyone else in the world. As the definitive source on Elliott Wave, he ran into many skeptics initially but then achieved virtual guru status himself in the 1980s with his uncannily correct projections (that term seems better than "predictions") for the stock, precious metals and interest markets, and his expectations for a disinflationary era.*

The following information is taken from articles that appeared in Commodities *and* Futures *magazines. It is not presented as a testimonial to show how great Elliott Wave and Prechter are but as an example of how complex Elliott ideas can be interpreted and applied to a market to make projections that might be useful to the trader/investor.*

END OF THE COMMODITY BULL RUN

From Commodities, *April 1981, when the CRB Index was hovering in the 300 area. The CRB Index sank to 200 in 1986 and again in 1992-93. Material is reproduced here with permission.*

Evidence is abundant that the gigantic rise in commodity prices that began in 1968 has ended, based on Elliott Wave perspective.

Under Elliott rules, any true bull market advance should take the form of five waves up and should channel between parallel lines so that waves 2 and 4 touch the lower boundary and waves 3 and 5 touch the upper boundary. Just as important, each subwave in the advance must also divide into five waves having the same characteristics.

In examining the long-term, intermediate-term and short-term charts of the Commodity Research Bureau (CRB) Futures Price Index, I conclude that, though an extension of the fifth wave cannot be ruled out, a perfect Elliott Wave bull market has taken place in the commodity markets.

The breakdown of waves is quite clear (see Figure 20.2), and the price channel is perfectly parallel. Each upward impulse wave subdivides into five waves, as per Elliott rules. The third wave is the largest percentage rise and is the most dynamic wave, as dictated by Elliott guidelines.

Fibonacci numbers and ratios are also present to a significant degree:

❑ Wave V is almost exactly as long as the distance from the beginning of the bull market to the peak of Wave III, a normal Elliott relationship.

❑ The points gained total 246, almost exactly 2.618 times the index's starting level at 92. This 246 also is just 13 points above 233, a Fibonacci number.

❑ The distance from the beginning of the bull market to the peak of Wave III and the length of Wave V are each approximately 0.618 as long as the entire bull market and 1.618 times as long as the distance from the peak of Wave IV to the peak of Wave V.

❑ The starting point at 92 is the measuring distance for the rest of the structure. So, within a small percentage error, the peak of Wave IV to the peak of Wave V equals 92. The beginning of the bull market to the peak of Wave III equals 92 times 1.618. The length of wave IV equals 92 times 0.618. The length of wave V equals 1.618, and the entire rise equals 92 times 2.618.

FIGURE 20.2   LONG-TERM WAVE: A CLEAR BREAKDOWN

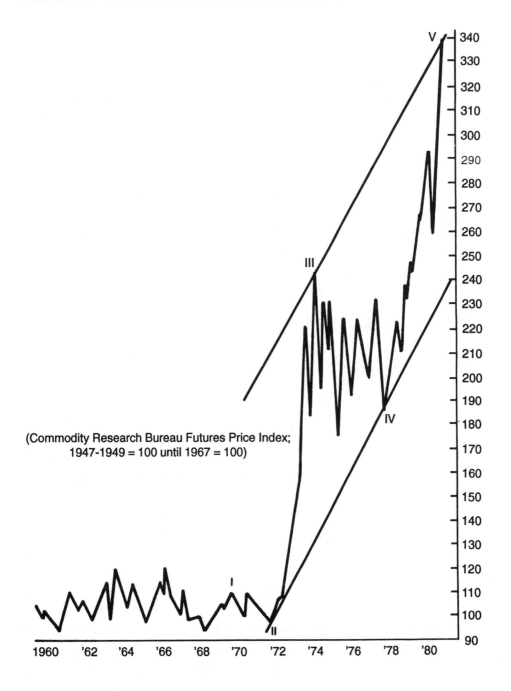

(Commodity Research Bureau Futures Price Index;
1947-1949 = 100 until 1967 = 100)

❑   The entire rise lasts just under 13 (Fibonacci) years or just more than (Fibonacci) 144 months.

In summary, current evidence supports the supposition that a new era of deflation has begun. This conclusion fits the expectations of deflation supported by the current position of the Kondratieff Wave, which still is in the middle stages of the "plateau period." Deflation sets in during this period, fostering a euphoric stage similar to the euphoria during the initial stages of inflation. That euphoria, of course, ultimately gives way to deflationary collapse.

I always have found it a fascinating exercise to take a look at the "big picture" at critical junctures in the wave count. An Elliott analysis at this time should help give the long-term investor an overall sense of perspective and the day-trader an excellent view of the forest while he's dodging the falling trees.

THE LAST WILD RIDE IN STOCKS?

From Futures, *September 1983, one year after the bull market projected by Elliott Wave analysis had begun. The Dow Jones Industrial Average was between 1,200 and 1,300 at the time, and it was quite a stretch to imagine the DJIA at 2,000, much less 3,000 or 3,700. Material is reproduced with permission.*

When A.J. Frost and I wrote *Elliott Wave Principle* in 1978, the prevailing attitude was that the Kondratieff Wave cycle was rolling over and would create the "Awful '80s."

Books like *How to Survive the Coming Depression* and *The Crash of '79* were on the bestseller list. Gold and inflation were skyrocketing. Jimmy Carter was battling the memory of Herbert Hoover for a place in history as the country's worst president.

In writing a book about how to apply Elliott Wave, it was virtually impossible to avoid making a forecast: A wave interpretation of the past almost always implies something about the future. At that time, the evidence was overwhelming that the stock market was at the dawn of a tremendous bull market.

Even at that stage, the Wave Principle revealed some details about what the bull market might look like: a classic five-wave form in the price pattern, a 400 percent increase in the Dow Jones Industrial Average in a short span of five to eight years and a Dow target close to 3,000.

While that figure was met with some derision at the time and a good deal of skepticism even today, Elliott Wave-based forecasts (even competent ones) can often appear extreme. The reason is that the Wave Principle is one of the tools that can help an analyst anticipate changes in trends, including trends that are so long-term that they have become accepted as the normal state of affairs.

By the time this bull market is ending, no doubt our call for a huge crash and depression will be laughed off the Street. In fact, that's exactly what to expect if there is to be any chance we're right.

If our ongoing analyst is correct, the current environment is providing a once-in-a-generation money-making opportunity. This opportunity takes on greater importance, however, because it may well precede not merely a Kondratieff Wave downswing but the biggest financial catastrophe since the founding of the Republic.

In other words, we had better make our fortunes now just in case "Elliott" is right about the aftermath. But, for this article, let's forget the crash part of the forecast and concentrate on the bull move, which could take the Dow to our recently refined target of 3,600-3,700 in 1987.

Unlike commodities, the stock market usually "announces" the beginning of a huge bull market. It does so by creating a tremendously overbought condition in the momentum indicators in the initial stage of the advance. While this tendency is noticeable at all degrees of a trend, the "annual rate of change" for the Standard & Poor's (S&P) 500 Index is particularly useful in judging the strength of "kickoff" momentum in large waves of Cycle and Supercycle degree.

This indicator is created by plotting the percentage difference between the average daily close for the S&P 500 in the current month and its reading for the same month a year earlier. The peak momentum reading is typically registered about one year after the start of the move, due to the construction of the indicator.

What's important is the level the indicator reaches. As Figure 20.3 shows, the estimated level of "overbought" at the end of July 1983, approximately one year after the start of the current bull market, is the highest since May 1943, about one year after the start of Cycle Wave III.

The fact that they each hit the 50 percent level is a strong confirmation that they mark the beginning of waves of equivalent degree. In other words, August 1982 marked the start of something more than the normal two-year bull market followed by a two-year bear.

On the other hand, it has not indicated the start of a glorious "new era" either. If a wave of Supercycle degree were beginning, we would expect to see the kind of overbought reading generated in 1933, when the indicator hit 124 percent one year after the start of wave (V) from 1932. There is no chance such a level can even be approached now. Thus, the highest overbought condition in 40 years signals that our Elliott Wave forecast for the launching of wave V is right on target.

Elliott Wave Principle made the following observation: "One of our objections to the 'killer wave' occurring now or in 1979, as most cycle theorists suggest, is that the psychological state of the average investor does not seem poised for a shock of disappointment. Most important stock market collapses have come out of optimistic, high-valuation periods. Such conditions definitely do not prevail at this time, as eight

FIGURE 20.3   MOMENTUM SIGNALS CONFIRM WAVE STRUCTURE

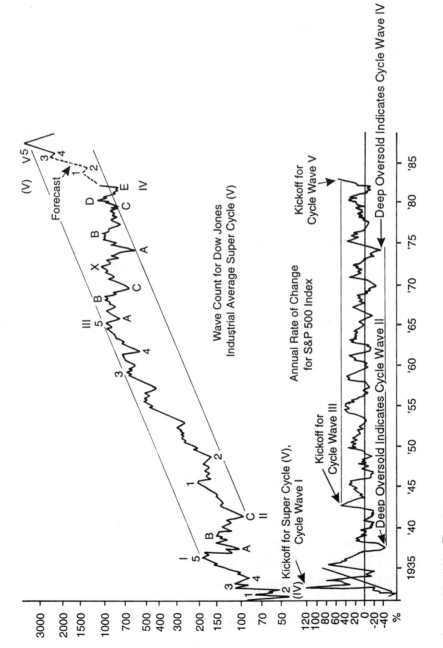

Source: *Elliott Wave Theorist*

years of a raging bull market have taught today's investor to be cautious, conservative and cynical. Defensiveness is not in evidence at tops."

So gauging investor psychology has been useful in the past. What about now? Why weren't the advisors who claimed that "everyone is too bullish" right in calling for a "major correction" last December? Or in January, March or May?

Again, it's a question of wave degree. Based on a conclusion that wave V had begun, I said in October 1982 that "sentiment indicators will get to absurd levels relative to the 1970s . . . traders should ignore them." That assessment has been proven by now, with the Dow over 300 points higher than when sentiment figures first gave sell signals based on old parameters.

All of the elements of the wave structure coming off the August 1982 bottom have been strikingly clear in contrast to the corrective wave ramble which preceded it. This strongly supports the case that a bull market is in progress.

With momentum, sentiment and wave characteristics all supporting our original forecast, is the environment on Wall Street conducive to a speculative mania? In 1978, an Elliott analyst had no way of knowing just what the mechanisms for wild speculation would be. "Where's the 10 percent margin that made the 1920s possible?" was a common rebuttal.

To be honest, we didn't know. But now look! The entire structure is being built as if it were planned. Options on hundreds of stocks allow speculators to deal in thousands of shares of stock for a fraction of their value. Futures on stock indexes (launched in 1982), which promise to deliver nothing, have been created entirely as speculative vehicles with huge leverage. Options on futures carry the possibilities one step further. And it's not stopping there.

Major financial newspapers are calling for the end of any margin requirements on stocks. S&Ls are leaping into the stock brokerage business, sending flyers to little old ladies. And New York banks are already constructing kiosks for quote machines so depositors can stop off at lunch and punch out their favorite stocks.

The financial arena is becoming the place to be. Remember, this is just the setup phase. The average guy probably won't be joining the party until the Dow clears 2,000. The market's atmosphere by then undoubtedly will become out-and-out euphoric. Then you can start watching the public's activity as if it were one huge sentiment indicator. At the peak of the fifth wave, the spectacle could rival Tulipmania and the South Sea Bubble.

Part of the character of a fifth wave of any degree is the occurrence of psychological denial on a mass scale. In other words, the fundamental problems are obvious and threatening to anyone who coldly analyzes the situation, but the average person chooses to explain them away, ignore them or even deny their existence.

This fifth wave should be no exception and will be built more on unfounded hopes than on soundly improving fundamentals such as the United States experienced in the 1950s and early 1960s. Because this fifth wave is known as a fifth within a larger fifth wave going back to 1789, the phenomenon should be magnified by the time the peak is reached.

Don't lose your perspective when the time comes. It will take great courage to make money during this bull market because, in the early stages, it will be easy to be too cautious. However, it will take even greater courage to get out near the top, because that's when the world will call you a fool for selling.

Despite the stock market's potential, the trip to the peak will not be a non-stop, one-way affair. No market ever is. The combination of intermediate- and long-term trend cycles is due to cause another run to new highs in early 1984. From then on, the market is likely to turn choppy and frustrating as Primary wave (2), a one-year sideways-to-down correction, begins.

Investor psychology, as is typical of second waves, may return nearly to the bearish extremes of the previous bottom. The pleasant surprise is that 1985, rather than being a "bear" as dictated by the widely recognized four-year cycle, should be a year for dramatic new highs in the averages as Primary wave (3) unfolds.

ELLIOTT IN THE 1990s

You can look at Figure 20.4 to see how Bob Prechter's early 1980s projections actually fared in the 1980s. After the October 1987 crash eroded confidence in Elliott Wave for a while, the stock market resumed its uptrend and reached Prechter's 3,700 target and beyond in 1993, a few years after his 1987 projection.

While this is a book on technical analysis and Prechter's articles are included mostly to show you how Elliott Wave and Fibonacci technical analysis can be applied to real market conditions, we don't want to leave you hanging in the 1980s. If you're a trader or stock market investor, you may be wondering, "Is this the time to be the fool and sell?" Here are a couple of paragraphs on the last half of the 1990s from Prechter's updated Elliott Wave analysis in the January 1995 issue of Futures (reproduced with permission):

Another financial sea change is taking place, one as important as that of 1980-81. Price patterns indicate the primary event will be a decline of historic proportion in stock and bond prices, which in turn will cause a depression. If an across-the-board deflation occurs, which is highly probable, then real estate and commodities will fall as well. A large downturn in the stock market average will be the big event that signals the major downturn in the economy . . .

FIGURE 20.4 DOW JONES INDUSTRIAL AVERAGE

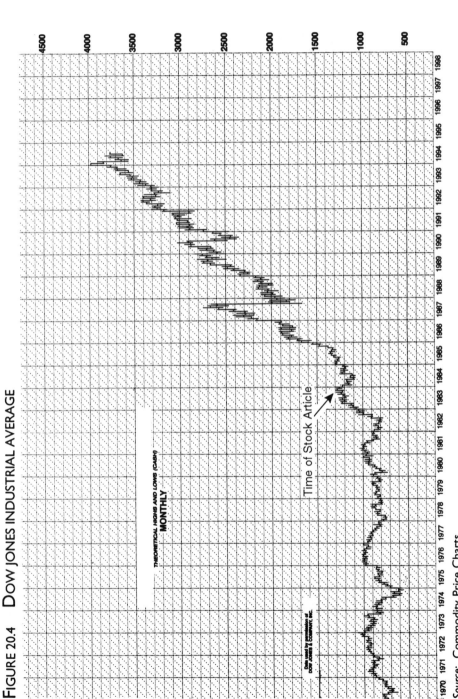

Source: Commodity Price Charts

(Cycle wave measurements in Supercycle wave (V) starting in 1933 show an almost ideal relationship for a Dow peak in the vicinity of 4,000.) And 1995 is a Fibonacci number of years from the most important market bottoms of the past two decades: 21 years from 1974, 13 years from 1982, 8 years from 1987 and 5 years from 1990, indicating the stock market cannot hold up beyond 1995 . . .

The magnitude of the financial calamity that will accompany the bear market in stocks, bonds and the economy will dwarf any difficulty this country has experienced. . . Your proper focus should be to preserve your assets in what will be the most challenging investment environment in our country's history.

THE NIKKEI TOP

By Rick Lorusso

Rick Lorusso, a technical analyst for Shearson Lehman Hutton Inc. in New York, illustrates the Fibonacci connection to time more extensively in this article on the Nikkei 225 Stock Average. The following is from an article that appeared in the June 1989 issue of Futures *when the Nikkei was around 34,000. It peaked above 39,000 eight months later. Note on the monthly chart what happened after that.*

Elliott Wave analysis, coupled with Fibonacci time measurements, suggests a high probability that Japan's Nikkei Stock Average will top sometime during the middle of 1989.

The monthly continuation chart of the Nikkei Stock Average began a rapid acceleration in 1983, coincident with the Japanese yen bottoming against the U.S. dollar. Using Elliott Wave analysis and Fibonacci numerical progression, it is possible to arrive at some new ideas about where this index is traveling and, even more important, when it will get there.

Time is more important than price. Only after time has run out can the main trend change. Some interesting conclusions on time and its relationship to the Nikkei Average can be drawn but only after a brief Elliott Wave analysis and interpretation.

Going into April 1989, the monthly chart shows four major or primary degree waves have been completed (circled numbers on Figure 20.5). Primary 5 began in late 1982 and is still in progress. It is divided into waves of lesser degrees. The focus at this point should be on the price movement from the late 1982 low to determine when and where the fifth wave will occur.

FIGURE 20.5 NIKKEI STOCK AVERAGE

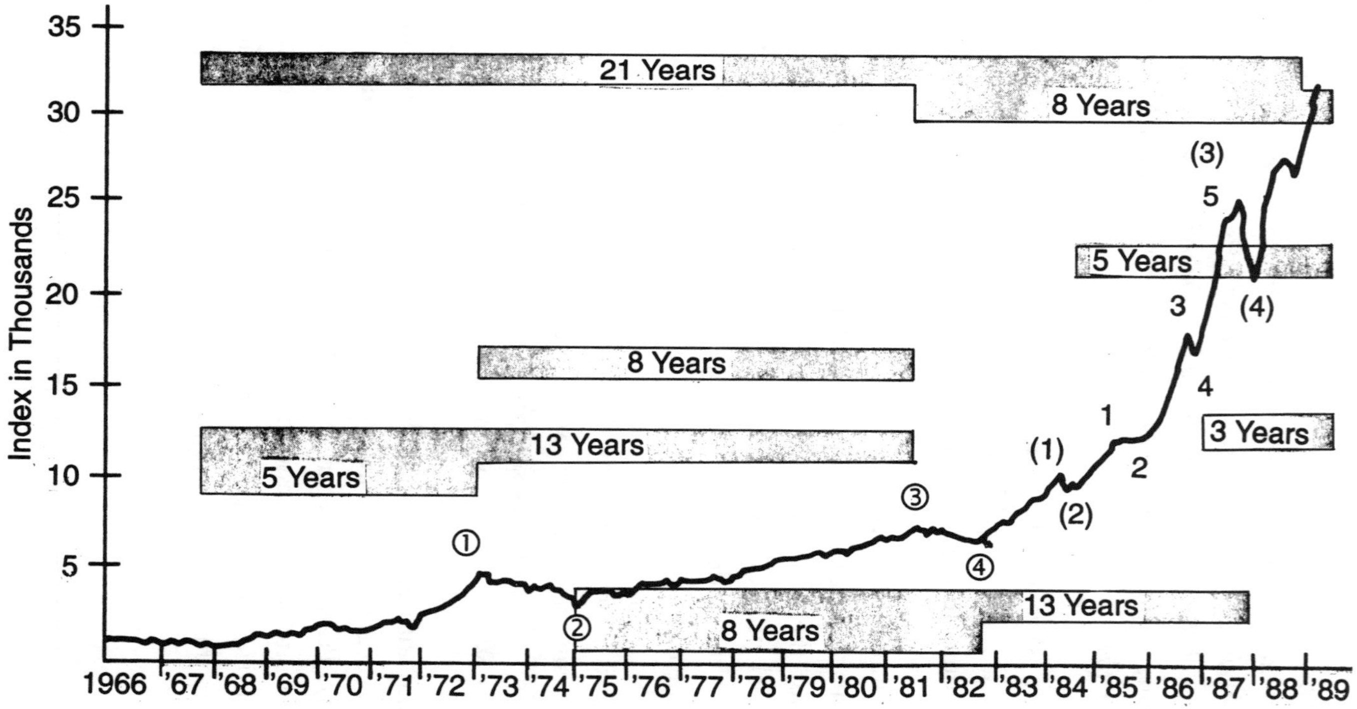

Source: Shearson Lehman Hutton, Inc.

Two possible counts can be made from 1982. Both counts are identical up to the first price peak in 1987. The chart shows the preferred count.

Intermediate wave 3 (in parentheses on chart) of Primary 5 is an extended wave, which presents some strong implications for what wave (5) of Primary wave 5 ultimately will be in size. When the third wave of a five-wave progression is extended, Wave 5 normally approximates Wave 1 in both magnitude and time, or it will relate to Wave 1 by a Fibonacci ratio.

A common relationship that produces a price target not far from current levels occurs if Wave (5) would wind up being 1.618 times Wave (1). Allowing for some approximation due to the lack of precision in this monthly chart, Wave (5) equals 1.618 times Wave (1) at 33,800 (monthly closing basis). The index closed in April at 33,713.35, topping 34,100 in early May 1989.

In major long-term moves, the internal wave relationships may be more a function of the percentage gained rather than a function of absolute points gained. For example, Wave (1) of Primary 5 (from 1982 to 1984) gained approximately 169 percent. If Wave (5) of Primary 5 equals Wave (1) of Primary 5 in percentage gain—the most common relationship when Wave (3) is extended—then Wave (5) of Primary 5 will peak at a monthly closing basis of about 36,445.

A most interesting web of Fibonacci time relationships exists between the waves on the preferred count. Starting at the beginning of this chart (approximately the third quarter of 1967), Primary Wave 1 tops five years later, a Fibonacci number. Primary 3 tops 13 years later, another Fibonacci number.

From the bottom of Primary 2 in late 1974, Primary Wave 4 bottomed eight years later. From the top of Primary Wave 1 to the top of Primary 3 is eight years, also a Fibonacci number. The bottom of Wave

(4) of Primary 4 in late 1987 occurred 13 years from the bottom of Primary 2, yet another Fibonacci number.

These are historical relationships that attest to the reasonableness of the wave counting exercise. But what about the future? The following observations certainly must bear some importance:

1. The middle of 1989 will be eight years from the top of Primary Wave 3.

2. The middle of 1989 will be five years from the bottom of Wave (2) of Primary 5.

3. The middle of 1989 will be three years from the top of Wave 3 of Wave (3) of Primary 5.

4. And, perhaps the most significant point from a truly longer-term perspective, the Nikkei Average will be 21 years past the 1967 low from the third quarter of 1988 through September 1989.

All of these are Fibonacci time periods and would seem to be more than mere coincidence.

The conclusion is that Wave (5) of Primary 5 should end—marking a major top—most likely in the period between early June and late September this year. In this analysis, the price for a potential top is less important than wave form and the element of time.

FIGURE 20.6   NIKKEI 225 CASH INDEX

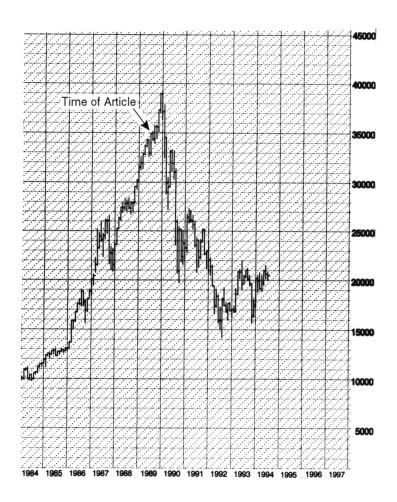

Source: Commodity Price Charts

CHAPTER 21

FINDING THE RIGHT ANGLE

Magazine articles by Phyllis Kahn of Gannworld Inc. in Seaside, Calif., Robert Miner of Gann/Elliott Educators in Tucson, Ariz., and Jim Hyerczyk of Gann Research and Trading in Chicago contributed to background for this chapter.

For all that has been said and written about W.D. Gann, you would think there wouldn't be much about him or his techniques that would not be known. Yet, his ideas and their application to trading remain a mystery to many traders.

Part of the problem is that there are so many aspects to Gann trading that it's hard to keep them all in mind. Consequently, analysts and traders have picked up on this idea or that idea from Gann, incorporated it into their own trading program and described it as a "Gann technique." But, to some other student of Gann, it may not be "real Gann."

Gann himself was not very clear about what "real" Gann trading was. He was an extremely successful trader and had some highly publicized trading results, including 264 winners out of 286 total stock transactions in October 1909 under the watchful eye of an investment magazine. He was renown for precise calls on how far a market would move. Yet, there is some disagreement whether he wound up a rich man.

He wrote a number of books and taught high-ticket stock and commodity courses ($5,000 for the weekend Master Time and Price Calculator Course) on his methods of analysis and trading. Yet, did Gann tell all? Depending on the source, Gann either revealed everything he knew and did, or he presented many interesting concepts but never gave out his real secrets of trading. Complicating the situation is that much of his writing is about minor points and details.

Some believe that if Gann did not write about something, it was not part of his analysis. Others contend that not discussing a subject in his work was probably the best clue that it actually WAS vital to Gann in his trading approach. One example is the Fibonacci numerical series described in the previous chapter. Gann apparently never mentioned it, even though it seems to fit perfectly with some of his own ideas and he must have been aware of Fibonacci concepts.

This indeed seems to have been a mysterious man, then and now, and if anyone has the plain and simple answers to Gann trading, they haven't let the world know yet, to my knowledge. We do know that he regarded time as being as important as price, that contract lows and highs and cycles were vital points to him and that he looked at some numbers as much more significant than others.

For those interested in pursuing Gann, there are a number of Gann specialists, advisory services and software programs available. We can't do justice to everything about Gann in a chapter; nevertheless, we'll tackle what seem to be the major Gann concepts.

GANN ANGLES

This may be one of the best-known Gann techniques and perhaps the most important for analyzing and forecasting prices at a particular time. The basic concept revolves around units of price and time.

Markets move up and down at various rates of speed. A market that goes from $1.10 to $1.20 in a month will look somewhat different on a chart than a market that goes from $1.10 to $1.20 in a day. What you want to know is the price difference divided by the number of units of time to find out what the size of the price increment or unit should be for each unit of time. Here, you face somewhat the same dilemma as the point-and-figure chartist (see Chapter 5): What should be the value or scale of the price box or unit?

Ideally, you want the price unit to equal the time unit. Then, if price moves up or down one unit as time advances one unit, prices would track along a line marked by a 45-degree angle. If price advances one unit but it takes two units of time, you have a 1 × 2 line at about a 26 1/2-degree angle. If price advances two units in one unit of time, you have a steeper 2 × 1 line at a 63 1/2-degree angle.

The basic diagram (Figure 21.1) shows how these lines fan out from a major bottom. The same types of fan lines can be drawn from major tops and then, of course, you have myriad other lines from lesser bottoms and tops that apply to shorter-term moves. A Gann chart with all those lines can look very confusing but, to a Gann advocate, very enlightening for identifying price or time targets.

The 45-degree angle is the most significant—of course, it won't be 45 degrees if you do not use the right price unit, but getting as close to that as possible is the goal. Typically, a rally above that angle is considered strong, one below that weak. If a market dipping below the 1 × 1 line is weak, then one dropping below the 1 × 2 line is weaker.

Jim Hyerczyk (*Futures*, March 1994) points out that these geometric or Gann angles "merely serve as extensions of bottoms or tops. Each angle represents the swing bottom or top moving up or down at a uniform rate of speed. Even if you miss a top or bottom, it's never too late to get in because the angles provide valid support and resistance points as

FIGURE 21.1   GANN ANGLES

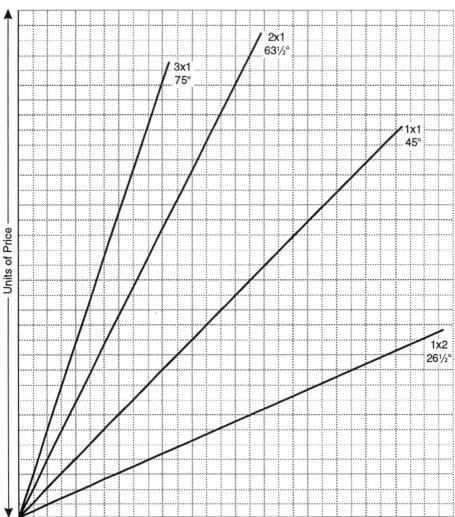

the market moves away from the top or bottom from which they originate.

"The angles drawn from the tops and bottoms created on swing charts will set up future moves in the market. This is especially true of angles drawn from contract highs and lows, and closing price reversal tops and bottoms. In the same sense, angles drawn from three-period tops and bottoms tend to be stronger than one- or two-period tops and bottoms. This is the core concept of Gann's theory that past tops and bottoms can forecast futures tops and bottoms."

Selecting the correct price unit scale that applies to each market is "the key to forecasting and developing trading strategies using geometric angles. The scale is important because it helps you determine the right speed the market should follow," according to Hyerczyk. The scale is subject to change, of course, but Hyerczyk's guideline for the equity market in early 1994 was:

Daily chart — 0.20 - 0.40
Weekly chart — 0.40 - 0.80
Monthly chart — 0.80 - 1.60 - 3.20

"One common factor generated by price and time is the phenomena of 'lost motion' or momentum," Hyerczyk continued. "To determine a change in trend from a bottom, you must see how far the market crosses a bottom before failing to continue lower. So buy and sell signals can be generated on the swing chart when the market exceeds these determined points. The rule applied to angles is when price penetrates an angle by an amount that exceeds a previous penetration, it shows a probable change in trend. This tells you where to place the stop-loss order."

The premise is that the market will either not drop low enough (in this example) to hit the stop before it returns to the trend of the angle ("regains the angle"), or, if the market does continue to drop, it will activate your stop and you will be on board for the decline to the next objective, the next lower angle line.

As you might imagine, Gann angles alone open up plenty of opportunities for analysis.

GANN SQUARE, CARDINAL CROSS, CARDINAL POINTS

If you know the all-time low price for a commodity, you can find other key points that serve as objectives, according to Gann theory (Figure 21.2). It may look more like a dart board than a trading aid, but the wheel of numbers illustrates how key numbers show up on the cardinal cross (the vertical C2-C4 and horizontal C1-C3 lines) and the fixed cross (diagonal F1-F3 and F2-F4 lines).

FIGURE 21.2

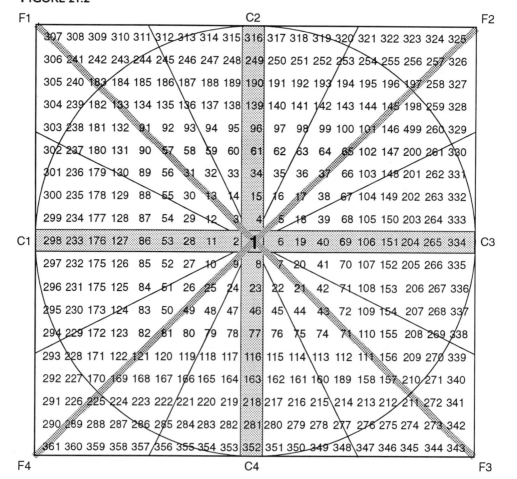

Source: Lambert-Gann Publishing Co.

(Note that the F4 end of the first cycle ends at 9, the square of 3; the next at 25, the square of 5; the next at 49, the square of 7, etc. Also, note that one line above the F2 row of numbers includes the squares of the even numbers: 4 is the square of 2, 16 the square of 4, 36 the square of 6, etc.)

Put the lowest price ever paid for the commodity in the center square at 1, and radiate other prices around it. For example, the all-time low for pork bellies was 19.75¢ in August 1971 so you put 19.7 in square 1, 19.8 where the 2 is to the left of square 1, 19.9 where the 3 is, 20.0 in square 4, 20.1 in square 5, etc., etc. around and around the square. (If you carry this out to the 15th cycle or "circle," incidentally, you will find the all-time high of $1.0510 in 1975 just one tick away from the C1 cardinal point).

Phyllis Kahn published the live cattle cardinal point table (Figure 21.3) with the most important price points in 1980, and you can still apply it to today. Numbers radiate around the lowest cattle futures price ever of $22.90. At the time of this writing, the contract high for June 1995 cattle futures was $72.50 and the low was $64. Those numbers are both just 20¢ away from the C3 cardinal cross point in the 10th and 11th cycles. In Gann theory, if the $72.50 price in the 11th cycle is exceeded, the price objective of the 12th cycle becomes $81.80 (the $81.60 from C3, column 12, plus 20¢).

Gann "Numbers"

Virtually every commodity has had its memorable price moves—the ones everyone remembers for years because they were so dramatic. Soybeans in 1973 is one example, and Gann advocates would tell you the key prices and times were obvious. Here's an example of applied Gann, written by Phyllis Kahn (*Commodities*, January 1980):

FIGURE 21.3

Live cattle cardinal points														
Cycle	1	2	3	4	5	6	7	8	9	10	11	12	13	14
C-1	229	238	255	280	313	354	403	460	525	598	679	768	865	970
F-1	230	240	258	284	318	360	410	468	535	608	690	780	878	984
C-2	231	242	261	288	323	366	417	476	543	618	701	792	891	998
F-2	232	244	264	292	328	372	424	484	552	628	712	804	904	1012
C-3	233	246	267	296	333	378	431	492	561	638	723	816	917	1026
F-3	234	248	270	300	338	384	438	500	570	648	734	828	930	1040
C-4	235	250	273	304	343	390	445	508	576	658	745	840	943	1054
F-4 END CYCLE	236	252	276	308	348	396	452	516	588	668	756	852	956	1068

© Copyright: Phyllis Kahn

"One of Gann's techniques for finding tops and bottoms is 'squaring' out price with time—when a unit of price equals a unit of time, it is 'squared.'

"The historic high price of July soybean futures prior to the June 1973 peak was $4.33 per bushel in June 1948. That was 25 years from peak to peak. One of the Gann courses has a table of weekly time periods which shows that the end of the 25-year cycle in weeks is 1300. The extreme high price of July soybeans in 1973 at $12.90 was just 10¢ less than an exact square of price and time.

"Tied to this, one of Gann's most powerful tools is the Master Price and Time Calculator, 'the square of 144.' The price of July soybeans in 1948 was $4.33:

"Three cycles of 144 equals 433.

"Three cycles of 433 equals 1296.

"(The square of 3) Nine cycles of 144 equals 1296.

"Could anyone who traded soybeans in 1973 believe that shorting soybeans below $13 was a low-risk trade? Yet, everything pointed to a culmination when price and time were 'square' in three different ways at once."

On top of that, 17 cycles on the soybean cardinal squares is $12.89.

A Gann devotee might say, "Prescient." You might say, "Coincidence." I am in the group that might say, "Hmmm, interesting."

For skeptics, it may seem that almost every number is a Gann something or the other. But Gann had some numbers that seemed to be particularly important, among them 8 and 144 (or 8 multiplied by 18?).

Gann divided the range of prices from top to bottom or bottom to top into eighths. The most significant point offering the strongest support or resistance was 4/8 or 50 percent. Then came the 5/8 level and the 3/8 level. Note that 5/8 at 62 1/2 percent and 3/8 at 37 1/2 percent are very close to the Fibonacci ratios at 0.618 and 0.382.

If prices advance or decline a total of $100, they can be expected to react back by roughly 50 percent of the move. If the reaction or retracement exceeds 50 percent, the next logical stopping point is the 62 1/2 percent or 5/8 level. If that level is exceeded, then 75 percent (6/8) becomes the target. And so on.

CONCLUSION

One should not conclude from this short chapter that this is all of Gann or even that this is the essence of Gann. There is much more to

Gann—and, for that matter, much more to Elliott, cycles, oscillators, charts and all the other topics we have covered in this book.

For some people and some topics, what you see in this handbook is all you want to know. But, for those who want to be serious traders and analysts, this book is only the beginning and just one source of information. Just analyzing the analysis techniques is a study in itself.

REFERENCES

Futures magazine, 219 Parkade, Cedar Falls, IA 50613 can provide back issues or reprints of the articles mentioned in this book as well as many others that would be useful to technical analysts.

BOOKS

Arnold, Curtis. *Timing the Market* (Chicago: Probus, 1993).

Bierovic, Tom. *A Synergetic Approach to Profitable Trading* (Wheaton, IL: Synergy Futures, 1992).

Bernstein, Jake. *Timing Signals in the Futures Market: The Trader's Definitive Guide to Buy-Sell Indicators* (Chicago: Probus, 1990).

DeMark, Tom. *The New Science of Technical Analysis* (New York: Wiley, 1994).

Edwards, Robert D. and John Magee. *Technical Analysis of Stock Trends* (Englewood Cliffs, N.J.: Prentice-Hall, 1991).

Elder, Alexander. *Trading for a Living* (New York: Wiley, 1993).

Frost, A. J. and Robert Prechter. *Elliott Wave Principle: Key to Stock Market Profits* (Gainesville, GA: New Classics Library, 1990).

Hill, John. *Stock and Commodity Market Trend Trading by Advanced Technical Analysis* (Hendersonville, N.C.: Futures Truth Co., 1978).

Kaufman, Perry. *The New Commodity Trading Systems & Methods* (New York: Wiley, 1987).

Krutsinger, Joe. *The Trading Systems Toolkit* (Chicago: Probus, 1994).

Murphy, John J. *Technical Analysis of the Futures Markets: A Comprehensive Guide to Trading Methods & Applications* (New York: New York Institute of Finance, 1986).

Murphy, John J. *Intermarket Technical Analysis: Trading Strategies for the Global Stock, Bond, Commodity & Currency Markets* (New York: Wiley, 1991).

Nison, Steve. *Japanese Candlestick Charting Techniques* (Englewood Cliffs, N.J.: Prentice-Hall, 1991).

Schwager, Jack D. *A Complete Guide to the Futures Markets: Fundamental Analysis, Technical Analysis, Trading, Spreads & Options* (New York: Wiley, 1984).

Steidlmayer, J. Peter. *Steidlmayer on Markets: A New Approach to Trading* (New York: Wiley, 1989).

Wilder, J. Welles, Jr. *New Concepts in Technical Trading* (McLeansville, NC: Trend Research Ltd., 1978).

Williams, Bill. *Turning "Chaos" into Cash* (New York: Wiley, 1995).

Williams, Larry and Michelle Noseworthy. *Sure Thing Commodity Trading* (Brightwaters, NY: Windsor, 1977).

Williams, Larry. *The Secret of Selecting Stocks.*

Williams, Larry. *How I Made a Million Trading Commodities.*

VIDEOS

Briese, Steve, *The Inside Track to Winning,* Financial Trading Seminars, New York.

Bierovic, Tom, *Synergetic Technical Analysis,* Futures Learning Center, Cedar Falls, IA.

Krutsinger, Joe, *Trading System Development,* Futures Learning Center.

Ring, Glen, *How to Profit from Trends in Futures,* Futures Learning Center.

Seehusen, Ken, *How to Profit from Chart Patterns and Technical Studies,* Futures Learning Center.

Williams, Bill, *Profiting from "Chaos"—A New Map for Traders,* Futures Learning Center.

Williams, Larry. *The Future Millionaires' Confidential Training Course,* Karol Media, Wilkes-Barre, PA.

INDEX